"LaSala, a well-known and admired social work educator and scholar, has created a highly readable and instructional book that is based on his 40-plus years of practice experience. It incorporates key theoretical concepts with recent research and practice wisdom and underscores the importance of self-reflection, the use of self, and a relational approach. I would highly recommend this book that also includes vivid case examples and engaging exercises for social work practice courses and early career clinicians who are interested in furthering their knowledge and skills."

Andrew W. Safyer, *Academic Dean, Institute for Clinical Social Work*

"In this time of Covid craziness, who doesn't need some healing? Making use of his 40-plus years of practice, supervision, training, and teaching Dr. Michael LaSala presents us in ten chapters with a volume that describes a model of clinical practice that focuses on healing relationships including the relationship the worker has with themself, with their clients, and the relationships between clients in couples, families, and groups. This is a wonderful book for clinical practitioners, for students of social work and for mental health professionals of all disciplines who may feel worn out and in need of regeneration and reminders about the healing nature of individual, couples, families, and group relationships. This book is an important reminder that the healers also need to be healed. It should be required reading for all clinicians – not just during these challenging times that we are living in, but for sustaining and replenishing our clinical practice in everyday life."

Gerald P. Mallon, *LCSW, DSW, Associate Dean of Scholarship and Research, Julia Lathrop Professor of Child Welfare*

"Drawing on 40-plus years of social work practice, supervision, training, and teaching, and his own life experiences, Dr. Michael C. LaSala's book, *Clinical Social Work with Individuals, Families, and Groups: The Healing Power of Relationships*, provides a unique perspective on clinical practice that focuses on healing relationships. The book is ideal for students and new practitioners as they begin their journey to understand the importance of relationships in all aspects of clinical social work practice through research, case examples and reflection exercises that also includes a focus on the impacts of the pandemic and racial justice issues. As dean of a social work program with a focus on preparing students for clinical practice, this book should be on the syllabus and required reading for any courses on clinical social work practice!"

Jo Ann R. Regan, *Ph.D., MSW, Dean, National Catholic School of Social Service at the Catholic University of America in Washington, D.C.*

Clinical Social Work with Individuals, Families, and Groups

The Healing Power of Relationships

Michael C. LaSala

NEW YORK AND LONDON

Cover image: © Getty Images

First published 2023
by Routledge
605 Third Avenue, New York, NY 10158

and by Routledge
4 Park Square, Milton Park, Abingdon, Oxon OX14 4RN

Routledge is an imprint of the Taylor & Francis Group, an informa business

© 2023 Michael C. LaSala

The right of Michael C. LaSala to be identified as author of this work has been asserted in accordance with sections 77 and 78 of the Copyright, Designs and Patents Act 1988.

All rights reserved. No part of this book may be reprinted or reproduced or utilised in any form or by any electronic, mechanical, or other means, now known or hereafter invented, including photocopying and recording, or in any information storage or retrieval system, without permission in writing from the publishers.

Trademark notice: Product or corporate names may be trademarks or registered trademarks, and are used only for identification and explanation without intent to infringe.

Library of Congress Cataloging-in-Publication Data
A catalog record for this title has been requested

ISBN: 978-0-367-82058-9 (hbk)
ISBN: 978-0-367-82059-6 (pbk)
ISBN: 978-1-003-01171-2 (ebk)

DOI: 10.4324/9781003011712

Typeset in Sabon
by Taylor & Francis Books

This book is dedicated to:
All of my teachers, including the hundreds of clients and students I have seen over the years.
My husband, Timothy S. Murphy, who has co-created a healing relationship with me for which I am eternally grateful.
And the light of the Creator, my coauthor.

Contents

List of tables		x
Introduction		xi
1	Social Workers' Relationship to Themselves	1
2	Clinical Social Work Defined: Psychotherapy Plus	13
3	Tips for Getting Started	34
4	Clinical Social Work with Individuals: It's About the Relationship	58
5	Healing Relationships with Each Other—Part I: Couples	104
6	Healing Relationships with Each Other—Part II: Families	134
7	Healing Relationship with Each Other—Part III: Groups	160
8	Healing Relationships with Clients from Diverse and Oppressed Groups	184
9	Ethics: Protecting the Healing Relationship	211
10	Healing Relationships in the Age of Covid	234
	Epilogue: Some Closing Thoughts	244
	Appendix: Questions for Individual Self-Reflection and Class Discussion	247
	Index	252

Tables

4.1 Example of a Completed Dysfunctional Thought Record   83
6.1 Client Complaints and Positive Reframes   154

Introduction

Between Covid, the overdue attention on racial violence, and the hostile divisions in this country, people are anxious and angry, and the future is perhaps more uncertain than ever. Thus, this is the perfect time to enter the field of clinical social work. People need the unique healing relationships that clinical social workers provide to help clients survive, thrive, and address the many challenges that confront us now and that we will surely face in the future. This book is meant to equip you with the tools you will need to heal clients and address the trials that no doubt lie ahead.

As the title alludes, this volume describes a model of clinical practice that focuses on healing relationships, including the relationship the worker has with themselves, with their clients, and the relationships between clients in couples, families, and groups. Worker self-knowledge, empirically-informed therapeutic relationships based on the common factors, Rogerian principles, strength-based interventions as well as systemic and structural thinking are highlighted in this book. There is also a good dose of clinical wisdom based on my 40-plus years of practice, supervision, training, and teaching.

The primary tool of clinical social work is the social worker themself, and this is explained in Chapter 1. People entering this work need to have a high level of self-knowledge in order to be successful and to also avoid burnout. In Chapter 2, clinical social work is defined and distinguished from other psychotherapy professions. Chapter 3 describes tips for the new clinician as they begin their career, and even their first day. Work with individuals is explained in the context of interventions within a healing relationship in Chapter 4. Chapters 5 and 6 describe couple and family work and how the relationships *between* clients are the targets of interventions. Chapter 7 on groups extends this theme as individuals come together to assess and alter their unhelpful relational behaviors. Chapter 8 describes how clinical relationships must be modified to address client diversity and their experiences of oppression, although this material can be found throughout the book. Chapter 9 illustrates how to apply the NASW ethical standards to protect these clinical relationships and finally, the impact of Covid-19 on our work is described in Chapter 10. As of this writing, the pandemic is thankfully no longer as fatal as it once was, but a highly contagious new variant is spreading like wildfire. It seems we will have to continue to deal with this pandemic indefinitely, and tele-mental health will play a significant role in the future.

About Me

For sure, knowledge passes through the lens of the messenger, so you should know who is writing. I am a white gay man of late middle age who has practiced social work for 40 years. I was the first person in my blue collar-rooted, Italian American family to go to college which my parents saw as a ticket to prosperity. As a sophomore, I volunteered to serve on the student crisis hotline, High Hopes, and became an intern at the university psychological services department. For sure, the bug had bitten. A social worker was a guest speaker at one of my psychology classes extoling the benefits of the MSW degree. I was attracted to the field by the promise of a career that would help make the world a better place.

Not incidentally, I had a difficult childhood marked by bullying from my family and peers. As you will learn later in this chapter, many of us got our initial social work training during our painful childhoods. As I staggered, bumped and bruised, away from my own childhood, I had issues to work on for sure. What I did not know at the time was that I harbored a secret wish to heal my battered self-worth through helping others. This is not an unusual initial motivation for people to enter the field, and many of you may have done so for similar reasons. However, my first few difficult cases quickly disabused me of the notion that my self-esteem could be repaired via others seeking my help. A seismic anxiety attack during the second year of my MSW program led to a period of self-growth (as good anxiety attacks invariably do). I enrolled in my first of many psychotherapies, beginning a lifelong journey of looking inward, repairing myself in the service of not only my own healing, but that of others.

I have many mentors, past and present, to thank for helping me get to the point in my career where I can write this book. First off is Dr. R. David Kissinger, who was the Director of Psychological Services at SUNY Binghamton, who supervised me when I was the Director of High Hopes, and also an internship where he taught me Rogerian, person-centered counseling techniques and got me started on my psychotherapy career. I would also like to thank the School of Social Welfare at SUNY Albany where I got my MSW and Ph.D. degrees. Bill Knupp, my second-year fieldwork supervisor gave me a grounding in cognitive behavioral therapy, aspects of which I still use to this day. Salvador Minuchin, Anne Itzkowitz, Carl Whitaker, Michael P. Nichols, Insoo Kim Berg, Monica McGoldrick, Steve de Shazer, Maurizio Andolfi, and James Hollis have all influenced my career, through their teaching, supervision, and guidance, and those in the know will be able to see their influences in my work. It is imperative that I thank the helpful editors at Routledge for helping me bring this project to fruition, as well as Rutgers University for supporting me in this endeavor. Finally, I would like to thank the hundreds of students and clients I have seen over the years, without whom this book would be possible. Thank you for blessing my life with meaning and purpose.

Each journey begins with a single step. Let us begin yours.

Chapter 1

Social Workers' Relationship to Themselves

Whether you were the person who family and friends turned to in a crisis, the child in the neighborhood who cleaned up trash, the teenage camp counselor, the kid in school who stood up for those who were bullied, you were a social worker in the making, way before the thought emerged into your consciousness. As director of the MSW program here at Rutgers University, as I interviewed applicants, I noted an interesting phenomenon. Prospective students were worried and apologetic that they did not have what they thought was the requisite, human service experience needed to be admitted. However, students who sought to become social workers had histories of engaging in social work-like activities such as child care, volunteering in soup kitchens, working in camps for disabled youth, and the like. This experience has led me to the conclusion that social workers are called to this profession, even before they realize it. Closely examine and reflect on the path your life has taken up to this point and you will find, in the words of Lady Gaga, "You were born this way!"

Self as Instrument

Throughout this book, I am going to periodically ask you to take a few moments to reflect on what you are feeling, thinking, and learning. Who we are, our feelings, and our relationships to ourselves are the clinical social workers' primary tools. So, for now, take a moment, sit in a quiet space, and close your eyes. In this silence, ask yourself the following:

1   Why did I choose to be a social worker?

    a   Why not a master's degree in marital counseling or counseling psychology, or a Ph.D. in clinical psychology?

2   Did I choose social work because it is the shortest route to a private practice as a psychotherapist? (No wrong answers here. If the answer is yes, that's ok for right now—but hopefully as your education continues, your vision will widen.)

DOI: 10.4324/9781003011712-1

a   Am I trying to heal my own wounds by helping others?

Write your answers down somewhere and keep them in mind as you proceed through this book.

The Path of the Wounded Healer

When the World Trade Center was attacked on September 11th, 2001, my husband along with hundreds of others fled lower Manhattan by foot and in terror, running from falling debris and bodies, and an overwhelming cloud of poisonous smoke. In retelling the story (a healthy act if one has experienced trauma), one of the many images that struck him were those of firefighters and rescue workers rushing headlong *toward* the danger. While less physically dangerous, social workers run toward emotional pain when most reasonable people flee in the opposite direction. What is it about *us* that we are willing to do this? Is it for the money? The prestige of the profession? Ha!

As previously stated, it seems people are called to social work early in their lives, sometimes in childhood. Does this mean we come into this world motivated and divinely destined to make it a better place? Do we carry a gene that makes us naturally altruistic? Perhaps, but there are research findings that suggest that the choice of social work as a profession might have more to do with nurture rather than nature, and our interests may have been shaped by our wounds.

Black, Jeffreys, and Hartley (1993) compared samples of social work and business students and found that the former had significantly higher levels of substance abuse, childhood histories of physical and sexual abuse, mental and physical illness, and in their families of origin, suicide completions and attempts. Rompf and Royse (1994) observed similar results with a comparison group of English majors. Coombes and Anderson (2000) found a higher incidence of alcoholism in the families-of-origin of social work students compared to that of business students. In a seminal study of 1,577 social workers by Lackie (1983), most respondents described themselves as the "good" child, the mediator, the burden bearer, or the parentified child in their families-of-origin, prematurely taking on adult caretaking roles. Based on these findings, it is not hard to imagine how those who were socialized to go beyond normal responsibilities in childhood find an occupation in adulthood that professionalizes this role. Paraphrasing Jungian analyst James Hollis (personal communication), you may think you have chosen this profession, but maybe you had no choice.

As most experienced psychotherapists know, parentification happens at the expense of a developing child's needs for nurturance, safety, stability, and identity development. This might explain the repeated findings that, as a group, we social workers are an anxious bunch. Among a sample of social workers, it was found that they tended toward low self-esteem, were self-critical, and employed self-blame a great deal, which could be a result of the previously described family psychopathology (Bedford & Bedford, 1985). In her sample of 751 North Carolina social workers, Siebert (2004) discovered that 60 percent had experienced episodes of depression at some point in their lives, which is three times the national average. Among a sample of 79 social work students, 42 percent reported experiencing four or more adverse childhood experiences (ACES) which is 3.3 times that of the general population (Thomas, 2016). A plausible, partial explanation for these findings is that we might be more likely to recognize our wounds and thus report them, and that is a good start. It's what we do about them that is important. As part of their classwork, I require clinical MSW students to complete a genogram (McGoldrick, 2016), which is a diagram of a family tree that illustrates the psychological and relationship problems in a family over several generations. I have been shocked and humbled to learn of the extensive family trauma that these students have experienced, much like that described in the previously cited studies. However, those findings do not demonstrate the persistence and resilience I see among these students who, despite their burdens, have made it to graduate school and have committed themselves to a life of service.

Hollis (2020) and others have talked about how people pursue a career of helping in an attempt to metaphorically fix their families. If we were parentified in our families, we likely took great pride in this role, and perhaps our survival depended on it. However, we also suffered as our own development was sacrificed as we attended to the Sisyphean task of healing our families. If, as a child, the clinician was only valued when they acted in accordance with a parentified role, their self-esteem as adults may be too tied to their success in helping their clients. This puts the worker in a precarious emotional position. Lackie (1983), Hollis (2020), and Hanna (1993b) have theorized that in our effort to heal our families as children, we inevitably fail, which leads us to feel unconsciously guilty but also resentful about the emotional toll these efforts cost us. Relatedly, our clients are stand-ins for our own families whom we could not heal—and if we are not careful, we risk acting out these feelings with our clients.

Could these troubled histories account for not only the choice of social work as a profession but also the high levels of anxiety several empiricists have noted? Does this mean that social workers are so wounded and so crazy that we are unable to help others? The answer is a qualified no. Childhood trauma can sensitize the sufferer, enabling them to develop compassion, empathy, and altruism toward others, and the world needs more people with these qualities.

At issue is, what we do with these experiences and their impacts? Do we paper them over in a misguided attempt to ignore them? Do we help others to distract us from our own wounds? Or do we face our weaknesses and vulnerabilities head on, trying to understand and learn from them and put what we have learned to good use? I would argue that ongoing self-examination is essential to the work.

Countertransference

Countertransference describes the feelings a therapist has toward their client based on their own unconscious, unresolved issues, which can impede treatment (Hanna, 1993a). The therapist is bringing their own experiences from past relationships into those with their clients. If the therapist is not careful and mindful of their countertransference reactions and impulses, they risk not only failing to be helpful but possibly doing harm.

> Rick, an African American clinician, grew up in a single parent, female-headed household where his mother ruled with an iron fist. He was taught never to question his mother's authority or talk back to her and on occasion, she would beat Rick with a folded belt, raising welts on his skin. As a child, he learned to survive by placating and appeasing her in order to emotionally and physically survive. At the same time, he learned to repress his anger and sadness. His supervisor noticed that when he worked with families he rarely challenged or confronted the mother, often siding with her against the children. As a result, the children's behavior along with family function, rarely improved.
>
> During his own therapy, Rick came to realize that he was the primary emotional caretaker for his mother. As a child, he was sensitive to his mother's needs, and because he was deeply intuitive, he understood the fragility beneath the anger and never challenged her as an adult. No doubt, these childhood experiences left him with an acute sensitivity to other people's feelings while ignoring his own. However, before this came to conscious awareness during his own therapy, he overprotected mothers in his client families, failing to confront them or even make suggestions when appropriate. His supervisor and his own psychotherapist helped him see how the way he was parented made it difficult for him to acknowledge concealed feelings of anger, sadness, and loneliness, a pattern he was inadvertently helping families repeat in his practice. Once he realized what he was doing, he was able to shift direction and help parents see the need to provide not only structure and discipline but also nurturance and affection to their children.

If we come from troubled families, we need to recognize our wounds and actively pursue our own healing if we are to be effective. Always, the priority is our clients and what helps them. Without being aware of our issues, we could be seeking something from our work that is not necessarily best for them. Like Rick, if we have been physically abused and bullied as children but fail to recognize it, we risk blindness to its effects on our clients' lives. Additionally, if your identity is too tied up in being a helper due to your family-of-origin role, you also run the risk of caring more about the client getting better than the client does. A cardinal rule is that if the worker is working harder than the client, the work won't work. If your self-esteem is tied up in being an expert helper, your emotional health is in danger and you are a prime candidate for burnout.

Relatedly, if we are unaware of what triggers us, we risk emotionally shutting down, or alternatively becoming too emotionally reactive without knowing why. We may overfunction, trying too hard to rescue clients, giving them fish rather than teaching them to fish for themselves. Even worse, when a client presents with an issue similar to one of our own that we have not dealt with, we may react in a way that is unhelpful. Here is another example:

> Belinda was a 45-year-old Latinx clinical social worker in recovery from addiction who was known in her local community as a compassionate, skilled professional that, along with her long-term sobriety, made her a therapist in demand. Belinda's client, Gloria, was a 60-year-old Latinx woman whose family was concerned about her drinking. Gloria's daughter gave her a copy of the Big Book and she occasionally attended local Alcoholics Anonymous (AA) meetings. However, she never participated or spoke up during these meetings. During a case consultation, Belinda, discussed wanting to accompany this client to AA meetings in order to coach her to participate.

For sure Belinda, a wise, sensitive, and talented clinician, was coming from a caring place as she wanted to make certain that Gloria got the help she needed. However, if Belinda had done this, it would have been an example of overfunctioning. No doubt, Gloria's underfunctioning elicited extra efforts on the part of her family and her therapist, who understandably worried for her. However, what happened in this case was an extension of Belinda's childhood experiences. In her family of origin, Belinda was indeed a parentified child, with an alcoholic mother and a depressed father. Frequently, she had been assigned the role of helping her intoxicated mother stagger up the stairs of their home after a night of drinking. She had also tried many times to convince her mother to get sober. At the time she was seeing Gloria, Belinda's mother was dying and was relocated to a hospice. At this point in Belinda's family's life, it was quite appropriate for her to be functioning beyond her usual role as adult daughter. However, it also activated old tendencies garnered from her experience as a parentified child trying, wishing, and failing to help her mother get sober, which showed themselves in her work with Gloria.

During supervision, Belinda came to this realization and was able to "pull back," and find ways to deal with her own anxiety. Belinda could not "save" her mother or Gloria; only *they* could decide to go into recovery. However, as her therapist, she could help Gloria explore her ambivalence. Belinda was able to also manage her own feelings about Gloria's reluctance—noting with some surprise and intellectual curiosity that her own parentification could still be activated, despite her age and the length of time she had been working on these issues. Ultimately, the decision to go into recovery from addiction lies with the person with the addiction, whether that is a client or family member. Recovery, even when a person is motivated, is hard work and I have yet to hear of an example of someone who recovered against their will. She could get Gloria to the starting gate, but going forward would be up to her.

The Cultural Zeal to Short-Circuit Suffering

Let's face it, most people, even those who have not experienced substantial childhood trauma, look for ways to avoid or distract themselves from the small and larger pains of living. Think of how unconsciously we greet each other with "how are you?" only to reply or receive a "fine" or "doing well" whether it is true or not. We try to anesthetize ourselves with things like alcohol, drugs, shopping, overeating, or other sensations to escape from pain. In line with "person-in-environment" ways of thinking that are endemic to social work, we are products of a society that seeks to avoid pain. So, it is no wonder that we are strongly tempted to do so in our work with clients. We become anxious when suffering inevitably rears its head in our work. However, we are meant to resist the socialized impulse to flee, and instead, like those 9/11 rescue workers, we must defy all of our natural impulses and run headlong toward trouble.

Further, the default reaction to hearing about a person's pain, especially if it is someone we care about, is to try to do something to take it away. This is an honorable impulse. However, the rush to rescue someone from suffering might lead the clinician to overlook its meaningfulness as well as the opportunities for growth that it provides. Thus, sometimes, in our wish to take away our client's pain, we might be doing more harm than good, trading possible short-term relief, or what Pema Chodron would call "idiot compassion" with the possibility for more long-term gains:

> It [idiot compassion] refers to something we all do a lot of and call it compassion. In some ways, it's what's called enabling. It's the general tendency to give people what they want because you can't bear to see them suffering. Basically, you're not giving them what they need. You're trying to get away from your feeling of *I can't bear to see them suffering.*
>
> In other words, you're doing it for yourself. You're not really doing it for them.
>
> (Pema Chadron, 2012)

As the quote suggests, offering such empty compassion is more about the needs of the giver than the receiver and is never effective in psychotherapy. In the following example, the client is a 10-year-old boy in foster care experiencing behavior problems who was referred to see a social work student in a mental health clinic. This is a first session, so the worker has yet to meet the child's biological mother. However, this child was placed in foster care because his mother and sole caretaker became addicted to drugs and, as a result, was neglectful of her son.

CLIENT: I wish I could go back home. I don't like living in the foster home. I miss my bed and my friends. I don't think my mother loves me anymore.
CLINICIAN: Oh no! Don't say that! I'm sure your mother loves you very much and wants you to come home soon.

I have seen similar situations played out as well-meaning students attempt to rescue their clients from suffering at the expense of recognizing and validating the painful feelings they have about their reality. The child is inducing from his mother's behavior the painful possibility that she might not love him. This awful realization might simply be too painful for the worker to recognize and then, of course, articulate. She could be acting out of a natural desire to avoid pain that could be aggravated by events in her own childhood. Did she ever doubt her own mother's love, doubts that were too difficult to face? Either way, in an effort to avoid her own feelings she misses a valuable opportunity to validate a client's reality and, what likely might be, deep anger or sadness. This inadvertently teaches the child that what he is experiencing is wrong and in fact unspeakable; a lesson that is profoundly damaging as it erodes the trust between the worker and the child, because the latter knows at some level that the worker is not being honest. Alice Miller (2008) has underscored the damage done to children when they are not permitted to recognize or emotionally react to parental abuse or neglect. One of our most important jobs is to directly face our client's pain and to help them do the same. We need to be able to hear and hold the parts that are truly awful, and at times we must reach for suffering when the client is (and even we are) frightened to go there. Again, approaching our own pain as fearlessly as possible provides fertile ground for helping our clients do the same. If you keep doing this, you will develop a type of emotional callus that will enable you to withstand painful situations without flinching or turning away. Following is a redo:

CLINICIAN: Wow, it sounds really hard not being home—and painful to not be sure of whether your mother loves you. You've been through a lot, that's for sure. For now, let's break it down a bit. What has happened that makes you wonder whether your mom loves you?

CLIENT: Well, she takes drugs even though she knows that means I won't be able to be with her if she keeps doing it.
CLINICIAN: That sounds like it hurts; it's awful to think she might want to do drugs more than take care of you.
CLIENT: (looks down, silently)
CLINICIAN: I have never met your mother so I cannot say anything for sure about how she feels about you. All kids, including you, deserve to be loved and taken care of by their parents. But I do know that people who are addicted to drugs often are so ill that the addiction takes over and they care more about drugs than anything else. When I meet with your mother, I will explore this with her. There are places that help people with their addictions and I plan on talking to her about these places. Addiction is a difficult disease and I can make no promises, but I will try.

As you can see, the social worker did not make any false reassurances to the child, nor any promises she could not keep. Instead, she validated his feelings and tentatively gave reasons for hope. The ultimate task of this client and his clinician is to get the client to believe he is deserving of love and care despite his mother's behavior—a very tall order and possibly a lifelong task. The first step is to begin the process of getting this child not to blame himself for his mother's problems or to think that he is constitutionally unlovable. As clinical social workers, we trawl in suffering as part of our job. To prepare, it is important to recognize how our discomfort and even anxiety can get in the way of understanding and pursuing the pain of our clients.

Know Thyself

This maxim, inscribed at the ancient Greek temple of Delphi, has great resonance for those embarking on a career as a clinical social worker. Take the time, if you have not done so already, to reflect on your childhood. Carefully review the Adverse Childhood Experiences (ACEs) inventory (Brown et al., 2009) and consider your score. Further, take an honest look at your family-of-origin experiences. Were you the parentified child in your family? What strengths did you gain from those experiences? What vulnerabilities have you inherited? In what areas of your life were you encouraged to grow and where were you impeded? How good are you at self-soothing when things go wrong? What about self-love? Do you love yourself? Truly? Do you act in ways that reflect that love? How might the impact of your history affect your work with clients? To reiterate, emotional difficulties related to childhood are not, in and of themselves, impediments to a successful career as a clinical social worker. However, to embark or even continue on this career path without getting one's house in order is comparable to a surgeon attempting to operate on a patient while blindfolded.

Find a quiet spot somewhere, close your eyes, take a few deep breaths and ask yourself the following questions:

1 What are the biggest wounds I have suffered in my life up to this point?
   a How have they affected me?
   b Am I prone to anxiety? Depression? Bad relationships? Distancing?
2 How might these wounds affect my work as a listener? A healer?
   a How might they help my work?
   b How might they hinder it?
3 What are the lessons about helping that I have learned from my family of origin?
   a Was it ok to seek help?
   b Was it ok to receive it?
   c Was it ok to give it?
      i Or was I required to give it whether I wanted to or not?
   d How did help come? Unsolicited advice? Were there strings attached?
4 Overall, what might my personal weaknesses be in helping others?
5 What actions can I take to get help with these issues?

This exercise is best done when you write down your responses. It is also advisable to do this periodically, as your answers may change as you continue your training and see clients. If you do not know the answers to these questions, that's ok, for now. Keep them in mind and the answers will eventually come to you. Running from our pain is a culturally-based impulse, as is the pursuit of a "quick fix" that provides the magic answer right away. Seeking self-knowledge is a lifelong endeavor. The good news is doing so will not only improve your life but will make you an increasingly effective clinical social worker.

Should Clinical Social Workers Be in Psychotherapy?

As an instructor, students ask me this all the time. Historically among certain schools of psychotherapy, one's own psychotherapy was a required component of clinical training and still is. If, after you graduate, you decide to pursue training as a psychoanalyst, a Jungian analyst, or a systemic family therapist, it is likely you will be required to participate in your own psychotherapy. The thinking behind this is that the clinician needs to be as conscious as possible of their own issues, and to have made some progress in resolving them before moving forward to help others.

Horton, Diaz, and Green (2009) have found that social work students are more likely than those from other fields to participate in psychotherapy.

This is a good thing, considering our backgrounds, and our need to defy cultural prescription by directly confronting our own and our clients' emotional pain. I would add that besides being personally useful, it is also a good professional experience to be "on the other side" of the therapeutic couch. This will enable you to be more sensitive to what clients experience. You will learn firsthand that, among other things, seeking such help takes courage.

I myself have been in years of psychotherapy. I did not initially enroll in therapy solely to make myself into a better therapist; I was in pain and needed help. However, once in therapy, I realized the great benefit it had for my work, and I never hesitate to seek it out when I experience symptoms, or some kind of block in my own development. Thus, if you are in any way inclined, I recommend you do the same. As you consider this, be vigilant for any feelings of shame on your part. Despite a decrease in the stigma, participating in psychotherapy does indicate a show of vulnerability that is generally frowned upon in our culture. If you are feeling shame, what does this say about your feelings toward your clients? If you can recognize and overcome these issues, you are well on your way to becoming an excellent clinician. The good news is that there is evidence that problems in childhood predispose clinicians to better engage clients (Wilcoxon, Walker, & Hovestadt, 1989).

As a young adult, I was fortunate to be surrounded by a group of talented stage actors. What I quickly came to notice was that no matter how accomplished or talented they were, they took ongoing classes in voice, movement, and character development. The "art" of doing psychotherapy/clinical social work requires continuous development and ongoing education. As stated earlier, people get designated as helpers in their families of origin, and this early socialization leaves them believing they had little choice but to professionalize this role. Others may choose the helping professions to make up for personal, emotional shortcomings. Once you are initially trained, you will work very hard to assist your clients, some of whom you will not be able to help, many of whom will not thank you for your efforts. Thus, tying your self-esteem or identity to helping clients is a sure recipe for emotional trouble.

However, starting this journey with motivations that are suspect does not mean you should not move forward. You will mature and grow through your professional development in ways you cannot fully imagine. You have made it this far because your professors, instructors, supervisors, peers, and even your clients saw that spark of promise in you. Try to remember this when the going gets tough—and it will. No doubt you care deeply about your work and understand the enormous responsibility that you are taking on, so anxiety is inevitable and, in fact, may be a useful tailwind, pushing you to do your best on behalf of those who will put their trust in your hands. You will need to be able to identify your anxiety as it emerges, know when it is worse or better, learn how to reduce it as much as possible, make room for the bits that you cannot eliminate, and most importantly, know how and when it is interfering in your work. The book you are now reading will assist you.

Our clients have been mistreated by caregivers, institutions, and society itself. As a clinical social worker, you have made a commitment to work directly with people who are suffering and seeking relief from their pain so that they can develop the strength to live in this world. Though I will probably never meet you in person, know that you all live deep in my heart. We are now of the same tribe, and I am honored and humbled by the privilege to share with you what I have learned.

References

Bedford, A., & Bedford, J. (1985). Personality and personal disturbance in social workers: A research note. *The British Journal of Social Work*, 15(1), 87–90. doi:10.1093/oxfordjournals.bjsw.a055062.

Black, P. N., Jeffreys, D., & Hartley, E. K. (1993). Personal history of psychosocial trauma in the early life of social work and business students. *Journal of Social Work Education*, 29(2), 171–180. doi:10.1080/10437797.1993.10778812.

Brown, D. W., Anda, R. F., Tiemeier, H., Felitti, V. J., Edwards, V. J., Croft, J. B., & Giles, W. H. (2009). Adverse childhood experiences and the risk of premature mortality. *American Journal of Preventive Medicine*, 37(5), 389–396. doi:10.1016/j.amepre.2009.06.021.

Chodron, P. (2012). The Buddhist notion of idiot compassion. *Elephant Journal*. www.elephantjournal.com/2012/12/idiot-compassion/.

Coombes, K., & Anderson, R. (2000). The impact of family of origin on social workers from alcoholic families. *Clinical Social Work Journal*, 28(3), 281–302. doi:10.1023/A:1005183718089.

Hanna, E. A. (1993a). The implications of shifting perspectives in countertransference on the therapeutic action of clinical social work part II: The recent-totalist and intersubjective position. *Journal of Analytic Social Work*, 1(3), 53–79. doi:10.1300/J408v01n03_04.

Hanna, E. A. (1993b). The implications of shifting perspectives in countertransference on the therapeutic action of clinical social work part I. *Journal of Analytic Social Work*, 1(3), 25–52. doi:10.1300/J408v01n03_03.

Hollis, J. (2020). *Living Between Worlds: Finding Personal Resilience in Changing Times*. Sounds True.

Horton, E. G., Diaz, N., & Green, D. (2009). Mental health characteristics of social work students: Implications for social work education. *Social Work in Mental Health*, 7(5), 458–475. doi:10.1080/15332980802467696.

Lackie, B. (1983). The families of origin of social workers. *Clinical Social Work Journal*, 11(4), 309–322. doi:10.1007/BF00755898.

McGoldrick, M. (2016). *The Genogram Casebook: A Clinical Companion to Genograms: Assessment and Intervention*. WW Norton & Company.

Miller, A. (2008). *The Drama of the Gifted Child: The Search for the True Self*. Basic Books.

Rompf, E. L., & Royse, D. (1994). Choice of social work as a career: Possible influences. *Journal of Social Work Education*, 30(2), 163–171. doi:10.1080/10437797.1994.10672227.

Siebert, D. C. (2004). Depression in North Carolina social workers: Implications for practice and research. *Social Work Research*, 28(1), 30–40. doi:10.1093/swr/28.1.30.

Thomas, J. T. (2016) Adverse childhood experiences among MSW students. *Journal of Teaching in Social Work*, 36(3), 235–255. doi:10.1080/08841233.2016.1182609.

Wilcoxon, S. A., Walker, M. R., & Hovestadt, A. J. (1989). Counselor effectiveness and family-of-origin experiences: A significant relationship? *Counseling and Values*, 33(3), 225–229. doi:10.1002/j.2161-007X.1989.tb00767.x.

Chapter 2

Clinical Social Work Defined: Psychotherapy Plus

Chances are, if you are in need of mental health services you will be treated by a clinical social worker. Social workers are the largest group of mental health providers in the U.S. (not psychologists, or psychiatrists, or licensed counselors) and have been so for many years (American Board of Clinical Examiners in Social Work, 2020; NASW 2005 https://www.socialworkers.org/LinkClick.aspx?fileticket=YOg4qdefLBE%3d&portalid=0). Over 200,000 social workers provide mental health services (SAMSHA, 2013), and we must bear that responsibility with competence and compassion.

Clinical Social Work: What It Is

Before going further, let's nail down what clinical social work *is*. This task is easier said than done. To start, take a look at the definition offered by the National Association of Social Workers (NASW, nd):

> Clinical social work is a specialty practice area of social work which focuses on the assessment, diagnosis, treatment, and prevention of mental illness, emotional, and other behavioral disturbances. Individual, group and family therapy are common treatment modalities. Social workers who provide these services are required to be licensed or certified at the clinical level in their state of practice.

Here is the definition from the American Board of Clinical Social Work:

> Clinical social work is a healthcare profession based on theories and methods of prevention and treatment in providing mental-health/healthcare services, with special focus on behavioral and biopsychosocial problems and disorders.
>
> (American Board of Clinical Social Work, 2020)

Further, each state licensing board has its own definition. For example, New York State:

DOI: 10.4324/9781003011712-2

Licensed Clinical Social Worker: The practice of licensed clinical social work encompasses the scope of practice of licensed master social work and, in addition, includes the diagnosis of mental, emotional, behavioral, addictive and developmental disorders and disabilities and of the psychosocial aspects of illness, injury, disability and impairment undertaken within a psychosocial framework; administration and interpretation of tests and measures of psychosocial functioning; development and implementation of appropriate assessment-based treatment plans; and the provision of crisis-oriented psychotherapy and brief, short-term and long-term psychotherapy and psychotherapeutic treatment to individuals, couples, families, and groups, habilitation, psychoanalysis and behavior therapy; all undertaken for the purpose of preventing, assessing, treating, ameliorating and resolving psychosocial dysfunction with the goal of maintaining and enhancing the mental, emotional, behavioral, and social functioning and well-being of individuals, couples, families, small groups, organizations, communities and society.

(NYS Office of the Professions, 2018)

And New Jersey:

Clinical social work services include, but are not limited to, the following:

1. Clinical assessment, defined as the process of evaluation in which an LCSW or an LSW conducts a differential, individualized, and accurate identification of the psychosocial/behavioral problems existing in the life of the individual client, the family, or psychotherapy group for the purpose of establishing a plan to implement a course of psychotherapeutic counseling. A clinical social work assessment includes, but is not limited to, a mental status examination and a psychosocial history. The clinical social worker may utilize currently accepted diagnostic classifications including, but not limited to, the American Psychiatric Association's Diagnostic and Statistical Manual of Mental Disorders, as amended and supplemented.
2. Clinical consultation, defined as ongoing case discussion and evaluation focusing on, but not limited to, client-centered advocacy provided as part of the psychotherapeutic process, clinical social work data, clinical goals, and treatment plans for the implementation of psychotherapeutic counseling with individuals, psychotherapy groups, and families. Clinical consultation may also include intervention with appropriate individuals and entities.
3. Psychotherapeutic counseling, defined as ongoing interaction between a social worker and an individual, family, or psychotherapy group for the purpose of helping to resolve symptoms of mental disorder,

psychosocial stress, relationship problems, or difficulties in coping with the social environment.

(NJ Division of Consumer Affairs, 2019)

These definitions vary by state and always have (Goldstein, 2007), so do familiarize yourself with your own state's licensing board definitions. The New York State licensing law definition along with NASW and the American Board of Clinical Social Work cast relatively wide nets in defining the scope of clinical practice. Hospital social work, hospice work, even child welfare could fit into their definitions, whereby New Jersey's standards are narrower and seem more limited to traditional psychotherapy. However, what is important to note is that social work, and clinical social work in particular, goes beyond the boundaries of traditional psychotherapy.

Clinical Social Work: Psychotherapy with a Wider Scope

> Rodolfo is a 27-year-old gay man who arrived in the US from Venezuela 10 years prior to his first visit with his clinical social worker. At the time of his intake, he worked as a waiter in an upscale restaurant, and because he had no health insurance, sought assistance from a public mental health clinic. He was considering breaking off his relationship with his boyfriend John, an Anglo 28-year-old because he found that John was having clandestine sexual encounters with other partners. He was seeking relief from anxiety and depression. As for his relationship, he was haunted by the questions, "What went wrong?" and "What do I do now?"

As this was a public mental health clinic, it is likely that he would be meeting with a social worker—and that social worker could be you. What are some of the ways you would start to think about this case? What are questions you might have? Contrast and compare the plans of Psychotherapist 1 and 2.

PSYCHOTHERAPIST 1: OK, well, first I would help him find ways to talk about anger, grief, betrayal, and trust. Then I would explore his relationship history. Next, I would need to determine how his parents got along and what he learned from them about relationships. Cognitive behavioral therapy might assist with negative thoughts that could be contributing to or adding to his emotional distress. Ultimately, we would need to determine whether or not the couple should stay together and if so, what he needed to do to move forward as a single man, should he decide to do so.

PSYCHOTHERAPIST 2: I would want to cover all of the things Psychotherapist 1 describes, but I would have additional questions. What is Rodolfo's current immigration status? What was his migration experience? Did he face homophobic oppression in his country of origin? If he is without relevant documentation, is he also coping with fears of deportation? How might this affect his relationship with John? Also, do cultural issues play a role in these problems? There is some evidence that Latinx families may have an especially difficult time accepting a child's gay or lesbian sexual orientation. I would want to know what kind of supports he has. Does he have family support at all? What are his wounds, and very importantly, what are his coping strategies? How might these issues affect how he thinks and feels about his relationship? Finally, many but not all gay male couples choose not to be sexually monogamous. What is his position on monogamy? Is he open to revising his relationship agreement with John or does he want to stick with monogamy? Where does John stand on this issue?

What are you noticing about the differences in the two therapist approaches? Your answers will likely address the legitimate question as to how clinical social work differs from psychotherapy. In psychotherapy, as traditionally practiced in psychology, psychiatry, and other disciplines, therapists generally seek to assess how internal factors affect a person's emotional state and behavior. A person's immediate or past history including previous family relationships, trauma, and their effects on the psyche are frequently explored, attended to, and become targets of intervention. If operating from a cognitive behavioral perspective, identifying and addressing dysfunctional thoughts are the focus (Beck, 2020). Followers of the behaviorist school carefully assess behaviors in terms of the rewards and punishments that shape them (Thyer, 2017).

However, as social workers we are always mindful of the effects of sociocultural factors on a person's well-being. Psychotherapist 2 is interested in how Rodolfo's experience as a gay Latinx migrant impacts his life and relationship. As clinical social workers, we consider and assess, as appropriate, for the effects of racism, sexism, homophobia, able-ness, poverty, and transphobia on our clients. Additionally, we also understand the importance of advocating for our clients, whether that is in their neighborhoods, at their schools, agencies, or at local, state, or federal levels. A while ago, clinical social work was described as "psychotherapy plus" (Lieberman, 1987) with its concern not only for the individual client but also for their interaction with the environment (Richmond, 1956), and this classic conceptualization remains applicable.

A word of caution is needed here. Professional categories are rarely if ever mutually exclusive and often overlap. For sure, there are psychiatrists and psychologists who attend to sociocultural factors. For example, Nancy Boyd-Franklin, a psychologist, has written a seminal book on family therapy with Black families, which emphasizes the impact of racism on individual well-being and relationships. (Boyd-Franklin, 2003). José Szapoznik is a psychologist with a long history of working with poor Latinx youth in ways that clearly address the influences of environmental challenges such as poverty and racism (Szapocznik & Hervis, 2020). Salvador Minuchin (1967), a psychiatrist and renowned family therapist, established his groundbreaking theories by working with and advocating on behalf of poor families of color in New York City and Philadelphia. However, while some members of other professions might address these issues, as social workers we are expected to *consistently draw upon and apply* knowledge of societal problems and the role these factors play in mental health functioning.

Definition

Therefore, I define clinical social work as the establishment of a healing psychotherapeutic relationship that addresses personal and interpersonal functioning in a flexible, culturally responsive, and empowering way with a social justice consciousness. This definition is comprehensive enough to encompass the various roles and functions that include but also exist outside of the 50-minute psychotherapy office session, including community mental health work, substance abuse counseling, child welfare work, social work in hospitals, hospices, prisons, or anywhere social workers are deployed to help clients improve their emotional health and ability to function. Although not traditionally seen as clinical social work, working with a family of a child at risk for foster care placement requires not only case management proficiency, but also family therapy skills that empower parents and strengthen parent-child relationships. The worker must bear in mind the pressures on families who are dealing with the impacts of poverty and racism as they help the families improve their functioning to the extent that the child is no longer at risk. A hospice social worker must not only ensure that the patient gets all the medical care they need but also that the family is assisted to cope with their loved ones' current condition and ultimate death. Though case management might be the primary function of workers in certain settings like hospitals, the psychotherapeutic skills of engagement, assessment, and intervention are vital for those who work directly with people outside of counseling centers and private practices.

Unfaithful Angels Revisited

Clinical social work has been roundly criticized for what is seen as an abandonment of the social justice mission of the profession (Kutchins & Kirk, 1988; Specht & Courtney, 1994). In their *cri de coeur*, Specht and Courtney condemned how social workers turned to psychotherapy at the expense of providing services to the poor, essentially selling out the values of the profession in order to line their pockets, and these ideas currently persist in academic circles. Ironically, the emphasis on psychotherapy that Specht and Courtney objected to was informed by the widespread myth that people in poverty could not benefit from psychotherapy (Kumar, 2012), or alternatively that psychoanalysis was a cure for almost every ill, including poverty. Such ideas stigmatized the poor, medicalized poverty, and placed the onus (and thus the blame) on individual psychopathology, minimizing the impact of social factors on a person's well-being.

In many ways, Specht and Courtney made important points. We cannot (and no longer) believe that people of low income cannot benefit from psychotherapy or that it is possible to use it to deliver people out of poverty. Homophobia, sexism, racism, transphobia, able-ism are real and play a role in our clients' emotional, financial, and physical well-being. Further, social workers, even those in full-time private practice, should always remain committed to serving underprivileged and oppressed people in some way. However, Specht and Courtney went too far in their argument by suggesting that social workers get out of the business of psychotherapy altogether. Instead, they called for social work-led community-based interventions such as psychoeducation and self-help groups, despite the findings that many psychoeducation groups are not uniformly effective (Pan & Bai, 2009) while others are not all that different from psychotherapy (Morris, et al., 2020). Further, what is missing from this argument are the views of social workers themselves (Maschi, Baer, & Turner, 2011).

As stated earlier, social workers are the primary deliverers of mental health services particularly to people with low incomes. Such folks suffer from anxiety, depression, and other psychiatric problems, and public and nonprofit mental health clinics are well staffed by social workers providing effective psychotherapy and other psychiatric services to people who could not afford to be treated elsewhere.

Jerry Wakefield, who has written extensively about the relationship between clinical social work and social justice, argues that even though social work did not start out to be a mental health profession, social workers address a wide range of problems such as child abuse, homelessness, domestic violence, and so on, that all call for psychological and behavioral interventions (Wakefield, 1998). Wakefield takes the position that clinical social work can fall under the conceptual umbrella of distributive justice and asserts that the outcomes of psychotherapy, namely self-respect and mental health, are social benefits subject to distribution or redistribution through the practice of psychotherapy. Using a distributive justice frame, he also contends that clinical social work needs to help people attain the mental health and resilience necessary to pursue equity and justice. Self-respect, self-esteem, self-confidence, self-knowledge, problem-solving ability, assertiveness, self-organization, and social skills are considered "psychological goods" and that, at minimum, should be fairly distributed to society. Clinical social workers armed with psychotherapeutic skills as well as an understanding of social justice are ideally suited to assist in this endeavor.

Clinical Social Work Defined 19

> My friend Tom asked for advice about his grandson Toby. Tom is a gay White man in his sixties. His daughter Carla, is a White woman in her forties and her son, Toby is 17 and biracial. Her son, who is the product of Carla's previous marriage to an African American man, has been failing in school for the past year, and according to Tom and Carla, has been more interested in smoking pot and playing video games with his friends than doing his homework. Carla had enrolled Toby in therapy, but she didn't believe the therapist was doing any good.

From a social work/social justice perspective, we would need to hypothesize that the explanation of Toby's difficulties may go beyond family dynamics or the stressors of adolescence, and that institutional racism could play some role in his difficulties. How is Toby being treated in school, in the classroom, and in his neighborhood? Do security personnel follow him around when he is in stores? Has he been stopped by the police in his neighborhood for no good reason? What does he think when he watches video footage of unarmed men his own age and slightly older getting murdered by the police? How aware is he of societal racism and relatedly, how young Black men are overrepresented in our prison systems (Gramlich, 2020) and experience murder as the leading cause of death (CDC, 2017)? Might any of these issues contribute to Toby's lack of motivation in school? A well-meaning White therapist, or even relative, might not have these important structural influences on their radar. Further, just because a family is biracial is no guarantee that these issues are identified or discussed in any meaningful way within the family (Killian & Khanna, 2019). Biracial families can avoid acknowledging or discussing the difficult topics of institutional racism to "keep the peace" just like any other family. In this case, Toby's mother was White and he had little contact with his African American father or his father's family. What adds to the mix is that adolescents and children with behavioral problems are rarely voluntary clients and are generally "sentenced to therapy," usually by their parents. This is one of the reasons why family therapy can be more effective for children and adolescents, which is addressed in Chapter 6.

Thinking systemically about the impact of social justice issues, it is important to imagine what it must be like for this boy to sit in a room with a White, middle-aged, female therapist trying to get him to talk. Considering his father's absence along with the particular stresses on Black men, it would be optimal for him to work with a young Black male therapist—someone he could identify with and who could role model how to deal with the multiple issues related to his race and gender.

The social work perspective demands a consideration of issues of oppression, race, and racism in this case. Now, this doesn't mean that there always needs to be a race match for clients and clinicians; in public and nonprofit settings, flexibility in therapist assignments is generally not possible. Despite the fact that there is no consistent empirical evidence that race matching improves psychotherapy outcomes, in this case role modeling could help, particularly if there is a lack of available Black role models in the family. Further, both the family members, and the therapist, no matter what race they are, need to be sensitive to the role of social factors on Toby's personal problems, so they can be articulated and resilience can be built around them. Attention to these important details is a hallmark of a social work frame for psychotherapy.

Private Practice

The previously described unfaithful angels' paradigm (Specht & Courtney, 1994) can result in a dichotomizing of social justice and mental health, and social workers in private practice have been particularly targeted. However, this does not need to be the case. What about social justice for social workers themselves? It is worth noting that as of this writing, the annual tuition at some schools of social work exceeds $60,000, which is significantly more than most starting social workers' salaries in their first few years of practice. Can we blame them for pursuing potentially more lucrative work in private practice in order to get out from onerous student loans? Further, it may be wrong to assume that clinicians who work privately have abandoned the profession's social justice mission. Slater (2020) interviewed a sample of social workers in private practice and found that they were indeed committed to social justice and were in fact engaging in practices such as advocating for bullied students in schools, accompanying and advocating for clients during social service office visits, and seeing impoverished clients on a sliding scale. Interestingly, it was not the desire to earn a high income that led them to pursue private practice but instead the personal and professional flexibility it afforded. This flexibility made it possible for social workers to work around parenting and other caretaking responsibilities. Unrestrained by agency policies and procedures that were not in clients' best interests, they were free to set affordable fees for clients with low incomes, do home visits, and accompany them to meetings at schools, welfare agencies, and participate in letter writing campaigns, voting registration campaigns, and Black Lives Matter protests. In the private group practice where I currently work, several of us have testified before the New Jersey State Legislature for a transgender rights bill and also sponsored a hogar or home for children waiting to be adopted in Guatemala, sending school supplies, food, and monetary donations. Slater's study was of a small sample, so we cannot assume that all who work in a private practice have such perspectives and incorporate such practices. However, this study does indicate that we must be cautious not to overgeneralize about the motivations and professional activities of social workers in private practice.

Unique Aspects of Clinical Social Work

Flexibility

The traditional way of doing psychotherapy is the 50-minute hour, in the therapist's office. I take no issue with this form of treatment, have participated in it both as a client and a provider and have found it to be effective, even lifesaving at times. However, as social workers, no matter where we work, we must be committed to serving clients for whom psychotherapy might not be easily accessible, such as those who are poor or have mobility issues. During my career, I have done psychotherapy in an empty church, on the stoop of a person's home, on a basketball court, and during a walk to McDonald's. During the Covid pandemic, all of my sessions were done online, and now, as we slowly emerge from it, undoubtably a larger portion of psychotherapy will continue to be online. Of course, when doing clinical work or any type of social work online or in open spaces, it is important to keep these discussions confidential, so it is vital to find places to talk where one cannot be overheard. This is especially important when working remotely (for further guidelines for teletherapy, see Chapter 10). However, the benefits of meeting clients where they are, particularly if they do not have sufficient transportation or are difficult to engage, are significant.

The Perez family was referred to a mental health program for children due to their 10-year-old son Alex's misbehavior at school. During a home visit with the family, the father, Juan, was absent. When working with children, too often a father's importance and involvement is marginalized. Fathers are either ignored or left off-the-hook, and are not included in family therapy sessions, case conferences, or teacher-parent meetings, placing the main burden of childcare on mothers (Parke & Cookston, 2019; Urry, 2018; Walters et al., 1988). When I asked about the father's whereabouts (which I always do, by the way), they replied that he was outside on the street working on his car. They warned me that he didn't believe in counseling. Fair enough, it is not uncommon for parents to be reluctant to participate in counseling for their children. Almost invariably, parents feel guilty and worry they will be examined as if under a microscope and blamed for their children's problems. For some parents, this manifests in reactive defensiveness that shows itself in sessions or in no-shows or cancellations. This tendency could be aggravated by feelings of distrust on the part of a Latinx family toward a White Anglo clinician. Thus, it is advisable to approach parents with the assumption that they are doing their best, are "the experts" regarding their children, and that you will work with them as part of a team to help their kids. It is also recommended to frame any parent-child difficulties as a result of a parent-child personality mismatch as opposed to anything wrong with the parent.

When I found Juan, I introduced myself, and proceeded to ask him about his car and how he was going about fixing it. I know little to nothing about the working of an internal combustion engine, so I was a good student—and after a little prodding, he was willing to give me a lesson right then and there. At about 20 minutes into the auto repair discussion, I asked him about his son. I told him that I recognized that he was the most important man in his son's life and so, as someone trying to help him, I wanted his input. What did he think would help his son with his current difficulties? What advice would he give to someone who is trying to assist him. Juan had some important insights around rewarding his son's good behavior and also opening lines of communication in the family. However, if he had not responded to these efforts, I would have continued to try other ways such as more meetings under the hood of his car, on the stoop outside of his home, or in the neighborhood bar he frequented (all of which I have done at one time or another with other clients). The point is that as social workers, we understand that clinical work does not take place solely within the parameters of the 50-minute office visit; we must be creative and flexible in our approaches.

Home Visits

From the times of settlement houses and Jane Addams (2007) in the last century, home visits have been a tradition in social work, and one that distinguishes us from other counseling and psychotherapy professions. In keeping with the flexibility and adaptability that are the cornerstones of clinical social work, home visits are one way we are called upon to enact these principles. No social worker should be reluctant to do home visits when indicated. Of course, they need to be feasible. Travel time must be allotted, because a worker cannot see as many clients as they would back-to-back in an office. I once worked in a mental health clinic that encouraged us to start to do home visits but still expected us to do seven sessions in an eight-hour period, which was clearly not workable, at least not without the aid of a Star Trek transporter. So, the conditions and expectations must be right, and if they are, home visits can be worthwhile.

There are many benefits to home visits, among them is the opportunity to observe the client in their natural surroundings (Stinchfield, 2004), and being able to serve clients who have barriers that make it difficult or impossible to attend outpatient psychotherapy (Tate et al., 2014) such as palliative care patients (Rudilla et al., 2016), those who lack transportation and people with mobility issues, such as the elderly or disabled (Cabin, 2010). Students often approach home visits with trepidation and sometimes even refuse to do them. Old timers like myself remember when it was considered blasphemous to even hesitate to do home visits, so forgive us ahead of time if you mention your reluctance to one of your elders only to be met by the scalding heat of our self-righteousness.

Anxiety at the thought of doing a home visit is normal and understandable (Lauka, Remley, & Ward, 2013). The first visit with a client is nerve rattling enough; heading to a stranger's home, not knowing what to expect, but expecting to be helpful is, no doubt, stressful. At least in the office, the environment is under the control of the worker; who knows what one will find in a stranger's home? What if the home is in a dangerous neighborhood and the worker gets lost? What if the family has big dogs, or a dirty, smelly home that is infested with bugs? If you do home visits, you will encounter all of these situations.

Clinician anxiety aside, people are more likely to behave naturally in their own environments and less likely to be on their best behavior as they would in an office setting, thus making assessment more accurate. Seeing where our clients live can help us get a better sense of the strengths and weaknesses of their communities and the obstacles they face in resolving whatever issues for which they are seeking help. Further, as social workers, we commit to address health disparities by either providing, facilitating, or advocating for services for underserved populations. Everyone deserves access to good mental health and the clinical treatment that enables it. Home visits to people who cannot get to a clinic or a private office are one way to provide this.

Nevertheless, you have a right to know what the dangers might be, if any, and how workers keep themselves safe. Home visits involve real risks, and social workers and the agencies that employ them need to be familiar with what they are (Lyter & Abbott, 2007; the National Association of Social Workers, 2020; Spencer & Munch, 2003). Social workers should not be made to feel ashamed for raising these concerns. However, rather than refusing to do home visits, social workers should get sufficient information so they can realistically assess the hazards as well as the protections in place. Here are questions that social workers should seek the answers to as they consider doing home visits:

1 What are the risks of doing home visits in this community?
2 Have any social workers been injured on the job?
3 What are the neighborhoods I will be visiting? How safe or unsafe are they?
4 What do workers do to keep themselves safe?
5 How many home visits are required per day/week? Is there adequate time for transit between visits? Is there reimbursement for gas and/or other travel expenses?

Consider these additional tips for home-visiting social workers:

1 Become very familiar with the neighborhoods you will be visiting. If possible, take a few "field trips" to get a lay of the land before actually seeing clients.
2 Have a well-charged cell phone with you at all times.

3 Know whether the clients you are visiting have engaged in illegal, violent, and/or gang related activity.
4 Stay apprised of activities in the neighborhood. Know if something dangerous has happened in the last 48 hours.
5 Wear comfortable clothing; avoid high heels or anything that can impede mobility.
6 Travel in pairs when feasible.
7 Know what times of the day are safest to visit.

Be open and honest about your fears with your superiors without putting your foot down and outright refusing to do home visits. Rely on your more experienced colleagues for practical guidance as well as how to manage your anxiety. Experienced workers who do home visits will likely have a good idea of the risks and also some additional tips. As an enthusiastic, new social worker, I arrived at my first day of work with a fresh military-style haircut and sporting a tie and a jacket. The agency executive director took one look at me and told me to lose the jacket and tie because, as a White man dressed like that in the neighborhoods where I would be working, I could be mistaken for a police officer or a child protective worker, which in turn would get in the way of engaging the community. He advised me to carry a page of letterhead with the agency name in a place that was visible during my visits. The agency was favorably well-known in the community where there were many adult graduates of its afterschool program. So, once people in these neighborhoods realized where I was from, they would often smile in recognition and start up conversations. At other times, when my coworkers thought they might be going into a dangerous situation, such as a family struggling with domestic violence, we teamed up in twosomes. It is almost a guarantee that experienced workers at agencies doing home visits have similar pieces of practical, sage advice; be sure to ask for it.

Home Visits: An Important Source of Data

During home visits, the information flows right from the start, before the session actually begins. Is the client's home located in a rural, urban, or suburban environment? Can you get a sense of the resources but also the problems in the community? As you first arrive in the neighborhood, note how accessible it is. Is it easy to get around? Is there public transportation like busses and trains? What does the neighborhood look like? Are the homes attractive, well kept, or run down? Does it look like most of the residents are of a certain race, ethnicity, or socioeconomic class? When you pull up to the home or arrive at the apartment, take a good look around. If it is an apartment, the door is the first thing you will see that is a possible source of important information. What is the condition of the door? Is it beat up? Does it look like someone has tried to break in? Is it open? For a house, the front yard will be important. Does it look cared for? If so, be sure to compliment the family. If there is a large growling dog to greet you, what might that communicate about family boundaries and those who approach (stay out!). These details can serve as signals about the family and the way it operates, so use them to form hypotheses that can be proven or refuted as you get to know the clients.

Once inside, compliment the home, with an eye toward client strengths, particularly if they seem hesitant or distrustful. Greet pets (ask first if they are friendly) and notice family photographs. If the home is neat, ask, "How do you keep things so tidy?" If they've planted a nice garden or there are healthy houseplants, recognize that and ask for tips. I have found few things engage reluctant clients more than putting them in an expert role in some manner. Clients and families in trouble enough to seek out services are usually focused on their problems, weaknesses, and vulnerabilities. For sure these things need to be discussed, assessed, and addressed, but the strengths are what you are going to build upon to help them overcome their obstacles, so be sure to inventory them. This goes double for clients and families who are mandated to treatment. Involuntary clients often see the clinical social worker as judge, jury, and executioner, which may be reflected in their level of enthusiasm when first meeting you. They are known to be defensive and may resist letting their guards down sufficiently for you to help them (more on this topic in Chapter 4). Thus, such clients and their families can be surprised and disarmed when the worker takes the time to recognize what they are doing well. I will never forget when a mother involved in the child welfare system relayed to me that I was the first person to tell her she was doing anything right. Compliments thus secured and sealed our therapeutic relationship. Keep this in mind when doing a home visit or any clinical work.

Never appear frightened or disgusted. It is important to engage not only the client but the community that surrounds them. Appearing scared or even mildly repulsed could attract hostile reactions from not only your clients but also neighbors and others who live in the community. Do your internal work by asking yourself the following tough questions: If you are afraid to go into these neighborhoods, how do you feel about the people who live in them? What does your fear say about your social class and your ideas about the class, race, and ethnicity of people in these neighborhoods? Have you lost the ability to see them as people with hopes, dreams, disappointments, and strengths similar to yourself? As social workers, it is certainly uncomfortable to know that you might harbor some racist, sexist, homophobic, and classist ideas. Neutralize this discomfort by giving yourself credit for being willing to uncover, examine, and change them. If you do not bring these biases to the surface of your awareness, you risk acting upon them unconsciously, which of course you want to avoid.

During home visits, you must learn to take charge, more so than if you are seeing clients in your office, which may require a change of mindset. You might have been raised not to be too bossy or pushy when visiting someone's home, but to be polite and complimentary. If so, your parents have done a good job teaching you manners. This is also a good way to start your home visit. However, you need to modify some of these ideas if you are going to be effective. In doing a home-based assessment or home-based therapy, you are entering a stranger's home with the task of taking some control over the environment and asking a lot of personal questions. Make it a part of your practice to set some boundaries by asking for the television to be off and for phones to be out of sight. I typically confess to clients that I am so distracted by television programs and phones, I am unable to concentrate on anything else when they are on or being used, and I really want to stay focused on helping them. As a result, they virtually always comply.

Food and Gifts

I know there are some social work instructors who say that if you are offered something from a client, never accept it. However, such a rule, if applied rigidly and uniformly, could actually be destructive. I'll never forget the reaction from an Italian American client when I declined lunch during a home visit: "What?! You are afraid to eat or drink from our table? Are we not good enough for you?" Quickly, I realized that the advice I received in social work school could not be uniformly applied in every situation. An offer of food may be a culturally-based way of engaging you (Stinchfield, 2004). So, unless your dietary restrictions prohibit it, by all means, accept the food, even if it is just a small amount to taste. Remember, as clinical social workers, thoughtful flexibility should be the norm. On a related note, it is usually ok to ask to use the client's bathroom if you must or to request a glass of water.

There are two possible pitfalls related to this topic. The first is if you go to the home expecting to be fed or asking for food which of course is a no go. Keep in mind that due to the power differential, clients might feel vulnerable and fear refusing you or doing anything that might displease you. This goes double if the client is mandated into treatment. Clients may not feel they have the freedom to refuse your request, whether that be for food, gifts, money, or sex. So, this must be kept in mind. Power must be recognized and used only in the service of the work, such as asking a family to gather without distractions for the duration of the visit. Second, extra caution must be taken when accepting food or anything from a client who is mandated to receive your services. The worker must determine whether the offer of food is out of hospitality, generosity, or a bribe. Whenever accepting something from a client, closely observe what happens to your relationship after you do so, to confirm whether you have made the right decision, and certainly go over this issue in supervision.

Important Others in Attendance

Sometimes I have shown up for a home visit to do family therapy and there were people present whom I did not expect. Early in my career, as a newly-minted family therapist, I was strict about only having *official* (nuclear) family members in the session. In my early career this was how I was trained. However, I quickly realized that if other people were in the house during a planned visit, such as neighbors, friends, or extended family members, that they were likely to be resources for the family. So, after asking my client or client guardian for permission to have them formally join us, I introduce myself, shake hands and ask them their names and their relationships to the other people there. Following these introductions, I then ask for their perspectives and advice. I find engaging these contacts extremely helpful, not only because it is a way to show respect for the family but also because invariably, they provide valuable insights about the client. African American families often rely upon strong relationships with extended members as well as non-blood "kin" for support and to assist them when problems present themselves (Boyd-Franklin, 2003), so including such persons might be culturally appropriate. As a clinical social worker, overlooking this potential assistance is unnecessarily wasteful. Instead, see these people as accurate observers, helpers, or even co-therapists because of the information they provide.

Client Resilience

Of course, a clinical social worker must assess for emotional, mental, or behavioral disorders. We seek to understand the various traumas our clients have faced, particularly those who have experienced poverty, racism, homophobia, child abuse, or any other stressor. There are theories that such trauma can actually alter our neurobiology (Courtois & Ford, 2009). However, trauma is only part of the story. We must also be students of resilience. What did or does the client do to cope with hardships and get through them?

Two popular approaches that capitalize on client strengths and resilience and developed by clinical social workers are solution-focused therapy originated by Insoo Kim Berg and Steve De Shazer (De Jong & Berg, 2012) and the strength-based approach developed by Dennis Saleeby (2006). What they have in common is the need for social workers to actively search for what clients are doing right, and, more specifically, what they have done previously to overcome obstacles. For sure, as part of our assessment, we must always ask about the negative, traumatic, and stressful things that have happened in our clients' lives. However, we also need to inventory clients' resources, both internal and external. A wise way to balance this is, even if you and your client speak almost the entire session about difficulties, be sure to not let the session end without asking the questions: "How do you cope? How did you survive?" When you do this, you will be surprised by their coping mechanisms.

When I worked at a mental health clinic, a single mother, employed full-time came in complaining that she was unable to get her four-year-old daughter to do any of the things she needed to do to prepare for bed. She put up a fuss at dinnertime, during her bath, when it came to brushing her teeth, and actually getting into bed. During the first two visits, I did a full psychosocial assessment, as was the requirement of the mental health clinic where I worked. At the beginning of the third session, she reported that her daughter's behavior had markedly improved. Perplexed, I asked her what she had done differently with her daughter. She responded by describing how she accidentally discovered that if she were to spend 15 minutes of uninterrupted quality time with her, sitting on the floor and engaging in conversation of her daughter's choice over dolls, or blocks, it made a difference in her daughter's level of cooperation during the evening. This resourceful mother came upon a solution that addressed her daughter's need for her mother's undivided attention after a day of school and day care. I, of course, praised the mother effusively for coming up with her own solution (the best type of solution there is) and for also teaching me something about caring for a child.

When I recently asked an African American client in her fifties who suffered from fibromyalgia what helped her cope with her pain, she replied with a single word: prayer. Exploring this further, she believed that God gave her the strength to cope. Her prayer group also gave her support and offered additional prayers on her behalf that she found helpful. During a group session for men who perpetrated domestic violence, when asked what tools they used when they were angry and actually avoided becoming violent, they described calming and reassuring self-talk: "Don't let this get to you; in the end it doesn't matter." "You don't want to lose this job so calm down." "Take a deep breath and try to relax." What they were doing would fit squarely into a cognitive behavioral textbook (Beck, 2020), despite never having been formerly exposed to this model. The strengths that clients report to us can be what we build upon when we get them to address and resolve their issues. So, commit yourself to becoming a student of strengths and search for them everywhere, in your clients, your agency, among your coworkers and colleagues, and most of all in yourself.

Advocacy and Case Management: Important Components of Clinical Social Work

As clinical social workers, we must stay abreast of the available services in our area and connect our clients to them. We are also expected to coordinate services and occasional case conferences. Generally, the more oppressed, troubled, or marginalized the client population, the more case management is necessary. For example, if you work in a public children's mental health clinic, you may find yourself needing to communicate and coordinate services with the child's teacher, school psychologist, school social worker, child welfare worker, parent's substance abuse counselor, and the child's probation officer. You might be a child's therapist, however one or both of the parents may have a therapist and there might be a family and/or a couples' therapist as well. When working with a client on parole, that client might have to see their parole officer and possibly a substance abuse counselor. If these services are not carefully coordinated, conflict over turf issues and splitting, or unhealthy conflictual relationships between the client and other helpers, can result. Thus regular, ongoing communication and updates (pending signed release of information forms from clients) are essential. We not only develop strong relationships with our clients, we are called upon to do so with other helpers as well, in the service of helping the people we serve.

Of course, psychotherapy will not help at all if a client is hungry, anxious about eviction, or dealing with violence in the family, workplace, or community. If a child is being bullied in school for being gay or transgender, no amount of therapy is going to help until the bullying stops. As I have written elsewhere (LaSala, 2006), in the event of bullying it may be necessary to go to the school and advocate on the child's behalf. It may also be important to ask for or initiate some change in the bullying environment of the school. Environmental interventions must always be considered, particularly when working with clients from oppressed groups.

Working with Other Professionals

When professional relationships go awry, it is often because the social worker's expectations of other agency professionals may be too high, or that they lack the same empathy for their colleagues that they have for their clients. Most, if not all of the professionals, paraprofessionals, and administrative staff with whom clinical social workers interact are well-meaning people who entered their respective fields with the noble intention to help others. However, they are frequently overworked, underpaid, flummoxed by nonsensical bureaucracies, and overwhelmed by the depth and enormity of client needs. Frustrated clinical social workers start to think and talk using a lot of *shoulds* as in, "this probation officer *should* call me back in a timely manner"; "this case manager *should* provide this service to my client"; "this teacher *should* treat my client better" and so on. When I have felt this way, I eventually found myself wondering if I was looking for a suitable scapegoat for my frustrations with my difficult clients. Either way, when we *should* in this way, empathy and the desire to understand flies out the window—a big problem considering that empathy is critically important in establishing good working relationships with these professionals. When dealing with these frustrating events, it is time to take a deep breath, and, in Larry Shulman's parlance, "tune in" to the worker and their experience (Shulman, 2015), and use empathy to plan ways to approach other workers. We all have bad days when the work gets to us and/or we are dealing with personal issues that temporarily leave us with less emotional bandwidth for our professional relationships. Doing social work during Covid times can be even more stressful (see Chapter 10). It is at these times, when you need to pause, close your eyes, take a deep breath, and another, and another, and get a pulse on what is happening inside. Is it time to take a break, even if it is just for a short while? Do you need a walk? A day off? A vacation? Sometimes a good supervision session or continuing education class that teaches us new skills can energize us and replenish our batteries. What kind of self-care do you need now and are you able to get it? Remember, when the oxygen masks come down on the plane, you must put the mask on yourself first before assisting others with theirs.

Once you have done your self-care, try to remember what those stressful times were like and think about how you would have liked to have been approached, then proceed accordingly. A snarky email or voice mail message that could be subtitled "That's showing 'em!" would certainly feel good, but will not likely get the result you want for your client. Instead, start out with something like: "I am guessing you're swamped at the moment—been there done that, but when you get out of the weeds, please call me about this client as it is quite important." Once you make contact, it might be a good idea to start out with: "Things are crazy these days, no?" The moral of the story here is for the clinical social worker to treat "the system" and everyone in it with the same skills as you would a client. Is this fair or just? Doesn't the colleague who fails to call you back, or worse yet, is hostile, deserves firing, discipline, or at least a nasty-gram response? Probably—but, as in any relationship, sometimes you can either be right, or effective. On these occasions, both are not possible. The idea is to always seek to lower the reactivity and emotional volume in these circumstances so that, in the end, the clients get the best help we can give them.

References

Addams, J. (2007). *Hull-house Maps and Papers: A Presentation of Nationalities and Wages in a Congested District of Chicago, Together with Comments and Essays on Problems Growing Out of the Social Conditions*. University of Illinois Press.

American Board of Clinical Examiners in Social Work (ABCESW) (2020). What is clinical social work?www.abcsw.org/what-is-clinical-social-work.

Beck, J. (2020). *Cognitive Therapy: Basics and Beyond* (3rd ed.). Guilford Press.

Boyd-Franklin, N. (2003). *Black Families in Therapy: Understanding the African American Experience* (2nd ed.). Guilford Press.

Cabin, W. D. (2010). Lifting the home care veil from depression: OASIS-C and evidence-based practice. *Home Health Care Management & Practice*, 22(3), 171–177. doi:10.1177%2F1084822309348693.

Centers for Disease Control (CDC) (2017). Leading Causes of Death—Males—Non-Hispanic-black—United States, 2017. www.cdc.gov/healthequity/lcod/men/2017/nonhispanic-black/index.htm.

Courtois, C. A., & Ford, J. D. (Eds.). (2009). *Treating Complex Traumatic Stress Disorders: An Evidence-based Guide*. Guilford Press.

De Jong, P., & Berg, I. K. (2012). *Interviewing for Solutions* (4th ed.). Nelson Education.

Goldstein, E. G. (2007). Social work education and clinical learning: Yesterday, today, and tomorrow. *Clinical Social Work Journal*, 35(1), 15–23. doi:10.1007/s10615-006-0067-z.

Gramlich, J. (2020). Black imprisonment rate in the U.S. has fallen by a third since 2006. Pew Research Center. www.pewresearch.org/fact-tank/2020/05/06/share-of-black-white-hispanic-americans-in-prison-2018-vs-2006/

Killian, C., & Khanna, N. (2019). Beyond color-blind and color-conscious: Approaches to racial socialization among parents of transracially adopted children. *Family Relations*, 68(2), 260–274. doi:10.1111/fare.12357.

Kumar, M. (2012). The poverty in psychoanalysis: "Poverty" of psychoanalysis? *Psychology and Developing Societies*, 24(1), 1–34. doi:10.1007/978-3-319-25718-1_4.

Kutchins, H., & Kirk, S. A. (1988). The business of diagnosis: DSM-III and clinical social work. *Social Work*, 33(3), 215–220. doi:10.1093/sw/33.3.215.

LaSala, M. C. (2006). Cognitive and environmental interventions for gay males: Addressing stigma and its consequences. *Families in Society: The Journal of Contemporary Human Services*, 87(2), 181–189. doi:10.1606%2F1044-3894.3511.

Lauka, J. D., Remley, T. P., & Ward, C. (2013). Attitudes of counselors regarding ethical situations encountered by in-home counselors. *The Family Journal*, 21(2), 129–135. doi:10.1177%2F1066480712465822

Lieberman, F. (1987). Psychotherapy and the clinical social worker. *American Journal of Psychotherapy*, 41(3), 369–383. doi:10.1176/appi.psychotherapy.1987.41.3.369.

Lyter, S. C., & Abbott, A. A. (2007). Home visits in a violent world. *The Clinical Supervisor*, 26(1–2), 17–33. doi:10.1300/J001v26n01_03.

Maschi, T., Baer, J., & Turner, S. G. (2011). The psychological goods on clinical social work: A content analysis of the clinical social work and social justice literature. *Journal of Social Work Practice*, 25(02), 233–253. doi:10.1080/02650533.2010.544847.

McLendon, T. (2010). *Understanding Social Workers' Experiences Utilizing the Diagnostic and Statistical Manual with Children: A Qualitative Inquiry* (Doctoral dissertation, University of Kansas).

Minuchin, S. (1967). *Families of the Slums: An Exploration of Their Structure and Treatment*. Basic Books.

Morris, A. S., Jespersen, J. E., Cosgrove, K. T., Ratliff, E. L., & Kerr, K. L. (2020). Parent education: What we know and moving forward for greatest impact. *Family Relations*, 69(3), 520–542. doi:10.1111/fare.12442.

National Association of Social Workers (NASW) (nd). Clinical social work. www.socialworkers.org/Practice/Clinical-Social-Work.

National Association of Social Workers (NASW) (2005). *NASW Standards for Clinical Social Work in Social Work Practice*. Author. www.socialworkers.org/LinkClick.aspx?fileticket=YOg4qdefLBE%3d&portalid=0.

National Association of Social Workers (NSAW) (2020). *Guidelines to Social Work Safety in the Workplace.* Washington DC. www.socialworkers.org/LinkClick.aspx?fileticket=6OEdoMjcNC0%3d&portalid=0.

New Jersey Division of Consumer Affairs (2019). State board of social work examiners Frequently Asked Questions www.njconsumeraffairs.gov/sw/Pages/FAQ.aspx.

New York State Office of the Professions (2018). LCSW license requirements. www.op.nysed.gov/prof/sw/article154.htm.

Pan, W., & Bai, H. (2009). A multivariate approach to a meta-analytic review of the effectiveness of the DARE program. *International Journal of Environmental Research and Public Health,* 6(1), 267–277. doi:10.3390/ijerph6010267.

Parke, R. D., & Cookston, J. T. (2019). Advancing research and measurement on fathering and child development: Commentary: Many types of fathers, many types of contexts: An agenda for future progress in fathering research. *Monographs of the Society for Research in Child Development,* 84(1), 132–146.

Richmond, M. (1956), *What is Social Casework? An Introductory Description.* Russell Sage Foundation.

Rudilla, D., Galiana, L., Oliver, A., & Barreto, P. (2016). Comparing counseling and dignity therapies in home care patients: A pilot study. *Palliative & Supportive Care,* 14(4), 321–329. doi:10.1017/S1478951515001182.

Saleeby, D. (2006). *The Strengths Perspective in Social Work Practice* (4th ed). Pearson.

Shulman, L. (2015). *Empowerment Series: The Skills of Helping Individuals, Families, Groups, and Communities, Enhanced.* Cengage Learning.

Slater, E. L. (2020). Private Practice Social Workers' Commitment to Social Justice. *Clinical Social Work Journal* 2(48), 1–9. doi:10.1007/s10615-020-00746-z.

Specht, H., & Courtney, M. E. (1994). *Unfaithful Angels: How Social Work Has Abandoned its Mission.* Simon and Schuster.

Spencer, P. & Munch, S. (2003). Client violence toward social workers: The role of management in community mental health programs. *Social Work,* 48(4), 532–544. doi:10.1093/sw/48.4.532.

Stinchfield, T. A. (2004). Clinical competencies specific to family-based therapy. *Counselor Education and Supervision,* 43(4), 286–300. doi:10.1002/j.1556-6978.2004.tb01853.x.

Substance Abuse and Mental Health Services Administration (SAMSHA) (2013). *Behavioral health, United States, 2012.* Department of Health and Human Services Publication No. SMA 13-4797. https://store.samhsa.gov/product/Behavioral-Health-United-States-2012/SMA13-4797.

Szapocznik, J., & Hervis, O. E. (2020). *Brief Strategic Family Therapy.* American Psychological Association.

Tate, K. A., Lopez, C., Fox, R., Love, J. R., & McKinney, E. (2014). In-home counseling for young children living in poverty: An exploration of counseling competencies. *The Family Journal,* 22(4), 371–381. doi:10.1177%2F1066480714530268.

Thyer, B. A. (2017). Social learning theory and social work treatment. In F. J. Turner (Ed.) *Social Work Treatment: Interlocking Theoretical Approaches* (6th ed., pp. 471–480). Oxford University Press.

Urry, A. (2018). The struggle towards a feminist practice in family therapy: Premises. In R. J. Perelberg, & A. C. Miller, (Eds.) *Gender and Power in Families* (pp. 104–117). Routledge.

Wakefield, J. C. (1998) Psychotherapy, distributive justice, and social work revisited. *Smith College Studies in Social Work*, 69(1), 25–57. doi:10.1080/00377319809517542.

Walters, M., Carter, B., Papp, P., & Silverstein, O. (1988). *The Invisible Web: Gender Patterns in Family Relationships*. Guilford Press.

Chapter 3

Tips for Getting Started

As an MSW student or a beginning social worker, you are starting a new chapter. You might feel relief, excitement, as well as a sense of homecoming as you begin studying the things you have always cared about. However, if you are like most students, as you get started and the first week of field approaches, excitement gives way to fear, even terror. As discussed in Chapter 1, social workers may have a natural predisposition for anxiety. When you actually consider the grave responsibility you are taking on, the anxiety increases exponentially. Things are about to become real; people are going to trust you with their most painful problems, and you have signed on to help them. Even if you have some previous experience as a helper, by pursuing your MSW and beginning a career in clinical social work, you are now called to help clients on a deeper level. Is it no wonder you are anxious?

Your First Day

It is the morning of your first day of field or on the job. Your anxiety/excitement/dread (can you tell the difference? Is there a difference?) kept you up last night or perhaps woke you up early. Now that it's time to get ready, decisions must be made. When we are nervous, it helps to feel one has decision-making control. So, let's start with the easy, practical stuff first.

"What Do I Wear?"

What is the right outfit for the first day? You understandably want to make a good impression on your supervisor, colleagues, and clients as you begin to establish professional and clinical relationships, and appearances matter. What you are wearing communicates important messages about yourself and how seriously you take this responsibility. Initial impressions tend to last, so you want to get that first sartorial choice right.

The image you want to portray is that of enthusiastic professionalism, so initially dress in a way that leans conservative. If you err, it is best to do so

DOI: 10.4324/9781003011712-3

on the side of formality. As a matter of fact, initially overdressing is forgivable. I once interviewed for a job during a freak heatwave in early April in the northeastern United States. I was wearing a wool suit and the institution's air conditioning had yet to be switched on. Halfway through our meeting, the search committee chair exclaimed in exasperation, "Ok, we get that you know how to dress for an interview. Now please take off your jacket and tie because you are making us hot just by looking at you!" The point is to start more formally, and adjust down if needed.

Keep in mind, a blazer or suit jacket invariably communicates professionalism, whether it is over a dress, blouse, slacks, or open-collared shirt. As for ties, if the other men (or male-identifying people) in the agency are wearing them, then you should as well; it is still a good idea for the job interview. Avoid revealing clothing, such as low-cut blouses, tight clothes, or short skirts; this is not the time to reveal your décolletage or show off your progress at the gym no matter how impressive. No worn or ripped jeans on the first day, and remove or hide body jewelry like nose or eyebrow rings, and conceal large tattoos. You should look clean and well-groomed. Supervisors and employers appreciate it when people come dressed up, at least at first, as it telegraphs respect for the job. That said, once you are in the position, ascribe to the old adage, "dress for the job you want" by mimicking the look of someone at the level to which you aspire.

Sometimes social workers are in positions where they need to communicate authority, such as during court appearances, when advocating for a client during a case conference, or discussing misbehavior and applying disciplinary consequences with an adolescent at a childcare institution. Sometimes in these settings, social workers are not taken seriously and accorded the respect they deserve. However, there are ways to correct this. Clothing can be a symbol of power. If you are in a situation where you need to exert your expertise, the blazer and briefcase signal authority. Students, particularly if they are young looking, are women, or are members of oppressed minority groups, can use these props to neutralize any unfortunate (and undeserved) impressions that they are not serious professionals. I once supervised a female MSW student who went to a school meeting to advocate for educational supports for one of her young clients. The male principal, who did not want to expend the requested resources, called her "Honey" and "Sweetie" several times during the meeting and ignored what she was saying. During a subsequent meeting, she wore a blazer, carried a briefcase, and wore her long hair tied up. In response to his first "Honey," she firmly but politely asked the principle to call her by her name. She also began to learn how to interrupt others, particularly men, who interrupted *her* when she spoke. Similar issues are faced by professionals of color who might get talked over or ignored at important meetings; civil but direct verbal ways of addressing them are also recommended. "Bob, I would really prefer you to use my name rather than 'buddy' as I find it more professional. Thanks for understanding." Or, when interrupted, a firm but polite, "Excuse me, hold on, I believe I was speaking. Thank you" is in order. Some people have an easier time doing this one-on-one with the offender and not in front of others at a meeting, which is fine. For sure, none of this is fair. People should be judged on their merits, not on how they appear, nor their gender, race, or ethnicity, or how they dress. Such a burden *should not* fall to the student or the beginner, but until society gets to that consciousness, these recommendations will help you procure and maintain the respect you deserve.

If these tips and the ones that follow leave you feeling more confused, or clash with what you have been told by others, you might now feel terrified you will make (or have already made) a mistake. Here is some advice that always come in handy. Remind yourself that you are new at this and you are learning. Do your best and know there will likely never be a more forgivable time than at the beginning of your career to make mistakes. Coming to field or work in the wrong outfit on the first day is unfortunate but fixable. If you notice everyone is in jeans and T-shirts, then that is how you dress for the next day. If you under-dress on the first day, but dress up on the second, people will notice and appreciate that you got the message. Further, ask your boss and colleagues for advice; most of the people you will work with will be helpers who, of course, love helping others. As a matter of fact, asking for advice, learning from mistakes, and correcting them as you go along is going to be a career-long endeavor that will strengthen your skills and help your clients. When your colleagues and superiors see self-correcting so early in your professional development, their hearts will be warmed.

I Have an Intake on Monday and I Don't Know What to Say!

If this describes you, know that you are not alone as this is a common concern for beginners. Of course, anxiety about this makes sense. You entered this field because you want to devote your professional life to helping others and making the world a better place. You are nervous because you care so deeply about what you are about to do. For sure, what comes with this noble cause is the realization of its burden. Many of the problems you run across will be quite serious—so of course, you are nervous.

However, when we feel anxious, we want a sense of control—so we can feel fully prepared for whatever comes our way. Clients are coming to us with difficult, complicated problems that they want us to resolve (which, as you will learn, we will not do). This is why instead of wondering what to say, the new clinician needs to work on *how to be*. For sure, the self of the social worker is the primary tool, and communication is how it is deployed. What may be initially difficult to understand is that the words spoken, in and of themselves, are not what are most important. In this work, you are called upon, particularly in your first sessions, to be warm, empathic, genuine, authentic, and, above all, a good listener. *Become* or *inhabit* these characteristics in your daily life and you will be able to manifest them with your clients.

In this work it is imperative not to underestimate the essential importance of providing a listening presence. We know that the most important aspects of psychotherapy, even beyond technique is the *relationship* which is a theme of this book and will be explored more thoroughly in the next chapter. For now, begin to think about this as you prepare for your first client meeting.

Find a Space for Reflection

Before meeting with that first client, find a quiet space to look over any intake information you get in advance. All good healers must first picture what it is like to be the person they are meant to help heal. See if you can imagine what it is like to be the client coming to their first session, putting yourself in their shoes. For example, if you are about to see the spouse of someone with dementia, try to imagine what that would feel like and what their concerns might be. Perhaps you would be anxious about the future, you might feel a sense of both current and impending loss. If you were suffering from panic attacks, you might perceive that your body or your mind were spinning out of control. If you have trouble doing this, think about times in the past when you have experienced a similar problem, even if in a milder form. For example, if preparing to see a depressed client, recall a time when you have felt depressed or even very sad. Take a moment to really feel what your client might be feeling and think about how you can communicate to them in a way that demonstrates an understanding of what they are going through, along with the kinds of support they might need. This is an effective way to prepare to empathize with your future client.

Set Up the Space

As you prepare the session, make sure there will be nothing, no furniture, in the physical space between you and your client. I groan when I see Hollywood portrayals of therapists where there is a coffee table between the client and the therapist—or a therapist at a desk with the client sitting on the other side. Such furniture placement could impede engagement; a coffee table suggests that you are in a living room, which is not sufficiently professional, and a desk makes it seem as if the client is being called to meet with a superior. Unlike movie and television portrayals, clients *never* walk around the office while talking, and would it not be unnerving if they did? The clinician and the client share an exchange of energy and so nothing should interfere with that. Lean forward in your chair to show interest, but not too close that they feel intruded upon. Take your cue from your client's body language; if the client backs away then you should also. Generally, 3–6 feet is a good range of distance. During Covid times, you and your clients might prefer the longer end of this range.

Sitting

Adjust your seat and posture so that your eyes are level with those of the client. Because, like clinical social workers, clients come in a variety of shapes and sizes, you may have to lower or raise your seat, or lean forward to lower your upper body sufficiently to have your eyes level with those of your clients. For tall folks, this might mean bending forward until you find that sweet spot. Social work students and new social workers are inherently good listeners, so you might find that you do this naturally. Some therapists see how their client is sitting and purposely adjust their body position to match that of their clients as a way to indirectly communicate connection. You also might find that your body language mimics that of your client without you giving it much thought. Good news, as this is a demonstration of being in sync with your client and that you are developing that all-important clinical relationship.

Engage

If you are seeking to become a clinical social worker, chances are you already have good engagement skills, and when considering your first meeting with your clients, it is just a matter of reprising them. For example, when you are meeting someone new, how do you usually interact with them? Chances are you greet them warmly, shake hands, and maintain eye contact. These same skills are effective during the initial clinical encounter. Whenever meeting a person for the first time, whether it is in a social or professional setting, a good way to break the ice is to comment on the environment you both share. If you are meeting your client in your office, you are experiencing the same weather, parking situation, or traffic, all of which can be referred to as you get started:

CLINICIAN: Did you have any trouble finding our offices?
CLIENT: No, the directions were good.
CLINICIAN: OK good. How is the weather? Is it still raining out there?
CLIENT: Yes, though it is slowing down.

If you are seeing your client remotely, you can ask about weather or anything else related to their location. As in a social relationship, small talk begins to break the ice and put the client at ease.

CLINICIAN: (online) I can see on the screen that you have some interesting pictures on the wall behind you. Can you tell me about them?

Then you can transition into offering a compliment. For example, when greeting an adolescent for the first time, "Hey, cool T-shirt," or a client during a home visit, "How do you keep the place so tidy," or, "Like you, I really like family photos. These are great. Tell me about these people."

More on Compliments

Any client who shows up is someone with the courage to be vulnerable and reach out for help. They have other strengths too, and it is your job to find them. Calling our clients' attention to their own strengths helps us build clinical relationships, aids in ameliorating their hopelessness, and increases their motivation. So, throughout therapy and definitely in the first session, get in the habit of uncovering strengths in your client and pointing them out. You could start by asking what they are good at, or compliment something they are wearing, like an interesting piece of jewelry or a flashy pair of sneakers. If you are having trouble identifying strengths in your client, remember, the act of seeking help is praiseworthy. If they are voluntary, praise them for knowing things could be better and having the desire to make them so. After making sure the client knows you understand their problems, ask them about how they are managing to cope. It is also advisable to ask what is going well in their lives that they would like to see continue. Even a client who is mandated into psychotherapy against their will can be praised for doing what it takes to stay out of trouble. That said, it is vital that compliments be grounded in truth. If they are not, the clinician runs the risk of seeming inauthentic and therefore untrustworthy. If during a home visit, you find the home is not so tidy, or during the first office session, the T-shirt is not that interesting, do not fake it. There will be opportunities once the session gets underway. Anxiety can fuel the excessive desire to please a client which can manifest in the overuse of compliments that are empty, insincere, and thus ineffective. Consider the following example:

SOCIAL WORKER: What are your favorite subjects?
ADOLESCENT CLIENT: Math and art.
SOCIAL WORKER: So, you're good in math; that's great! How are you getting along in school?
CLIENT: Ok.
SOCIAL WORKER: Really, that's wonderful!

But, is it wonderful? *Really?* Compliments like this can come across as phony, particularly to an adolescent, especially if you have no evidence that they are true. Solution-focused therapists like Insoo Kim Berg (De Jong & Berg, 2012) have mastered the art of the compliment whereby they attach them to a skill or asset that the client has demonstrated. The clinician must name that skill and compliment it accordingly.

CLINICIAN: Tell me what do you like about math?
CLIENT: Well, I'm really good at it. I got 100 on a quiz last week.
CLINICIAN: Wow, a lot of people struggle with math, including myself. How did you manage to become good at it?
CLIENT: I pay attention a lot in class. I think it is interesting.
CLINICIAN: So, you've figured out that if you like something and really focus on it, you can succeed. That's really an important lesson you've learned; not everyone gets that, especially at your age.

From this example, you can see that questions such as: "How do you manage?" "How did you figure that out?" or "How did you accomplish that?" can be compliments in and of themselves.

A note of caution, do not comment on clients' bodies, as this can seem intrusive or misconstrued as sexual. If a client is wearing something revealing or sexy, avoid complimenting that as well. A guiding rule is to make the compliment authentic but not in any way seductive or flirty. Compliments are used throughout therapy and are described throughout this volume, but particularly in more depth in the next chapter.

Goal Setting

Once the casual talk is over and you have some identifying information (or completed your required forms), avoid questions like, "How can I help you?" Such a question seems standard and innocuous, but it incorrectly suggests that *you* are going to take on the responsibility of helping the client get better. In reality, the bulk of the work is going to need to come from the client. So, a better way to start is: "People come to see me because they want to change something in their lives; what is it *you* want to change?" This communicates to the client that the onus will be on *them*. If you are working in a child welfare setting, a parent whose child was removed might respond, "I want my kids home" and such children would likely say, "I want to go home." A man who is separated from his wife might say, "I want my wife back." A depressed person might reply, "I want to feel better." Along the same lines, ask your client "What would make our first meeting worthwhile? What needs to happen that would lead you to say, 'Yes, this was the right thing to do?'" Because you want to know as much as possible about the client's problems, try asking: "What have you tried already to solve this problem? Did anything work, even a little bit?" This might prevent you from making a suggestion that simply reinvents the wheel. It also might give you a clue as to the client's problem-solving skills. You can use the answers to these questions to generate goals. (Goal setting is described in more depth in Chapter 4.) Finally, at the end of your session, ask: "What was that like for you? What do you wish went better? What was most helpful?"

These questions should get you through the first session. A sign that your session is going well is if the client is talking, and most importantly, talking more than you. If you ask a question, and the client begins to unload in multiple, uninterrupted sentences, you are asking the right questions and the formation of the clinical relationship is well underway. Once they get started, sit back, do not interrupt. Do not worry about fixing anything, especially right away. The client unloading their issues during the first session is an important initial step and is healing in and of itself.

"Do you have children?" The issue of therapist matching

Here is a trigger for anxiety (as if you need another). Imagine that you are a newly graduated, 25-year-old social worker meeting with a parent of two adolescents to discuss their misbehavior. You have no children and have not yet had a chance to be in a long-term relationship. Or picture yourself meeting with someone from a different ethnic or racial identity than your own. Perhaps you are heterosexual and are about to work with a lesbian couple. The questions: "Do you have children?" from a client who is a parent, "Are you gay?" from a lesbian client, or "Are you in recovery?" from a client struggling with substance abuse can strike at the heart of a new worker's insecurity, leading to painful self-doubts: "Because we are so different, maybe I cannot help them!" How similar do you have to be to assist a client? Do you need to be from the same demographic or having experienced the same problems to be able to help them? The answer is no. However, courage, thoughtfulness, and sensitivity are required.

The first step is to recognize and acknowledge the anxiety and to understand that one does not have to experience the same stresses and strains of a client in order to help them. The second is to recognize that this question reflects client anxiety. The worker has to be careful not to let their own nervousness obscure the clients' real plea which is, "I need your help. Can I trust you? Will you be able to help me?" These pleas need to be kept in mind as you develop your response:

CLIENT: You look so young; do you have children?
CLINICIAN: No, I don't. What makes you ask?
CLIENT: Oh, nothing; never mind.

A beginning therapist might have just let this go while thinking, "Phew, I'm off the hook." The question reflects the client's anxiety about whether or not she is sufficiently competent to help the client. Thus, it is too scary for the beginner who is secretly wondering this about themselves and, therefore, they believe it might be better to just ignore it. Such a question is an important opportunity for engagement. If the clinician does not grab this opportunity, they are overlooking the client's worries in the service of their own anxiety and thus will have lost the chance to begin an authentic and meaningful therapeutic relationship. It is important for the clinician to take a deep breath, realize this has nothing to do with their competence but is more about the client's vulnerabilities and concerns.

CLINICIAN: No, I do not have children. But tell me, do you have concerns about me not being a parent and therefore being unable to help you?

(Side note: For the therapist to be able to ask this, they need to be aware of and okay with *their own* concerns about not being a parent.)

CLIENT: Well, yes, a little. How will you know how to help me with my kids if you've never been a parent yourself?
CLINICIAN: That's an important question and I am glad you are asking it. You are wondering and worried as to whether I can really help you, particularly because I have not had the experience of being a parent. That sounds understandable. What are your concerns? What might I miss?
CLIENT: Perhaps the stress of raising kids, not knowing if you are doing the right thing, fear of making a mistake; that sort of thing.
CLINICIAN: Thank you for your honesty on this. It's hard to get started with a new person and it is reasonable to wonder if you can trust me to help you with these problems. However, I would really like to give it a try. I have quite a bit of training in child development and my supervisor, with whom I consult quite a bit, is a parent. But if I miss something or there is something I don't seem to understand, let me know so we can discuss it. Are you willing to give this a try?
CLIENT: Yes, ok.

It is important to remember that some clients feel especially vulnerable, particularly in the beginning, and will not want to challenge the clinician. So, it is essential for the clinician to follow up when the client hints at such concerns. Obviously, the worker cannot conjure parenthood or any other unique experience of the client. However, note how the worker not only responds to the question, but acknowledges and validates what the likely concerns are, namely that the worker will not understand her challenges and therefore not be able to help her. By naming these worries, the therapist validates them and this goes a long way in forging the relationship necessary for healing.

By the way, clients who seek a match in their therapist are almost invariably disappointed. When I was beginning my career and working with children and families, I nervously raised the children issue with my colleagues, many of whom were parents. They shared with me the following "typical" vignette:

CLIENT: Do you have children?
SOCIAL WORKER: Yes.
CLIENT: Well, I'm sure you don't have as many as I do.
SOCIAL WORKER: No, I have 3, just like you.
CLIENT: Well, I bet they are not adolescents.
SOCIAL WORKER: They *are*; 13, 16, and 19.
CLIENT: Well, I'll bet they are not as difficult as *my adolescents*.

No two people's experiences are exactly the same, no matter how similar they appear on the surface. If you share certain similarities with your client, this could help you get a leg up on engaging them. However, sooner or later, you must ferret out and address the uniqueness of your client, how they are different from you and everyone else. Once the client senses you understand, they will be willing to trust you.

If possible, it is also a good idea to offer an escape clause. This takes the pressure off of both the client and the clinician and also honors client self-determination, an important ethical principle.

CLINICIAN: Of course, we have had and are going to have different experiences. I know you are concerned that I might not be able to help you or even understand you if I do not fully share yours. So, let's make an agreement, that when you feel I am not getting something, you let me know right away so we can address it. Ok? If we both find that this isn't working, I can help you find another social worker.

As always, when a client asks or does something that engenders anxiety or self-doubt in the worker, it is important to acknowledge and attend to it, but to then refocus on what this says about the client's concerns. In these situations, it is the job of the clinician to address their own anxiety sufficiently to put their client's concerns front and center.

You Are the Instrument: Know Who You Are

As you develop professionally, it is important to maintain an ongoing understanding of your own unique characteristics and qualities. Start with what you bring with you when a client first sees you. A man, particularly a large man is going to be advantaged in a situation that requires authority, such as getting a child to behave properly or advocating for a client during a meeting. Sexism is likely rearing its head here but there is an impression that women are softer, and more understanding. Though the research is equivocal on this matter (Black & Gringart, 2019), I have noted that both women and men believe they will be more comfortable with women psychotherapists due to what is perceived as their *natural* nurturant qualities. This may or may not be true but that is the impression clients have and it is important to be aware of it.

If you are young, older clients may doubt your abilities, or might initially feel embarrassed that they have to ask for help from someone who is clearly behind them in age. However, if you properly engage these clients, such doubts will diminish. Youth can be an advantage when working with children and adolescents as parents and kids themselves may believe it is easier to bond with a younger therapist. Conversely, age can also be an advantage. I have worked with older students from their 40s to their 60s who were concerned that they would face discrimination in the field due to their age. However, in practice, age carries with it a certain authority, and clients assume that older people hold the wisdom of experience, even if they are still trainees. The important thing is for clinicians to recognize who they are, how they come across, what perceptions clients might have of them, and how to use these perceptions to their advantage.

We must not forget that the clinical encounter takes place embedded in societal context. So, it is not free from sexism, racism, homophobia, or classism. I have seen women professionals belittled in subtle and not so subtle ways and have watched wonderful clinicians become flustered as a result. I have witnessed family therapy sessions in which single fathers ask female therapists for a date. When male clients sexualize a professional by flirting, attraction and the wish for companionship may be part of the motivation; however, it also demeans and symbolically removes a woman from a position of authority, demoting her to a sex object. The good news is that if the clinician can stay calm, they can turn these situations into potential learning opportunities for clients, and perhaps themselves.

It is not only the appearance of a clinician that can affect the client; the feelings the client engenders in the clinician can also be impactful. I once supervised a therapist who had a client who kept talking about the size of his penis. She asked him to stop but he persisted. This may come as a shock to the reader but this man had difficulties in his relationships with women. If a clinician feels uncomfortable or unsafe with a client, it should always be their prerogative to refuse to see them and arrange to have the case transferred. The clinician's initial reaction to this sex talk was to freak out and seek to transfer him to another therapist. However, sometimes these circumstances provide opportunities for therapeutic interventions that are in vivo, and thus immediate and powerful. In supervision this clinician realized that as long as she believed she was not at risk for assault or any other type of danger from this client, she would actually be able to orchestrate a therapeutic experience for him. She went back to the client and reflected what his behavior felt like for her.

CLINICIAN: You know, you keep talking in a sexual way in here and I'm not sure why. However, it is making me feel uncomfortable, annoyed, and wanting to distance from you.
CLIENT: Oh, come on! I'm just kidding. Can't you take a joke?
CLINICIAN: Sure, if it's funny. I don't find this funny and I'm willing to bet other women wouldn't either. So, I am giving you feedback as to how you are coming across. I know you want to find ways to have a serious relationship with a woman. However, if you treat other women this way, I can see why they might back away.

Note that her confrontation with the client was not reactive, but calmly linked his behavior to his goals for treatment, which was to better understand why his relationships with women failed. This incident was emblematic of the insensitivity with which he related to women. Eventually he took her feedback to heart, bonded very closely with this social worker and was able to get better insight and self-awareness as to how he came across to women. Like everything that goes on between therapist and client, "Do you want to see my penis?" was grist for the mill of clinical social work.

Minority Therapist

There are pressures inherent in being a member of an oppressed minority and also a clinician, particularly for those working with members of the majority. Clinicians from oppressed groups I have supervised report that, unsurprisingly, their clients bring their prejudices with them into the helping relationships, so much so that clinicians experience their microaggressions.

Take this example from early in my career. I was a family therapist for a foster care prevention program that served inner-city youth who were at risk of foster care placement due largely to their behavioral difficulties. The program consisted of an afterschool component during which youth had group therapy, recreation, and assistance with their homework. All families of enrolled youth were required to participate in family therapy.

Unfortunately, the program was short staffed and thus not well supervised, and horrifically, a 7-year-old boy was sexually assaulted by Cliff, aged 13. The younger boy's family pressed charges and the case was making its way through the family court and child welfare systems. The perpetrator's family was my client and I visited them soon after the assault.

As we sat down in the kitchen, Cliff's mother, Lynette, noted that she left her lipstick on the table. Jokingly, she asked if it was my shade. I had a hunch that the joke was an allusion to my own gay sexual orientation which I'm sure she suspected though I had not yet revealed it to anyone in my professional life in order to avoid the stigma (it was the early 1980s). Sadly, my surprise and fears got in the way of what was really needed, a discussion of the family's feelings about sex, aggression, and sexual orientation. Instead, due to my anxiety and defensiveness (and lack of experience), I focused strictly on the child's behavior, helping Lynette set limits on her son's aggression and assessing Cliff for sexual abuse.

I once worked with Molly, a young African American MSW fieldwork student with a natural ability to empathize and connect to people, but who complained about racist behavior from her White clients. Up until that time, I was ignorant of this possibility, no doubt due to my White privilege, and had not previously thought to ask my supervisees or students of color about such experiences. One such client expressed microaggressions to Molly during her session, making comments like: "All the staff in the welfare office are Black so they don't want to help me. They just want to take care of their own" and, "All this [Black] worker cared about was her braids." During supervision, Molly and I were able to recognize obstacles that got in the way of confronting her client, including, but not limited to, feeling as if she had to be consistently and uniformly empathic in her responses as well as the fear that her client, supervisor, and colleagues would view her through the lens of the "angry Black woman" trope. Further, Molly also worried that if she brought up issues of racism, the client would get so angry and upset that the relationship would break down due to her White fragility (D'Angelo, 2018). However, a discussion of racism was definitely needed. A therapist does not have to put up with racism or any other abuse from a client. Yet, it is important to recognize that if a client is talking like this, they might be unconsciously asking for help while at the same time setting up a transference that is hostile (see next chapter) without realizing it. Gently confronting such a client with firmness but also empathy in the context of a trusting relationship is the way to proceed.

Through supervision and her own self-reflection, Molly came to the correct conclusion that this client's racist statements were not acceptable and that she did not have to withstand them. How to go about dealing with them was a bit more complicated. To start, I suggested that this client may have been raising these issues as an unconscious way to show her therapist she needed help with them. By stating these things so brazenly, she was sending a message to her therapist, one of anger but also an indirect request for help. Molly found a way to gently confront the client:

MOLLY: I noticed you say a lot of negative things about Black people you encounter. I am wondering how you think I feel when you say these things.
CLIENT: What do you mean?
MOLLY: When you say Black people only care about themselves or you talk about someone's braids. As you can see, I also have braids.

CLIENT: I don't mean anything by it. By the way, you are different.
MOLLY: Still, I wonder if you are angry or even annoyed with me over things that have happened in therapy. Perhaps you are frustrated with me as well for not helping you enough.
CLIENT: No. I think you are reading into this too much. I have no trouble with you; it's about the people who are supposed to help me and don't.
MOLLY: Well, I am guessing you did not intentionally want to hurt my feelings, but have you thought about how these comments would have an impact on me?
CLIENT: No, I guess I didn't. I'm sorry; I didn't mean to hurt your feelings.
MOLLY: I appreciate that. However, I am wondering how your feelings and statements about Black people are impacting your relationships, particularly among people who are trying to help you. Let's also keep talking about your impressions that Black people don't care about you and also the ways that *I* might be falling short in trying to help you.

This initiated a meaningful discussion about how her racist projections hurt Black people but also hurt *her* by pushing away the very people who were trying to help her. Together they explored where these ideas came from, including the client's family of origin, peers, as well as the media. The therapist had to consistently reinforce that it was ok to talk to her about race and the client's racist ideas, but that she also needed to be open to changing them. Don't be misled; psychotherapy does not cure racism. However, in cases like these, if handled well, a racist perspective can be challenged by pointing out not only its origins but also its consequences. Molly helped neutralize some of the emotional charge of this confrontation by externalizing the blame for these ideas onto the culture of the nation as well as the community and family in which the client grew up. Nevertheless, now the client needed to take responsibility for changing these ideas. It was also vital that Molly understood the possible indirect messages her client was communicating about the transference of their relationship along with the impacts her client's statements had on her (countertransference).

Another colleague had a speech impediment that he used as a barometer for what was happening in the families he was treating. He would explain to families right off the bat, that his stutter acted up when the families were experiencing intense emotion especially if it was concealed. It is important to note that this clinician needed to have worked through any nervousness or potential shame he had about his stutter in order to utilize and actually *honor* it as an assessment tool. When he stuttered, he would stop the session and get family members to reflect on what was occurring and take notice of any charged issues that might be emerging. The way he used what could be perceived as a disability was brave and brilliant, and ultimately helpful to clients, which after all, is what it is all about.

It is important to recognize that just like the social work axiom, person-in-environment (Kondrat, 2013), we need to consider that clinical practice takes place in a societal context that makes discussions about race and other differences uncomfortable. Clinical social workers must be brave enough to go forward, challenge taboos, and have these difficult discussions particularly in the service of the client's growth and development.

Therapist Feelings as Clinical Data

Sleepiness

As a group, I have found that social workers and other psychotherapists tend to be hard on themselves and as a result, they tend to overlook, dismiss, and pathologize their own feelings and reactions. Keep in mind, whatever feeling you have during your session with a client, whether it is fear, sadness, sexual arousal, or (horrors!) sleepiness, these are all potential sources of clinical information. Sleepiness during a session can happen and as a matter of fact, is not uncommon. Therapists and students can be very self-punitive when they experience it. However, there might be important, clinically-related reasons for drowsiness that relate to the client and what is happening or not happening in the session. Clients who keep their clinicians at a distance by rambling on about something irrelevant or avoiding the invitation to deeply explore their feelings can invoke sleepiness in the clinician. Remember, we are socialized not to talk about or even think about our negative feelings, and also to find ways to anesthetize ourselves when we experience them. So, it is no surprise that clients who come to see us might try to avoid talking about their pain; some without even knowing they are doing so!

CLINICIAN: I'm noticing myself getting sleepy. This usually happens when things are staying too "surfacey," that we are not really getting at the important stuff. What are your thoughts about what I am saying?

Note the big difference in alertness once a client who usually makes you sleepy starts to express emotions. Do not be surprised if the distance and sleepiness disappear. Of course, if you are feeling sleepy regularly during sessions, take an inventory of your own circumstances. Are you getting enough sleep at night? If not, what is getting in the way? Are you eating a heavy lunch before your afternoon session? Do you need to ramp up the self-care? However, if the sleepiness is occurring during a particular session with a certain client, and dissipates when the session is over, it is likely related to what is happening with the client.

Other Clinician Feelings

If a client tells you a scenario and you are feeling angry on their behalf, it is often because the client might not be owning this emotion. They are telling you about a situation in which they should be angry but are not expressing it, thus leaving you with the anger that they are harboring but not expressing.

CLIENT: My husband yells at me and calls me "idiot" and "good for nothing" when dinner is not on the table when he gets home from work. I try to have things ready for him, but between the kids' homework, and the housecleaning, and the laundry, sometimes I don't get to it.
CLINICIAN: I hear you express this so calmly, but I am wondering where your anger is about all of this?
CLIENT: I really don't feel angry to be honest; more like exhaustion
CLINICIAN: Hmmm ... sometimes when anger is repressed, it can make us tired. As I hear you talk, I am getting angry on your behalf. I often feel this way when clients are not owning their own anger. Do you think that is happening here, in this situation that you just spoke of?

Sometimes, you might even feel angry *at* the client for not owning their anger. It is also possible that when you are feeling angry at a client, they are doing something to invade your boundaries. Additionally, the client's issues might be touching upon your own. What is important is that you do not dismiss these feelings but welcome them as opportunities to learn about your client and also yourself, and to use the information they yield to assist your client.

If you are feeling sexually aroused, reflect on what is happening between you and your client at the moment you are having these feelings. Is your client somehow being provocative, giving off sexual messages, either consciously or unconsciously? Early in my career, during home visit sessions, an older adolescent told me possibly fictitious but definitely arousing stories of how she seduced her stepbrother. In supervision, I was alerted to two things: 1) that this client who was regaling me with tales of seducing her stepbrother into an inappropriate relationship might have been trying to do the same thing to me. This could indicate how she interacts, or feels she must interact with the men in her life and; 2) I needed to not meet alone with this client in her home but instead should insist she come to the office. Mind you, there was no chance I was going to engage in sexual or romantic behavior with this client, but she clearly indicated that she might make up stories about her sexual exploits, so some protections needed to be put into place.

Sometimes, we might be working with a client with poor hygiene. For many social workers, nothing is more disturbing or distracting than working with a client (or in a client home) that smells badly. Many workers suffer in silence as they gamely go forward, trying to ignore the attack on their olfactory senses. However, it must be remembered that what you are perceiving, others are as well and having a similar reaction:

CLINICIAN: When I am with you, I notice that you have an odor about you. It makes me want to back away and distance from you, which is unfortunate and I know is something you do not want. I am wondering if others feel the same way.

Targeted self-reflection followed by gentle self-disclosure in the service of helping the client gain insight into themselves is the appropriate response to these scenarios. In each of these situations, the clinician is using their feelings and reactions as a tool in the service of assisting their client. In addition, they are inviting the client to go deeper into their own experiences and lives so as to make the therapy more meaningful and effective. This topic will be further addressed in the next chapter where the issue of countertransference is addressed.

As You Go Forward, Know the Rules, and When to Break Them

In a lot of your classes, you are probably learning some "rules" about clinical social work. As an anxious new worker, you want to show your colleagues, your supervisor, and your clients that you are doing a good job; you want to follow the rules and wouldn't dream of breaking them, right?

The National Association of Social Work Code of Ethics (NASW, 2021: www.socialworkers.org/about/ethics/code-of-ethics) is a document that should be intimately familiar to all social workers and social work students, and is fully addressed in Chapter 9. Rules can provide comfort, particularly in stressful situations, like the beginning of field, a new job, or the first clinical encounter. However, there are other "rules" that students learn or perhaps overlearn in their social work classes that are at times useful but, I would argue, should not always be blindly followed. Such rules might include: never ask close-ended questions, and never accept food or other gifts from clients. These guidelines all have sound logic behind them. However, sometimes strict adherence to the rules without thinking them through can actually work against clinical engagement and effectiveness.

Closed-Ended Questions

These are questions that can be answered with a yes or no. Beginning students are often taught they are taboo and should be avoided at all costs. I have had students present process recordings and apologize after asking close-ended questions, as if they were about to be penalized. Certainly, open-ended questions are helpful whereby they yield more information. Examples of such queries include: "Tell me about …," "Help me understand …," "Say more about …," or "What are your thoughts/feelings about …?" and these questions should be the mainstay of your clinical repertoire.

However, sometimes yes/no questions are unavoidable. For example, when a client *does not* want to elaborate on an emotional or otherwise difficult issue, a well-timed yes/no question can be just the thing to begin to open them up. Take the following case situation, for example:

SOCIAL WORKER: I heard you got into a fight today at school. What was that about?
ADOLESCENT MALE CLIENT: (hood up, sunglasses on, shrugs in silence)
SOCIAL WORKER: Did something that other guy do today piss you off?
CLIENT: Yes
SOCIAL WORKER: And that made you want to hit him?
CLIENT: Yeah, he really started it.
SOCIAL WORKER: Really? How exactly?
CLIENT: First he tripped me, then he started talking sh—t about my girl. Nobody does that and gets away with that. So, I taught him a lesson. I don't know who he thinks he is.
SOCIAL WORKER: I can really see why you got so angry. He seemed like he was trying to humiliate you, and I can understand why you retaliated. Let's keep talking about this; I want to really understand how you were feeling.

Once the client says a few more words, especially after a series of short answers, you know you are onto something and are beginning to engage the client in a helping relationship. The general rule is, the more the client talks, the more they are engaged. However, yes/no questions can start the rock rolling down the mountain.

Accepting Gifts

Though it is unlikely that you will be offered gifts during your first days or weeks in your field placement or new job, as the holidays approach, this might become an issue. Social work students are taught never to accept a gift from a client. Some agencies prohibit it. The rationale is that the gift is communicating some meaning or feeling that is antithetical to therapy. Perhaps the client might be somehow trying to manipulate the therapist, or the client feels indebted to them, or maybe the client somehow believes the therapist expects it. For sure, the easy way to avoid any entanglements about gifts is to simply not accept them. If the agency has a rule about this, the clinician can simply point to the rule and claim it is out of their hands.

However, it is worth noting that there are occasions when a client giving a gift may have a positive therapeutic meaning. Clients may want to show appreciation and say thank you. In these circumstances, if the therapist turns down the gift, it could result in a rupture in the therapeutic relationship.

Sylvia was seeing a particular family for six months. During the holiday season, the mother in the family gave Sylvia a gift of a sweater. Sylvia prided herself in her sense of fashion, and the sweater was not at all her taste. However, what concerned Sylvia more was what she had learned in social work school, that she was not to accept gifts from clients. So, she handed the gift back at which point the client became tearful. She claimed she wanted to show her appreciation to the clinician, who was helping the family deal with the troubling behavior of their child in school. Sensing that returning the gift would do more harm than good, Sylvia took the box, opened it, expressed appreciation, and wore the sweater on the day of their next session.

In a different scenario, Christina had a male client, Jim, who gave her what appeared to be an expensive necklace. Christina had access to her client's income information in order to establish a sliding scale fee, so she knew that her client could not afford this piece of jewelry. Jim had come to treatment because he was having trouble maintaining a long-term relationship with a woman. A truck driver and an affable man in his mid-40s, Jim had no trouble meeting women but had difficulties maintaining a relationship. Through therapy, Jim and Christina learned that, once in a relationship, Jim's feelings of unworthiness and low self-esteem led him to struggle with jealousy, possessiveness, and the need for constant reassurance that his girlfriend cared for him and was not seeking other partners. There were moments during the treatment where he seemed to blur the professional boundaries between Christine and himself. He asked her about boyfriends, and what restaurants she liked, and made comments about her appearance. Christine had to set limits with him several times, pointing out the difference between a therapeutic and a dating relationship. When he persisted, she reflected that these behaviors were an indication of his unwillingness to respect the boundaries of women, including those he dated, and this might be what was "turning them off."

Therefore, in this instance, it would have been inappropriate for Christine to accept the gift, a gift that Jim could ill afford, and that also came with possible meanings and misunderstandings about the relationship:

CHRISTINE: Wow, I'm really taken aback by this gift. Tell me, what gave you the idea to buy it for me?

JIM: Well, you have been so nice and have really helped me. You always look pretty and the stone in the necklace reminded me of your eyes. I wanted to express my appreciation.

CHRISTINE: Well Jim, I certainly appreciate the sentiment; that you wanted to do something nice for me. However, I am concerned that this gift might represent a misunderstanding on your behalf about our relationship. This is the type of gift that you would give a girlfriend, not your therapist or any women with whom you have a professional relationship.

JIM: Oh, c'mon, what's the big deal? Do you really need to analyze everything?
CHRISTINE: Well, yes, as a matter of fact, that's what you are paying me to do, no? (slight chuckle). We have spoken many times about how you deal with women and their boundaries. Clearly, we need to discuss this further, but for now I am going to return this gift to you. You should save it for a future girlfriend who will appreciate it as an expression of your affection.

As these examples demonstrate, the challenge is to determine the meaning surrounding each gift that is offered. Occasionally, a client may offer a gift to try to manipulate or bribe you. For example, if a client needs a letter for court, to get off probation, or wants you to advocate for them to child protective services, it is probably best not to accept their gifts. However, if this is an ongoing client, particularly one who does not pay a fee and who is not seeking a formal favor beyond your usual counseling assistance, it is probably ok. Notice any changes in your client or clinical relationship after you accept the gift to assess whether doing so was a good idea, and of course, always review the issue in supervision. It is your job to try to figure out if the gift has a negative or otherwise special meaning, or simply that the "cigar is just a cigar."

I, like Sylvia, have found that making a big deal out of a small token of appreciation can do more harm than good. Like most clinical dilemmas, there are no pat answers. Ultimately, what is right is what is in the best interest of the client. If you can keep your anxiety under control, it is possible to use these incidents as important sources of clinical data.

Self-Disclosure

Too often students are told by well-meaning teachers and supervisors that they must never self-disclose to their clients. Unfortunately, this can result in an anxious reaction when students and beginners are asked a personal question, leading to the awful, stereotypical response: "What makes you ask this question?" or worse, the meaningless, formulaic: "My supervisors say I am not allowed to answer personal questions."

In fact, some self-disclosure on the part of the therapist might strengthen the therapeutic relationship by helping them appear more genuine, thus enhancing treatment outcomes (Hill, et al., 2018). However, an important caution is necessary here. Some people, particularly extroverts (like myself), enjoy talking about themselves and their own experiences (see, I just did it there). We do so as a way to process and clarify our own ideas and to energize ourselves. However, a cardinal rule of clinical work is that all interventions and utterances are to be in the service of the client, not because it feels good to talk. So, first off, be healthily suspicious of your motivations. Why do you want to disclose something personal? How will it help *them*? If it is a story of how you have handled a certain situation, have you considered the possibility that it could make the client feel inadequate and unable to meet your standards? Will the self-disclosure help you feel better? Or will it help the client feel better? Is it a way to avoid the stress of having to slow down and listen to the client?

> Rick and his partner were arguing about whether or not to get a dog. His partner badly wanted one while Rick was hesitant. Neither had ever been dog owners. During our conversation, I revealed that I owned a dog and I knew from experience that housebreaking a puppy could be quite a lot of work. Initially they needed to make room in their schedules, a solid two weeks, to help the puppy settle and to initiate training. I avoided the temptation to go into a long diatribe about how to raise a puppy; there are plenty of more qualified experts out there (if you met my dog you would know this to be true). Instead, this disclosure was meant to add important information as the couple worked to resolve their conflict and arrive at an agreement.

The clinician must also be on the lookout for demands from the client for self-disclosure that divert attention away from painful issues the client is experiencing. During a recent session, a politically-minded client was discussing the stress she was under while leaving a job and starting a new relationship. It was during a presidential election year and at the time we were in the midst of a raucous Democratic primary season. She talked about how, on top of everything else, she was stressed by the current politics, the content of which we started to discuss. After a few moments, I quickly realized that doing so was a mistake as it steered the conversation away from her issues. I needed to refocus us back to her therapy concerns: "It's so easy to slip into politics and avoid more painful, personal issues. How does what is happening politically affect, if at all, what you are dealing with personally?" The client revealed that the confusing flux of her life in the context of the political upheaval of the country only added to her sense of anxiety about her occupational and relationship concerns.

Another type of self-disclosure is that which is directly related to the relationship. I had been working with a man in his 30s for several sessions as he described a number of problems including his conflict with his wife and his work stress. Previously, I had felt bored and sleepy in the session, which as stated previously, happens when clients are not digging deep enough and are keeping the conversation superficial. At one point in therapy, he became tearful as he spoke about how his wife was unresponsive to his request to spend time with him, stating that it felt like he was invisible to her. At that moment, I became more awake. I remarked that he was finally showing me some deep emotion and felt closer to him as a result.

Here are some guidelines around self-disclosure:

1   Do not think of it as all-or-nothing. Consider that at times it might be a good idea to do some small, carefully circumscribed self-disclosure, especially with clients who have struggled with feelings of abandonment or isolation.
2   Before you do so, carefully assess whether and how self-disclosure will help your client. Be conscious as to why you are doing it now and for what reason. At times, it might be best to let the client know your reasoning.
3   After the self-disclosure is discussed, quickly return the focus back to the client.

A Note on Advice Giving

Have you ever told a friend or family member about a personal problem that was particularly difficult and been given a piece of advice that made you squirm with irritation? Did you find yourself responding with a "yes, but" statement? "Yes, but that won't work because ...", "Yes, but I've already tried that." Chances are, you were given advice prematurely and/or without you asking for it. Perhaps your report of your problem made your advice giver so anxious that they wanted to rush in and try to solve it. One of the most potentially unempowering things a therapist can do is give advice at the wrong time, in the wrong way. Advice presumes that the worker knows best, which is sometimes true but certainly not always, and definitely not before the worker has established a therapeutic relationship with the client, or has sufficient information about the problem, its history, and what the client has done to solve it. Premature advice indirectly imparts the idea that the client's problem is easily solvable and is an indirect putdown. The client will quickly let the therapist know this was not the right move. Fortunately, like almost all clinical missteps, this one is also fixable.

CLINICIAN: (to the parent of a child who doesn't do his homework) You might want to try to do a chart. You can check off every time he does his homework, and give him a star sticker when he does it.
CLIENT: Yeah, I've already tried that. It didn't work.

Maybe the client tried it, maybe they didn't follow through on it. You can certainly check with the client to see if perhaps they did the chart incorrectly. However, before giving advice, get a full inventory of what the client has done to try to solve the problem. Compliment their attempts and be sure to comment on how the problem has been difficult to solve. If it was an easy issue to resolve, they would not be coming to you with it. Carefully review their attempts with an eye toward anything they have tried that worked, even a little bit. As a clinician, you really want to jump on and reinforce anything the client has done to solve their problems successfully. This will leave the client, who already may be demoralized by their lack of ability to solve their own problems, feeling empowered, and that of course is a good thing.

Please Tell Me What to Do!

Sometimes our clients *ask* for advice. When we demur with responses such as, "What do you think you should do?" or "I'm here to help YOU figure out what is best for you" some clients can become distressed, feeling as if we are withholding something. When pushed against a wall, I suggest this comment or something similar, "Well, here is something to try that I know other clients have found helpful. You might give it a try, as an experiment, and, during our next session, let me know how it went." Do not be surprised if the next week the client reports, "Yeah, that didn't work either."

Use of Supervision

In their anxiety, new clinicians, may be looking for answers and certainty from supervisors, teachers, lecturers, and even some of the current psychotherapy superstars via videos and conference presentations. For sure, consulting with these people can be helpful. Further, it is a good idea to consult with your supervisor before you decide to "break" any of the previously described rules. It is also advisable and in fact good practice to have multiple people to reach out to for help. However, you don't want to reach out to too many, as you could get lost in the crossfire of multiple opinions. Be sure to limit how many people you seek advice from, particularly for one case. Sometimes less is more.

How does one decide with whom to consult? Think carefully about the expertise of the person whose guidance you are pursuing. For example, if you are working with children, "collect" experts on children's behavior problems and development whom you can call upon for advice. Comb your network for people who have expertise, interest, and training in various areas upon whom you can rely. Note, if in your place of employment you have a regular supervisor, be sure to let them know you are getting advice and consultation outside of supervision sessions and it is advisable to share the input you get with this supervisor. This will help you avoid any trouble, including a triangulation of yourself between two experts. A wise supervisor will encourage you to seek out other sources of expertise, but if they are overseeing your work, they are ultimately responsible for your performance and will need to keep abreast of what is going on with your cases.

Ultimately, YOU have to decide how to move forward with your cases, even the difficult ones. No one has all of the answers and ultimately, after you get the information, training, and some more experience, you will notice that the models you learn will, at times, yield information that is inconsistent with your own developing clinical wisdom. Eventually you will need to plant your flag somewhere, and as you get more experience it will be easier to make these decisions. Beware of anyone who claims to have all of the answers. There is an old saying: "If you meet the Buddha on the side of the road, kill him." Make no mistake, this is not a call to violence but instead is a caution not to worship too zealously at the feet of any master. Be committed to your own intellectual growth and the development of your own storehouse of clinical wisdom that you will learn from trial and error, personal and professional experience. But also know that on this path you must continue to commit to self-growth and perseverance. Right from the start, learn and be as open as you can to the various models. As you become more experienced, you will drop some theories, add new ones or combine theories or components of theories in ways that you find useful and effective. Stay open and keep learning!

Hopefully, after reading this chapter, you are ready to begin that new job or field placement. It is time to learn various clinical skills in more depth, starting with working with individuals, which is what follows in the next chapter.

References

Black, S. C., & Gringart, E. (2019). The relationship between clients' preferences of therapists' sex and mental health support seeking: An exploratory study. *Australian Psychologist*, 54(4), 322–335. doi:10.1111/ap.12370.

D'Angelo, R. (2018). *White Fragility: Why it's So Hard for White People to Talk about Racism*. Beacon Press.

De Jong, P., & Berg, I. K. (2012). *Interviewing for Solutions*. Cengage Learning.

Hill, C. E., Knox, S., & Pinto-Coelho, K. G. (2018). Therapist self-disclosure and immediacy: A qualitative meta-analysis. *Psychotherapy*, 55(4), 445–460. doi:10.1037/pst0000182.

Kondrat, M. E. (2013). Person-in-environment. *Encyclopedia of Social Work*. Oxford University Press. doi:10.1093/acrefore/9780199975839.013.285.

National Association of Social Workers (NASW) (2021). *Code of Ethics of the National Association of Social Workers*. NASW Press. www.socialworkers.org/About/Ethics/Code-of-Ethics/Code-of-Ethics-English.

Chapter 4

Clinical Social Work with Individuals: It's About the Relationship

As you embark on a career as a clinical social worker, you are committing yourself to very unique relationships. Unlike any others you have experienced, the healing relationship is intentionally one-sided, existing completely in the service of the client. In short, it is all about them, and not at all about you. Of course, you will likely get some pleasure out of the relationship; as a social worker you will know the sweet satisfaction that comes from helping another human being. However, as already discussed, you may harbor some unconscious motivations to address your own personal issues that you will need to monitor and address. Without exception, the relationship with the client must consistently be front and center.

Healing Relationships

For those who continue to worry about not applying the right intervention in the correct way, there is good news. Though many psychotherapeutic treatments have been empirically proven to be effective in individual work with clients, repeated research has not crowned any singular model as superior (Lambert, 2013; Norcross & Lambert, 2019). Instead, it is the clinical relationship that matters most. Whatever model a clinician is working from, the client will not accept the intervention unless they believe the therapist hears them and understands or is attempting to understand their problems. Sometimes interventions can involve leading and even pushing a client into some uncomfortable territory. Nonetheless, clients will not be able to receive this guidance until they feel that their pain is understood. When this is achieved, the clinician has established the all-important healing relationship.

There are many schools of thought that describe how negative early childhood experiences, especially with parents, set the stage for emotional, psychiatric, and relationship disorders later in life. For example, attachment theory describes how if a child does not experience a secure relationship with their primary caregiver, they can develop a variety of problematic relationship behaviors in adulthood such as avoidant distancing, anxious clinging, or acting out (Bowlby, 2012). Bowenian family therapists point out

DOI: 10.4324/9781003011712-4

how mental health and substance abuse problems get passed from generation to generation via faulty marital and parent-child relationships (Bowen & Kerr, 2009). Freudian and post-Freudian therapists see trauma in any of the early stages of development as problematic, and the earlier the trauma, the more profound the psychopathology in adulthood (Danto, 2017; Freud, 1939).

When a child is an infant, they can feel overwhelmed by their own vulnerability. Thus, they need to have a strong omnipotent caretaker to rely upon to feel safe. Winnicott, a British post-Freudian, coined the term *holding environment* to describe the ideal relationship a mother establishes with her infant that enables them to feel safe as they explore the world around them (Winnicott, 1988). However, if that caretaker is abusive, neglectful, or otherwise emotionally or physically unavailable, the child fails to develop a sense of mastery, security, and confidence in their environment, and as a result, may become overwhelmed with feelings of fear, sadness, and frustration. Sometimes the child may grow up repressing their own feelings in the service of trying to appease their parents, hoping that in exchange they will be protected and cared for. In the process, they sacrifice their own identity development and instead develop a false self. (Note the similarity between this theory and those of Hollis, (2021), and Hanna (1993), in describing clinicians' childhoods, mentioned in Chapter 1). When the therapist establishes a good holding environment for the client, childhood wounds and trauma can be healed as the client learns about their self-worth as well as new relating behaviors. Within this reparative holding environment, the clinical social worker can reteach the client important lessons on an affect level about their value and lovability. This helps the client grow and develop beyond their symptoms. Carl Rogers, founder of person-centered psychotherapy, was one of the first voices in the field of psychotherapy to empirically identify the required elements for healing relationships, but others have done so as well (Lambert, 2013; Norcross & Lambert, 2019; Rogers, 1957; 1961). Imagine your client as a seedling; these elements represent the sunlight, water, and fertile soil that enables the plant to grow strong. As stated by Carl Rogers:

> In my early professional years, I was asking the question: How can I treat, or cure, or change this person? Now I would phrase the question in this way: How can I provide a relationship which this person may use for [their] own personal growth?
>
> (Rogers, 1961: 32)

Following are the therapist qualities that establish healing relationships based on Rogers' above referred philosophy, the common factors of effective psychotherapy empirically identified by Lambert, Norcross, and their colleagues, and the clinical knowledge I have gained from my years of practice.

Be a Highly Focused, Deep Listener

True listening is a lost art and absent from many of our day-to-day social interactions, leaving most people hungry for it. If we listen carefully to people, we begin to be able to understand who they really are, and in my experience, people in our society are literally starving for this understanding. Have you ever heard a popular or magnetic person referred to in this way: "They make me feel like I was the only person in the room?" If you develop good listening skills, demonstrating that you can really "see" others (or at least are trying to see them), you will not only be a good clinician, but a good partner, spouse, parent, friend, or colleague.

Before each session, take a moment to clear your mind. Try to empty it of the worries of the day in order to prepare yourself to be fully present and engaged with your client. As a species, many of us are much better at talking rather than listening, particularly if we are extroverts. True, deep listening manifests as maintaining uninterrupted eye contact, leaning forward, occasionally nodding, and of course eliminating distractions like cell phones. The tricky thing is that we can inadvertently or subconsciously throw up obstacles that get in the way of good listening. For example, being distracted by other thoughts like what we will eat for dinner, or other tasks that need completion can interfere with listening. Clinicians can also get side-tracked by performance anxiety; worried about saying the "right" or "perfect" thing rather than the client's feelings and concerns. If your agenda is to "fix" the client and demonstrate your competence, this can get in the way of true listening. If you have trouble staying focused on listening to the client, it is important to discern whether your inattentiveness is due to your own emotional issues, feeling overwhelmed with other responsibilities, or is because the client is somehow pushing you away or avoiding the work. All of these are common possibilities.

Unlike how it is portrayed in too many movies and television programs, psychotherapy is not about performing one "Eureka!" intervention that opens the door to permanent healing. Instead, it is about slowly building a healing relationship and engaging the client in the painstaking, piecemeal process of changing their emotional and behavioral patterns and, in turn, their lives. No matter what model you are working from, you are putting interventions out there and seeing how they land based on the client's responses. Inevitably, some will work better than others while others will not work at all. However, an essential skill is the ability to listen. Remember, above all, a good clinician is a good listener. So, make good listening not only a professional skill but also a lifestyle that you continuously practice in all of your relationships.

Empathy

Empathy is the ability to emotionally understand and communicate what another person is experiencing, and is the hallmark of deep listening. It is more than just walking in someone else's shoes, but is getting inside their heart and seeing the world through their eyes. When the clinician has achieved an empathic connection, the client feels understood. Research underscores the profound importance of empathy in the clinical relationship and its association with successful clinical outcomes (Elliott, et al., 2018).

Communicating empathically is one of those things that is harder than it looks and takes practice. A common beginner's mistake is to simply parrot client comments in a formulaic manner.

CLIENT: When my husband yelled at me and called me stupid, I felt so defeated and sad.
CLINICIAN: So, when your husband yelled at you, you felt sad, also defeated.

This all-too-common attempt at empathy is well meaning, but does not demonstrate that the worker understands or is even attempting to do so. It is as if the worker is checking off a box without really getting to the heart and soul of the endeavor. Though they might not tell you as much, the client will see this as mechanical and empty rather than demonstrating understanding or curiosity.

Better:

CLINICIAN: Defeated ... that sounds so painful. Tell me more about what happened and how you felt.

Another component of establishing the empathic connection is to show interest in client feelings by asking them to elaborate.

CLIENT: I've been feeling terribly anxious lately and I have no idea why. It's awful!
CLINICIAN: Wow, that sounds distressing but also mysterious. Tell me whatever you can about what it feels like for you and let's try to solve this mystery together.

As you can see from the responses, the clinician is being thoughtful about what the client is saying, processing it and then requesting elaboration. In addition to directly naming the client's feeling, notice that "tell me whatever you can" also communicates that the clinician has heard the client's confusion and wants to hear more. Demonstrating interest in the feelings and experiences of the client in this way forges the therapeutic bond. As stated in the last chapter, if after your intervention your client continues to further elaborate, talking for an extended period without interruption or prompting from the clinician, it is a good indication that they feel you've gotten it right. When the client recognizes, either consciously or unconsciously, that they are (finally) in the presence of someone who cares enough about them to carefully listen, they can feel as if they have reached an oasis of cool water after a long, hot, lonely journey. Such empathy is the cornerstone of a good clinical relationship.

Do your best to understand and reflect the client's feelings but try not to worry too much about getting them exactly right all of the time. This is not an exam where you lose points for the wrong answer. If the client believes you are incorrect and they trust you enough to correct you, this is the mark of a successful, potentially healing relationship. The *attempt* to be empathic in and of itself can be therapeutic because it demonstrates the clinician's desire to understand the client, that the client perceives and appreciates and which can in fact facilitate healing:

CLIENT: When my husband yelled at me and called me stupid, I felt so defeated and sad.

CLINICAL SOCIAL WORKER: Yes, to be treated that way certainly sounds painful.

CLIENT: Painful?! Oh boy, this goes beyond painful! It was devastating! Oh my God, I was so upset, I couldn't eat or sleep for two days. I don't know why I get so upset when he does this, but I just do. I really would like it not to hurt so much when he criticizes me, but it does. I don't know what to do, I really don't. You know, he reminds me of my own father, who was so critical of me and my mother. I just feel like I've had enough and can't handle it anymore when he gets this way.

As you can see from this example, the clinician did not get the affect exactly right but still, the attempt communicated that they were trying to track the client's feelings, which tells the client "I'm interested." Once the client pauses, the clinician can continue to intervene in ways that demonstrate empathy:

CLINICIAN: Clearly, I did not get that quite right. I'm glad you clarified that for me. I certainly want to hear more about the devastating impact of this for you.

It is important to note that in order to admit they are wrong, therapists need to be able to handle the anxiety and neutralize any self-criticism about failing to meet useless and irrelevant perfectionistic standards. You might be the first or perhaps only person in the client's life who has shown an interest in their feelings. If you are open to correction, you are actually helping to heal a client who might never have had anyone say to them, "Yes, I was wrong; I didn't hear your experience accurately, and I really want to understand." Never underestimate the healing power of those words.

It bears repeating that whatever model a clinician is working from, the client will not accept the intervention unless they believe the therapist actually grasps or is attempting to understand their problems and who they really are. Sometimes interventions can involve leading a client into some uncomfortable territory and even confronting them. Clients will not be able to go there unless they feel that their pain is first understood.

Pushing for Concealed Feelings

When we ask our clients to express their feelings, we are entreating them to approach the gateway of recovery. "Tell me what that feels like for you" is an antidote to continuous messages they might have gotten not only from their families but also society, that negative feelings are not a normal part of the human condition and therefore not to be acknowledged. The frequency of people with depression and anxiety who come to our offices as well as the myriad of stress-related health problems that are so common in our society is no doubt due to this tendency. Further, avoidance is one of the main ways people sidestep difficult feelings, particularly those related to trauma (Courtois, Ford, & Cloitre, 2009). Compulsive behaviors, whether they be drug or alcohol use, binge eating, sex, gambling, or any other addiction are some of the myriad of ways people escape these painful feelings. So when we are soliciting our clients to express their feelings, we are asking them to swim against the tide of personal, family, and societal disapproval. Unsurprisingly, it may feel unsafe to express affect after repressing it for so long; or the repression has worked so well, the client cannot call up feelings on command. So don't be surprised if clients seem to resist at first.

CLINICIAN: Do you remember what it felt like when as a child your mother would hit you?
CLIENT: I don't remember. I didn't really feel anything. She was just doing her best to try to be a good parent.
CLINICIAN: Hmmm ... I'm guessing there are some feelings there. They might be too painful to face at this time—or perhaps you don't trust me enough yet, which is understandable. But that's ok, we will keep chipping away until we can get to them.

When you see a client tearing up, it is essential to follow up on it—always. If a client is expressing feelings either directly or indirectly, they are not to be ignored as this all is material to be utilized in the treatment.

CLINICIAN: I notice a wave of emotion spread across your face as you talk about that argument you just had with your dad. Can you tell me what you are feeling right now?

Also:

CLINICIAN: I can see your eyes fill up with tears. Tell me, what's happening for you? What are those tears about?

I will never forget when a large male bodybuilder was telling me the story of how his mother routinely criticized and ridiculed him as a child. As he spoke, he tilted his head back, and peered at the ceiling which I initially found to be strange. When I asked about this, he told me he was looking up so that the tears would not fall from his eyes but instead get reabsorbed into his tear ducts. (By the way, this does not work.)

Another client, a young transgender woman, would wave her hand in front of her face when discussing rejection from her family. Upon inquiry, I learned that this was an attempt to dry her watering eyes before the tears leaked out and ruined her eyeliner and, more importantly, revealed her profound sadness. It is always a good idea for the clinician to notice and ask about any strange behaviors in the session. Never, never ignore the elephant in the room; whatever is happening in your session is clinical data.

The acknowledgment and expression of feelings are so taboo that I have had clients on several occasions cancel sessions, telling me that they were "too depressed" or "too upset" to come to their therapy. This makes about as much sense as saying one is too sick to go to the doctor. However, such action reflects our clients' profound shame and discomfort with feelings and strong reluctance to express them. What I tell my clients is that it is my mission to help them with their feelings. I joke that tears are part of the job for me. If you cannot cry in your therapist's office, where can you? Eventually, my gentle joking combined with my sincere interest and unconditional acceptance of their feelings gets them to the point where they feel safe enough to share them in my presence. In turn, this helps build the healing relationship so central to effective clinical social work.

Goal Consensus

A meta-analysis of 54 studies (Tryon, Birch, & Verkuilen, 2018) confirms what seems logical; therapy works best when client and clinician agree on goals. In addition to being mutually agreed upon, both the clinician and the client must believe that the goals are worthwhile and achievable. How can therapy work otherwise?

Good goals in clinical social work are observable, measurable, and feasible. It is generally good practice to establish goals with these properties, and nowadays agencies, funders, and insurance companies require it. Goals should be positively stated, meaning that instead of a goal of "I would not be so depressed" the goal should be stated as something that *would be* happening, "I will feel happier." De Jong and Berg (2012) point out that negatively stated goals can drain client energy and channel it in a negative direction. It is easier to imagine and work toward something that you *would like* to happen as opposed to the absence of something.

As I state in the last chapter, I like to start my first session with "People come to see me because they want to change something in their lives. What is it you would like to change?" I like this statement because it is client-centered and also communicates that it is the *client* who will be responsible for doing the changing, not the *clinician* (even though the clinician will be on hand to assist as much as possible). As an additional benefit, it also generates goals that are in the client's own language.

CLINICIAN: People come to see me because there is something they want to change in their lives. What is it that you want to change?
CLIENT: I want to be happy.
CLINICIAN: Ok, good; that's very reasonable and understandable. Of course, you want to be happy. But happy means different things to different people. Tell me, how do you define happy?
CLIENT: Happy is not being sad, enjoying my life more.
CLINICIAN: Yes, that certainly makes sense. But I want to know more. If I saw you being happy on a video, what would I see?
CLIENT: (after a pause) I'd be smiling more. I would be exercising. I would not be arguing so much with my girlfriend. I'd have a better job.
CLINICIAN: Ok, got it. So how about if we set up these things as beginning goals: 1) You will be exercising more; 2) Your relationship with your girlfriend will improve; 3) You will be in a better job. Tell me, how will you know your relationship with your girlfriend is better? What will be happening that is not happening now?
CLIENT: We would be spending more time together, talking more, and also having more sex.
CLINICIAN: So, can we agree that under the overall goal of improving the relationship with your girlfriend, we add the goals of spending more time together, communicating more, and having sex more often?
CLIENT: Yes, ok.

Other good goal setting questions to ask include:

"If I were a fly on the wall seeing you when you are (happier, not depressed, feeling better) what would I see?"

"If I was watching a video of you (after you met your goal), what would I see?"

"What is something you would like to see different at the end of therapy?"

"What needs to happen for you to be ready to fire me; to end therapy?"

Instead Questions

One way to get clients to positively frame goals is to ask *instead* questions (De Jong & Berg, 2012).

CLINICIAN: You say you want to fight less with your husband. When you and your husband are fighting less often, what would you be doing instead?
CLIENT: We would be getting along better, spending more time together—having conversations that were not arguments, perhaps going out on weekly dates like we used to.

Here, with the help of instead questions, the client is establishing goals that are behavioral, more easily tracked and, thus, more achievable.

Sometimes agencies and funders want goals to be as behavioral as possible, and in such cases adding "client will report" as in "client will report that they are exercising three times per week" or "client will verbalize a new understanding of their feelings about being abused as a child" will be necessary. Further, the client could be encouraged to include steps that lead to the goals. For instance, if a client's overall goal is to get a better job, the clinician might ask, "What steps are you willing to take right now to begin to work on this goal?" If the client's response is to apply for a couple of jobs, you then might agree on the following objective to serve the overall goal: "Client will apply for two positions per week." If a client is overwhelmed by the prospect of meeting a goal they see as lofty, a good question might be, "What are you willing to do between now and the next time we meet that would be baby steps toward your goal of getting a new job?" These baby steps could be regarded as objectives.

It is important to note that goals are not something that are only established in the beginning of treatment, but should be reviewed and revised as needed, on an ongoing basis. As a matter of fact, when therapy has become directionless or when a clinician feels lost or stuck, it is invariably a good idea to suggest: "Let's review what we're working on here and take another look at our goals." This directive provides a helpful opportunity to assess and update goals as needed.

Assessment: Getting a History

For sure, when a client complains about a symptom or a problem, it is important for the clinician to get historical details. For example, with depression, we will want to know how severe it is, how long it has been, what it feels like to the client and anything else related to the complaint. The same thing goes for problematic behaviors. It is also advisable to get a family history. Insight into family-of-origin issues will provide important clues as to why the client acts the way they do in relationships. In addition, especially for depressed clients, it is a good idea to do a suicide assessment which is addressed later in this chapter.

At the risk of committing heresy, I admit I am biased against long, comprehensive psychosocial assessments as I find that they are not nearly as helpful as intended. In fact, sometimes getting a client to recite a long list of all of the terrible things that have happened to them, reminding them of all of the horrors they have been through, can leave them sad and deflated. Additionally, keep in mind that clients might not initially feel ready or safe to reveal painful and traumatic events from their histories (Courtois, Ford, & Cloitre, 2009). Invariably, in establishing the healing relationship with your client and dealing with their presenting problems, they will eventually tell you all you need to know. However, your agency, funders, or insurance companies may have specific requirements regarding the assessment information you will need to collect. By all means, fulfill these requirements, but before the end of the session remember to ask your clients how they survived and coped with whatever hardships they had experienced in their past. This will end a long description of misfortune in an upbeat way that can leave your client feeling resilient and empowered.

Unconditional Positive Regard

This aspect of the healing relationship is about demonstrating that you as the clinician respect, value, genuinely like, and are always on the side of the client (Farber, Suzuki, & Lynch, 2018). Positive regard is operationalized when the clinician demonstrates a sincere, nonjudgmental interest in the client's experiences, while at the same time, curates their strengths.

CLIENT: I was so afraid to bring up this issue with her. I thought she would become angry with me. I was nervous as I was doing it.
CLINICIAN: Yes, I can see how scared you were, but it was also really courageous that you did not let the fear stop you. How did you manage to do so in spite of your fear?

Notice how in this example, the clinician expresses positive regard in the form of a sincere and well-placed compliment. Consider this intervention with a long-term client:

CLIENT: I can't seem to get myself to act more assertive in my relationship. I have good intentions, but when there is a disagreement, I always back down and give in. Ugh, it's so frustrating. What's wrong with me?
CLINICIAN: I can see your frustration, but I know you well enough from having worked with you for a while now that you do not go forward with a plan until you are ready. So, let's work on you being patient

with yourself and also exploring why now might not be the time for this change.

Here the clinician demonstrates positive regard by communicating interest, curiosity, and understanding about the client's affect state while withholding judgment and not joining the client in their harsh self-criticism. In this example, the clinician quickly evaluates the situation in a way that puts it in a positive light. Many (most?) of our clients are extremely self-critical and therefore experience difficulty accepting compliments, no matter how mild.

CLINICIAN: So, what's been going on?
CLIENT: Well, I went six days without drinking.
CLINICIAN: Really? Wow, that's a real accomplishment considering that you were worried that you were drinking every day. How did you manage that?
CLIENT: It was no big deal. It was only six days.
CLINICIAN: Well, I disagree with you on that. I know your goal is to drink less and this certainly is a step in the right direction. Tell me, how did you avoid drinking this week?
CLIENT: Well, I just made up my mind to not drink and to find other things to do. I've started working out and I thought this could be a time to do other things to improve my health.
CLINICIAN: I know you see this accomplishment as very small, but I see this as an important step in the right direction and thus not to be underestimated. How confident are you that you could continue this?

Here the social worker does not let the client invalidate the acknowledgment of strengths. However, they do not arm-wrestle the client into seeing things their way; that never works. Instead, the worker pushes gently, gives more data to back up their assertions, and if the client still cannot accept the compliment, the social worker could state: "Ok, let's agree to disagree on this for now. At some point, we need to take a look at why it is so difficult for you to receive compliments."

An important component of positive regard is unconditional acceptance of the client and their problems and behaviors. As clinicians, we seek to understand the client's problematic behavior, and at least initially, try to see its value for the client.

> You must believe you have a good reason to (keep drinking, hit your child, cheat in your marriage, etc.). Let's work together to figure out what that good reason is.

Keep in mind, we do not *condone* these behaviors, but we do not negatively judge the client for them either. Rather than labeling the client as lazy, resistant, or mean, we assume they believe that these behaviors are helpful in some way and we are curious as to how. Once we figure out the needs or problems the client is attempting to solve with these behaviors, we can help them find alternatives that are less harmful, such as finding ways to manage anxiety other than drinking, discovering less damaging ways to discipline a child, or figuring out what needs are not getting met in one's marriage.

Research suggests that clinician positive-regard might actually *be the cause* of positive outcomes (Farber, et al., 2018). This, along with common sense, suggests that maintaining and communicating positive regard is a vital skill for the clinical social worker to cultivate.

Genuineness

Of all the stated qualities for a successful therapeutic relationship, this one seems the most abstract. Rogers (1957) discussed how being genuine means to be clearly oneself without trying to act like someone you are not, and also to be self-aware of how you come across. Gelso and Hayes (1998) described it as being open, honest, authentic, and present with the client in the here and now. I will add, be natural, be yourself, and don't be phony.

I have seen enthusiastic, well-meaning beginning clinicians go off the rails in their efforts to express genuineness and lose authenticity in the process. In an anxious effort to communicate positive regard, we might overdo it to the extent that we come across as insincere, simply blowing smoke up our client's ... chimney. A sign that the client is not buying it is when, for example, after you pay a client a compliment, you get a response like "Yeah, you *have* to say that because you are my social worker," or, "You say that because you are being paid to be nice." In order to demonstrate genuineness, the clinician needs to compliment without overexaggerating. In addition, giving a bit of self-disclosure that demonstrates that you admire the client, helps establish genuineness.

CLINICIAN: You're right; being a nice guy is part of the job. I mean, after all, who wants a mean therapist? But what I have learned from you so far is that you are a true survivor. Your mother's alcoholism, the deaths of your entire immediate family in the past five years, growing up with disabled siblings ... You might not believe this about yourself, but you are quite strong, which I find admirable. Let's talk about how you made it through all of that.

The case situation was real and so is the therapist's response. The psychotherapist is also shedding light on something that the client is overlooking about themselves and their experiences, namely their resilience in the face of trauma. This can be built upon as the work continues. Being real is about always telling the truth. Many of us have been taught to repress, and therefore not express or even recognize certain feelings. As a matter of fact, psychoanalyst and author Alice Miller (1990) points out that when a child is abused, they are taught to see the abuse as "normal"; whatever negative emotional reactions the child is experiencing is because there is something wrong *with them*, and this might be the most damaging effect of the abuse. So, one of the most healing things you can do is really listen for and hear a client's true feelings, bearing witness and thus validating their full experiences in a sincere manner.

Cultural Curiosity

If you are working with a specific population, become curious. For example, if working with a certain age group, get to know what their interests are as a group. Who are the popular musical groups they listen to, or in the case of middle aged and elderly adults, *had* listened to and perhaps still do? For children, what are the toys and videogames that they play with? If you are working in a community or neighborhood that is different from your own, part of your job will be to get to know that community.

If you ever wonder how a client judges our authenticity or genuineness, meet with a recalcitrant teenager. Adolescents can smell phoniness a mile away, so let them guide you. When I worked with adolescents in the past, many of my clients were wearing rock and roll t-shirts featuring groups popular in the 70s, like Led Zeppelin and the Doors. I could partially relate because I was familiar with those groups when they were originally popular, and therefore could hold an informed conversation about them. At the time, several of my young White clients were fans of Marilyn Manson. I was not a fan, but I was curious as to how my clients perceived him. Marilyn Manson (well before recent allegations against him of interpersonal violence) seemed to be a clever, innovative entrepreneur who, like many rock musicians before and after, tapped into youth's rebellious urges (and parental fears and disapproval). Referring to myself as an old man (I was in my mid- to late thirties at the time) I asked my clients to explain why they liked him. I can't say I ever got answers that were terribly enlightening (e.g. "He's cool" accompanied by a shrug); but the point was to show interest in the client's world. During this time, I knew that Snoop Dogg put out a controversial album that was popular with the teens I was seeing. (This was years before he adopted his current tamer, friends-with-Martha Stewart-persona.) Though he was a Black hip hop artist, his music had crossover appeal to the impoverished, rural White youth I was serving, which made him rather unique in the 90s. He had put out a controversial compact disc (CD) cover that depicted images of violence and misogyny and, of course, parents were appalled. I was not so familiar with his music at the time, so it would have been a mistake to act as if I were. However, I was genuinely interested in what youth thought about the controversy. So, in breaking the ice with a kid who liked the artist, I could ask: "Parents are concerned that his music encourages violence and the mistreatment of women. What do *you* think?" Note, this question was asked without communicating any negative judgment, which would have likely shut down any honest discussion. My young clients tried to reassure me that they understood that the man and his image were make-believe and scoffed at the idea that a cartoon would encourage them to become violent. I also used the CD cover to generate parent-child discussions about violence and respect for women. Communicating familiarity along with curiosity about your client groups' culture (without judgment or attempting to adopt it yourself) can be a springboard to engagement. In doing so you are showing an interest in seeing them for who they really are. Further, cultural images and their potential influences on youth can be a good topic for family discussions about family and societal values, and expectations about behavior.

Don't fake it and risk appearing inauthentic. Educate yourself as much as you can and be curious about what you do not know. Ask your clients for clarification; they will appreciate your interest. Remember, you yourself are an instrument for this work, the most important one at that. Your unique personality is vital to the psychotherapeutic endeavor and there's no need to try to leave it at the session door; you couldn't even if you wanted to. As stated previously, it is likely you were drawn to this work because of your ability to draw people to you. You are fine just the way you are and there is no need to act like someone you are not.

Working with Transference

The skills of empathy, warmth, genuineness, and goal setting are all important in establishing the healing relationship. In addition, it is vital to acknowledge that both the client and the clinician bring the ghosts of previous relationships into their current ones. We all first learn how to relate to ourselves and others by the way our families cared for us as children. In addition, we absorb powerful lessons about how worthwhile we are from our peers, past and present. Finally, as children we learn how people got along by watching the adults in our lives relate to each other. Many theoretical perspectives describe how if we were surrounded by stable, loving, and consistent care during early childhood, we developed the ability to establish trusting relationships as adults. Conversely, if we experienced abuse or neglect in these relationships, or were bullied by other children, we learned that we were not worth much, or that we had to fight or distance ourselves because closeness was dangerous. Clients project these ideas and accompanying feelings onto their adult relationships, including their relationships with their therapists, and this phenomenon is known as transference. This term was originally derived from psychoanalysis (Freud, 1939) and has since been referred to in some form and in a variety of ways such as the imago (Hendrix, 2007), the family projection process (Bowen & Kerr, 2009), and the shadow (Jung, 2014). What is important to recognize is that in adulthood we unconsciously seek to repeat interactions from our childhood relationships (Strean, 1986). The clinician establishes a relationship in which the client begins to project their issues onto the therapist and act as if the therapist was their mother or some other important person or people in the client's life. No matter the model you are working from, transference is unavoidable in helping relationships and is actually the target of intervention in virtually all psychodynamic and interpersonal models of psychotherapy.

> José was working with a 24-year-old female client, Jenny, who had experienced a history of incest. She was working in therapy on her anxiety along with sexually compulsive behaviors that left her feeling ashamed and depressed. During therapy, Jenny wore tight revealing clothes, sat with her legs spread open, and asked José personal questions that he refused to answer. In the first session, Jenny revealed that as a middle schooler, she was sexually molested by an uncle who would caress her buttocks and genitals. After such incidents, he would take Jenny for ice cream. José quickly realized that Jenny presented herself as sexually provocative most likely because this behavior had been rewarded as a child.
>
> Wanda was seeing a 60-year-old client named Roger, a gay man, who was having relationship problems with his younger partner. Based on Roger's accounts, he was being bullied by this partner who would ask him to buy him things and pout and give the silent treatment when Roger refused. The silence put Roger in a panic that was relieved only if he gave into his partner's demands. Roger had been raised by strict, controlling parents. As a child, they chose what recreational activities and sports he would play, whether he liked them or not. As a young man, they chose his college, his major, even where he would live. From an early age, Roger was taught not to assert or even recognize his own needs and preferences. As an adult, this difficulty evidenced itself in his relationships in that he consistently put the needs of others over his own, even when doing so interfered with his own well-being.
>
> Clara was a 45-year-old mother of two receiving public assistance and disability benefits. She was known among local service providers as a difficult client. She had an explosive temper which would frequently erupt when she was frustrated by service providers who she believed (sometimes accurately, sometimes not) were dismissive of her. Several service providers feared her wrath; she was never violent, but the heat of her anger intimidated people and they refused to work with her. She was referred to Mitch, who was known in the community for his ability to engage clients with difficult personalities. When she first entered his clinic, she was asked to complete paperwork and pay a nominal fee, at

which point she began shouting at the support staff. When doing a family history with Clara, it was clear she was raised by profoundly abusive parents who used rage as the primary means to control their children. When they weren't yelling and fighting, they were ignoring Clara. For her, fury was a way to defend herself and also be noticed.

In each of these cases, clients were demonstrating relating behaviors derived from their childhoods. In Jenny's case, she was reinforced as a child for being sexual. As she was an attractive adult woman, when men approached her with sexual or romantic interest, she would be pleased but at the same time uncomfortable for reasons she did not understand. When establishing a relationship with her male therapist, she acted seductively because she had learned that this was how to get attention or affection from the men in her life. She needed a safe place to learn that these behaviors would never get her the real validation she craved and deserved, and that she had value beyond her sexuality. Establishing a healing relationship with clients by incorporating the elements described earlier in this chapter can help them identify and resolve transference issues and unlearn their damaging lessons from childhood.

José was not taken in by Jenny's seductive behaviors. He needed to find ways to convince her that she was lovable, especially by men, for reasons beyond her attractiveness and sexual availability. He did this through direct, nonjudgmental interpretation of her behavior ("I notice you are a bit flirty with me; I am wondering what that's all about"). José refuses Jenny's invitation, in a way that is firm but also compassionate. At the same time, he frames it as an opportunity for self-insight and growth.

> I can see you are an attractive woman, but you need to know, you and I will never have a sexual or romantic relationship. In here, you do not have to give me your body for me to like you and want to work with you. In fact, a romantic relationship between us would not help you at all. After all you have been through, you need a relationship with a man that shows you your value beyond your sexuality, and you have an opportunity to work on that here. I know this type of relationship will feel strange to you, particularly at first, but let's keep exploring this issue and your feelings about it in our work together.

Once Jenny truly believed this, she was freer to find out who she was besides her sexuality. In keeping with the idea of the healing relationship, José is like a good mother, providing a holding environment for Jenny to explore her ideas about her worth in relationships.

In Roger's adult relationships, he always seemed to be putting other's needs ahead of his own, doing favors, even when he did not want to. What Wanda also noticed is that every time she gave Roger feedback or direction of some kind, he would enthusiastically nod his head yes and agree even before Wanda finished her sentence. Wanda realized early in her relationship with Roger that he had a habit of placating people while either concealing or remaining unaware of his true feelings. By complaining how he was bullied in his current relationship, he was almost provoking the therapist to push him to be more assertive, getting her to repeat the behavior of his controlling, overbearing parents. Eventually, Wanda realized that the needed reparative work was to help Roger figure out *his own* feelings about what was going on, as well as his own needs. In this case, the therapist needed to refrain from offering suggestions or interpretations and encourage the client to come up with his own.

> That's a tricky problem and I can see how hard it is to figure out what to do, but based on the way you've dealt with some of your past problems, I can see you are good at figuring things out. What do you think is going on? How might you like to proceed with this?

Wanda needed to be careful not to impose what *she* thought Roger should do, but instead (and in contrast to his parents) help Roger figure that out *for himself*. This was the real healing for Roger.

Clara's angry behavior was a way to protect the wounded parts of herself that were damaged during childhood. Sadly, her rage alienated people who were trying to help her; setting up relationships in which her needs were not met because people either distanced from her or met her anger with their own. Her clinician needed to find a way to show he could handle Clara's anger without running away. At the same time, Mitch needed to establish a relationship with her that was sufficiently trusting so that he could get her to talk about her intense rage, and give her feedback as to how it served and did not serve her. With the right healing relationship, Mitch got her to trust him enough to reveal the sad, abandoned, neglected child behind the anger. This child is invariably hiding inside any rageful adult.

Winnicott would call these interactions corrective emotional experiences (1988). It is important to recognize that once you establish this holding environment, a sudden cure does not automatically follow. The healing relationship that includes accurate empathy, and unconditional positive regard can seem very foreign to our clients and can engender discomfort, anxiety, even anger and acting out. Clients might push back by escalating certain behaviors in a renewed effort to get the therapist to act like their abusive, seductive, or controlling parent. For example, Roger might appear more helpless and confused, and Jenny might up her game in terms of trying to seduce her therapist. In the face of these escalations, the therapist needs to maintain a calm, accepting, but firm presence and continue to be mindful of the transference and what needs to be done to heal it.

The Clinician's Issues

Sometimes, no matter how experienced we are, a client's issues can collide with our own. In keeping with the classic view of countertransference, a client's difficult transference behaviors can dredge up powerful feelings in the clinician which, if unrecognized, can interfere with treatment (Hanna, 1993). Truth be told, initially Wanda advised Roger, "Hey, you need to buck up and stand up for yourself" and assigned him tasks in which he was to assert himself—understandable in light of Roger's difficulties. However, each week Roger would report that he had failed to complete these assignments. If Wanda became angry and more directive with Roger, she ran the risk of repeating the unhelpful patterns Roger had experienced in his childhood and adult relationships. Wanda had grown up in a family that prized assertion and fighting back in the face of unfair treatment, and to feel shame when she acted in any other way. As a result, she became agitated when she saw the vulnerability in people who did not stand up for themselves. Thus, her own issues could interface with Roger's. Like magnets and steel, a client's transference and a clinician's countertransference can lock together and work in tandem ways that are unhelpful. Initially, Wanda felt the need to push Roger to act as she would without understanding that Roger needed to figure out what he needed and how to get it.

It is important to note that when a clinician finds themselves repeatedly applying an intervention that is unsuccessful, countertransference is likely at work. A basic rule in psychotherapy (and life, come to think of it) is that if what you're doing is not working, stop doing it; do something else. There is also the rule of three: if you tell somebody the same thing three times, by the third time they are not listening. It is up to the clinician to determine why the intervention is not working. In this case, did Roger really need instruction on how to assert himself? Were Wanda's repeated suggestions simply mimicking that of the "do it my way" parenting Roger received? Had Wanda fallen into Roger's transference trap in which he unwittingly recreates his problematic relationship with his parents? The answers to these questions are no, yes, and yes. What Roger really needed was encouragement to find *his own way*, and Wanda needed to manage her own feelings in the process.

Mitch felt anxious and threatened by Clara. He had been raised by an aggressive mother who was frequently angry and at times, physically abusive. As a result, when confronted with anger, particularly from women, he would distance or emotionally shut down. However, if he acted this way with Clara, she would reexperience her abandonment feelings as a child and perhaps be even more angry, leading the therapeutic relationship nowhere. Clara set up relationships throughout her life in which people not only refused to help her but withdrew in the face of her fiery rage. Mitch needed to find a way to contain Clara's anger, meeting it in an atmosphere of calm acceptance and with appropriate limits but without backing away. Mitch continuously reflected Clara's anger and frustration while at the same time let her know that she needed to find better ways to express it.

While preparing for his upcoming session with Clara, Mitch overheard her yelling at the office reception staff about her fee. Upon hearing the commotion, Mitch left his office and calmly approached Clara.

MITCH: Hi Clara, wow, I can see you are very, very angry, and I want to hear about what it is that is pissing you off so much. Ok, so let's step into my office and talk about it.

I have found that when a client is in an explosive state, leading with comments like "knock it off" or even "calm down" do not work. The client needs to get that you understand the depth and breadth of their emotion, so an empathic reflection is needed, and can actually deescalate a situation before it spins out of control:

MITCH: Wow Clara, you seemed furious out there. Tell me all about what happened that got you so angry?
CLARA: That secretary got nasty with me. I did not realize there was a fee and paperwork, and when I asked about this, she got rude. I don't know who the f–k she thinks she is talking to!

Mitch is showing he is interested in her feelings, which begins to counteract Clara's impression that no one understands or accepts them. Mitch simultaneously empathized with Clara's anger and coached her not to yell at office staff.

MITCH: I can see how enraged you are, but I am concerned that when you act in certain ways with our office staff, they will not give you the help you are seeking. So, let's talk about what is getting you so angry and at the same time, strategize ways to get what you need.

More often than not, anger is the cloak worn by sadness and powerlessness, and to a lesser extent, fear and hopelessness. Mitch was able to see that this was the case with Clara's rage. After weeks of Mitch withstanding the hot blast of Clara's litany of angry complaints about her husband, children, extended family, and helpers, Clara's anger in sessions began to subside. She could see she had an ally in Mitch who was not scared off by her. The stick-to-itiveness of the therapist along with his calm openness to her anger, helped Clara to calm down. Soon she became so loyal and trusting of Mitch, that she could accept his correction and direction, such as instructions to pause and breathe deeply when she was starting to rage.

It was important that Wanda and Mitch underwent their own psychotherapy which helped them be sufficiently self-aware to avoid the pitfalls of their clients' transference. As I recommend in Chapter 1, participating in your own therapy could help you identify issues from your past, begin to address and resolve them, and most importantly for the clinical encounter, recognize when they are rearing their head in your work. Because we are working so closely with people, our own issues can get churned up, no matter how experienced we are. That is why continuous self-reflection is vital

Sexual Attraction to Clients

If you are familiar with my research, you will know that I am sex positive. However, sexual relationships between clients and clinicians must never happen, period. Such relationships are taboo and for important reasons. Of course, they are a violation of the NASW Code of Ethics (NASW, 2021) and such behavior could lead a clinician to lose their license or be sued. However, it is vital to drill down on the important reasons why sexual relationships are an abuse of the clinical relationship and a cruel betrayal of our clients' trust.

When we have sex with someone, we seek to have our physical and (often but not always) our emotional needs fulfilled and to hopefully do the same for our partner. Even if it is a casual encounter, both partners are making themselves physically and at times, emotionally naked and vulnerable in ways that go beyond the flesh. However, as stated previously, the relationship between client and therapist needs to be one-sided and completely in the service of the client's healing. This agenda clashes with the drive toward mutual satisfaction sought by partners in a consensual sexual encounter. A therapist having sex with a client is exploitive in the same way as if a parent or older authority figure has sex with a child. Despite any occasional appearance of compliance, the great power differential between the child and the adult means the child cannot ever fully consent to sex. The similar dependence and power differential on the part of the client means that when it comes to consent, the client–clinician relationship is far from a level playing field.

There is an alarming report that suggests that up to 20 percent of all therapists have had sex with their clients (Hetherington, 2000). In that article, the offending therapists give a variety of reasons to justify their behavior, including being in love with the client and believing that what they are doing is curative. These writers go on to discuss these therapists' psychodynamics from their own childhood that might contribute to these behaviors, such as having emotionally neglectful caretakers, so once again clinician issues resurface but in a very destructive way. When therapists ethically step out of line, they rationalize their own actions by claiming that *their* circumstances are in some ways special and warrant an exception to the rules. Holding this notion is dangerous and as a clinician, if you are ever tempted to have sex with a client or commit any ethical violations, be on the lookout for this rationale in your self-reflection.

That said, we are all human and sooner or later you will run across a client to whom you are sexually attracted. In spite of your commitment not to engage in a sexual relationship, be on the lookout for indirect or unconscious ways you might act such feelings out, such as voyeuristically encouraging clients to talk about their sex lives, even when the topic is not directly relevant to the treatment. Take a quiet moment to reflect and ask yourself, "Am I having sexual feelings or thoughts because my own sexual needs are unfulfilled and need attending?" Sometimes sexual feelings can represent a desire to merge with or even nurture someone. Note: if you are repeatedly having these feelings across clients, this would be good material for your own therapy. Wanting to have sex with your client might mean that you have some omnipotent fantasy to take care of them in what you think would be a deep and meaningful way, which in a real relationship, would be exhausting, and frankly impossible. Or, it simply could signal your feelings of closeness. So, the takeaway here is do not act on these feelings, but do not penalize yourself for having them either. Instead, see them as portals to sources of insight about your client and yourself.

Symptom-Focused Treatment

The relational model described previously can be sufficient in helping a client meet their goals, however, there are focused models of treatment that are more appropriate for targeted relief of symptoms such as acute anxiety and depression. It is still vital to establish the right relationship with a client using the above principals and techniques. However, these models can be integrated into the relationship-oriented methods previously discussed.

Behavioral Therapy

Behavioral therapy is arguably the most symptom-focused psychotherapy. Strict behavioral therapists are solely concerned with behavior change, and problematic behavior is assessed and analyzed in terms of how it is reinforced and how alternative behavior is punished.

Classical Conditioning

Pavlov, a Russian behavioral scientist and founder of what is known as classical conditioning, would give his dog a treat and ring a bell at the same time (Franks, 1969; Skinner, 1965). He soon discovered if he rang the bell but delayed the treat, the dog would begin to salivate in anticipation. Classical conditioning is one way to understand anxieties and phobias. The problem is when the person associates the nervousness with the setting in which the anxiety occurred and then avoids the setting. Let's say a person has an anxiety attack in a supermarket. Their nervousness may have little or nothing to do with the supermarket but as a result, each time they enter such a store, they become anxious. Fear of anxiety or anxiety about anxiety sets in and as a result, people become hypervigilant for bodily signs that they are about to get anxious. Sometimes this is a self-fulfilling prophecy as they develop anxiety in an increasing number of settings and start to consistently avoid multiple places that do not feel safe. In extreme cases, people develop agoraphobia believing that the only safe place is home and thus they find themselves housebound. Successful treatment of this disorder is getting that person out of their home and back into situations that frighten them, so they can learn there is nothing really to fear. (For a compelling poetic rendering of this treatment, read the poem *See Paris First* by M. T. Cooper.) The only way out of this dilemma is to force oneself into situations that scare them. A colleague of mine who specialized in treating people with agoraphobia pushed clients to go to the supermarket. When clients objected, "I can't go! I'll pass out!" he would reply, "Carry my card with you with instructions to have someone call me when that happens." Of course, it never did.

Systematic desensitization exposes the client to what they are afraid of in increasing increments while also teaching them how to manage their physical symptoms (McKay, Davis, & Fanning, 2021). First, clients are taught relaxation techniques such as deep breathing and progressive muscle relaxation. Then they are instructed to visualize the object or situation that raises their anxiety. For example, a person who is afraid of escalators might be first instructed to close their eyes and visualize an escalator, report their anxiety levels, and be prompted to apply relaxation techniques. Then they might be instructed to visualize approaching the escalator. As they become better able to apply the relaxation methods during visualizations, at subsequent sessions they might be instructed to approach a real escalator and slowly progress to eventually getting on it. Pure behavioral therapy focuses on eliminating problematic feelings and behaviors, however, following such interventions, the client and therapist might choose to explore the thoughts that fuel the anxiety (Thomlison, 1986).

Operant Learning

A—>B—>C
(A)ntecedent Events—>(B)ehavior—>(C)onsequences.

People react to particular events with a certain behavior that is either punished or reinforced by whatever follows. Psychotherapy based on the principals of operant conditioning seeks to change the relationship between behavior and consequences (Thyer, 2017). For example, a client who has suffered the loss of a relationship (antecedent event) might begin to drink excessively (behavior). At first, drinking seems to provide relief for the client's grief (a consequence), however, being hungover the next day is also a consequence. A behavior therapist might help the client change their behaviors in ways that would maximize the positive outcomes; in this case, relief from grief while minimizing the negative effects. Behavioral philosophy undergirds punishing a child for misbehavior. By applying a punishment, parents, and others who care for youth hope that their problematic behaviors will be extinguished. However, there is good reason to believe that rather than punishment, reinforcement of desired behaviors is more powerful and more likely to achieve the desired outcomes. Even better is what is known as *intermittent reinforcement* when the desired behavior is not consistently reinforced but instead is done so only periodically (Thomlison, 1986). The idea is that the client whose behavior one is trying to change, keeps manifesting the behavior in the hopes that *this time* the reward will come.

When teachers or parents use charts to track behavior and stickers to reward it, they are doing behavior therapy. Giving a child a dollar for every A they get on their report card is another way of applying behavior therapy. What is important to recognize is that children, particularly those younger than 10 or so, cannot cognitively link their behavior to a reward or consequence if the gap of time in between is too long. So, for example, to tell an 8-year-old that they will get a bicycle if they get all A's on their report card might not be effective because the report card (and thus the bicycle) is too far in the future. The most effective rewards (and to a lesser extent, punishments) are applied as quickly as possible after the targeted behavior. Thus, it is better to reinforce the steps the child needs to take to achieve the A, such as rewarding a good grade on a homework assignment or even spending 1 hour of studying.

Behavior therapy is typically a component of clinical social work with children. In working with families, parents and caretakers need to have the authority to be able to set reinforcement schedules. This will be further discussed in Chapter 6, which describes working with families.

Cognitive Behavioral Therapy

So many of our clients treat themselves horribly. They say things to themselves out loud and silently that are harshly self-critical often without any awareness that they are doing so. This self-talk can be about not being *enough*: smart enough, attractive enough, nice enough, empathic enough, successful enough, hardworking enough, and so on. This punitive self-narrative escalates when the client is faced with disappointing or stressful events, such as failing an exam, being mistreated by a loved one, or fired from a job. These thoughts might stem from historical experiences previously mentioned in this chapter, but for sure, they make the feelings and reactions to negative events worse and are often a major player in an individual's anxiety or depression.

Cognitive behavioral therapy (CBT) is a model that has a strong empirical basis for addressing anxiety and depression (Mor & Haran, 2009; Tolin, 2010). In this model, the central idea is that feelings follow thoughts, and emotional and behavioral problems are based on the notion that what needs to change for these clients is their irrational or automatic thinking (Beck, 2011). Clients who are experiencing depression or anxiety are thinking incorrectly, especially when faced with a stressor or a challenging situation. Problematic thoughts tend to be unforgiving and cruel and can include, but are not limited to, self-talk statements such as: "I'm so stupid," "I'll never succeed," "Everyone hates me," "I'll never get this task done," "They think I'm crazy." For sure, it is impossible to feel good about oneself if one is talking to themselves in this way. So, the task is to get the client to identify these thoughts and change them. The A—>B—>C—>D model is used to identify the core principles of cognitive behavioral therapy.

A—Antecedent or Stressor (Failing an exam)
B—Problematic thought following the stressor ("I'm so stupid." "I'll never get through college.")
C—Emotion (Depression, feelings of worthlessness)
D—Behavior (Sleeping too much, overeating, avoiding exams)

Cognitive behavioral therapy is distinguished by its use of charts, notes, and homework assignments. The main target of intervention is what is known as the clients' automatic or dysfunctional thinking. First off, the therapist needs to slow down the ABCD process, particularly if the client can only recognize the feelings and not the thoughts, as is often the case. Once the thought is identified and brought into the clear light of day, it is evaluated and replaced with a thought that is less emotionally crippling and more realistic (McKay, Davis, & Fanning, 2021).

According to Judith Beck and her father Aaron who developed this model, its cornerstone is the dysfunctional thought record or the DTR (Beck, 2011). The DTR consists of several columns that correspond to the ABCD model. Each of the following has its own column: the date or time and description of the antecedent situation, the automatic thought, the emotions that follow, the adaptive response and the outcome. Some DTRs include a scaling of the problematic emotion from 1–100, (100 being most intense), which can be helpful for clients who have trouble identifying and talking about their feelings. In addition, some CBT practitioners encourage clients to label their dysfunctional thoughts as part of the process of assessing and repudiating them (McKay, Davis, & Fanning, 2021). Following are some examples:

Filtering: Overfocusing on the negative parts of a situation or event at the expense of the positive: "Even though my guests said they liked the meal, some of the meat was tough and that really ruined the evening. They were probably lying to me to make me feel good."

All or Nothing: A situation is either all good or all bad—there's no room for a combination of both or any nuance; related to filtering: "The meat was dry so the meal was a failure."

Magnification: Making a problem out to be bigger than it is: "I failed this exam. This must mean I am too dumb for this program."

Fortune telling: Predicting the future but with a negative or even disastrous spin: "I just know the biopsy will come back with bad news and I will discover I am terminally ill."

Personalization: Taking everything personally and feeling at fault, even in the absence of any clear evidence: "My spouse is in a bad mood, I must have done something wrong to cause it."

Mindreading: Believing you know what others are thinking and that their thoughts are usually negative: "I know the clerk at the welfare office is judging me because I am unemployed." "My wife *says* she is not angry, but I know she really is!"

All or nothing thinking: When things are all good or all bad: "I am a failure" or "I am great!" What is missing is the nuance of being a flawed but mostly ok human being with strengths and weaknesses, which is in fact, a good description of each of us.

Shoulding: Maintaining and at times enforcing hard and oppressive rules about one's behavior or feelings leading to harsh judgment of self and others: "I should have known better." "He should have called me back when he said he would." When clients do this, it is good to point out: "You really are shoulding all over yourself."

It is less important to know the exact label than it is to identify that the thought is dysfunctional, and will inevitably lead to emotional distress. Cognitive behavioral therapy teaches clients how to replace these thoughts with those that are forgiving, kind, and realistic. Table 4.1 is an example of a completed DTR.

During the initial sessions, the clinician is training the client in the model, and this can be broken down into steps. For the first session, the client is assigned to only complete column 1 and identify the situations and their emotional reactions and rate them. Once they master this, they can begin to identify the thoughts that precede their emotions and to label them. As they become more proficient, they can complete the balanced thought column and then rerate their feelings. By the time they get to this point, clients should begin to feel better.

Cognitive behavioral therapy, despite its strong empirical basis, may not be for everyone. Clients struggle with identifying the thoughts that initiate feelings. They often say: "I'm not thinking anything—I'm just feeling bad." It can be rather difficult to identify thoughts, particularly in the midst of an

Clinical Social Work with Individuals 83

Table 4.1 Example of a Completed Dysfunctional Thought Record

Situation	Feelings/Rating out of 100	Automatic Thought	Label	Behavior	Balanced Thought	Re Rated Feelings
Can't sleep	Tired 80 Bored/Frustrated 60	I'm tired; I should be able to sleep. I'm going to feel awful tomorrow.	Shoulding Fortune Telling	Restlessness	Well, I do wish I could sleep, but in the meantime, I will try to just rest and not worry so much about sleeping. I cannot predict how I will feel tomorrow. Maybe it will be a good day to take it easy	Tired 70 Frustrated 30
Argument with Dad	Angry 85 Frustrated 90	He never listens to me. He should be more understanding. He's so rigid.	All or nothing Shoulding	Alternating between angry yelling and withdrawing with no contact.	Sometimes he listens when he's calm and in a good mood. Sure, it would be nice if he could be more understanding and flexible, but I cannot control that, only myself. Maybe I need to figure out when to approach him when he's in a better mood.	Angry 25 Frustrated 35

overwhelming emotional situation like a panic attack. In fact, research findings suggest that the inability to identify thoughts, holding a pessimistic viewpoint, and having difficulty staying focused as factors that contraindicate its use for some clients (Renaud, Russell, & Myhr, 2014). At times, this model can seem superficial in that targeting a client's thoughts only skims the surface when what is needed is a deep exploration of attachment issues, old wounds, and trauma. For example, in my experience some people are not only seeking symptom relief but also where their punitive thinking originates, and how their past history impacts their current problems, which this model does not provide.

That said, it is clear that negative thinking, in terms of self-talk, creates painful feeling states. A client's severe self-talk tape must be identified and stopped. Referring to the frame found earlier in the chapter, once the client has formed the proper relationship with their clinician, they can come to this conclusion on their own and start changing their thinking. Nevertheless, cognitive behavioral therapy may provide an effective shortcut for some clients.

Solution-Focused Therapy

In the 1980s, Steve deShazer and Insoo Kim Berg developed a model of psychotherapy that was meant to codify and disseminate the brilliant but-difficult-to-replicate work of the talented hypnotherapist, Milton Erickson (1991). Using a constructivist perspective, they developed a model of therapy that is straightforward, empowering, and humane. Following is a list of precepts from the model:

1. The solutions to clients' problems lie within themselves. The therapist's job is not to provide solutions but to help clients recognize and apply their own strengths and problem-solving abilities. It is assumed that in the past, people have successfully utilized solutions to their own problems, but overlook or have forgotten them. The therapist's task is to unlock these solutions and bring them to the fore. All clients have strengths and have developed solutions, and the clinician's job is to unearth them.
2. All environments, no matter how bleak, contain resources. It is the clinician's job to help the client identify them. For example, people in a distressed, high-crime neighborhood where a client lives might share a sense of comradery, helping each other out during hard times.
3. Focusing on these strengths as the clients define them increases their motivation. If therapy overfocuses on what is going wrong in a client's life, it can leave them feeling dehumanized and depressed, while focusing on strengths can energize clients sufficiently to actively solve their difficulties.

4   Strength identifying renders helpers less judgmental and less likely to burnout. That is because looking for what is strong, resilient, and resourceful in people is inevitably inspiring for the clinician, while staying focused on all that is going wrong (which clinicians are meant to fix) can be overwhelming and draining.
5   Change is constant and inevitable. When people say, "things will never change" or "he'll never change" they are espousing a myth. Continuously, people change through aging and life events that alter their perceptions, and they gain new insights. The idea is to steer clients to change in directions that lead to solutions and improvements in their lives.
6   Small change is all that is necessary; a change in one part of the client's life affects changes in others. As a tip, next time you see a new (voluntary) client, ask them what other changes they had recently made in addition to seeking therapy. Don't be surprised if they talk about starting an exercise or weight-loss plan, enrolling in a course, or making an appointment for a long overdue physical exam.
7   Clinicians operate from a position of not-knowing. Clients possess the solutions to their problems. The client, not the social worker, is the expert. The counselor assists the client in uncovering and rediscovering resources they already have.
8   If it works, don't fix it. If it worked once, do it again. If it doesn't work, don't do it again. Do something different.

Solution-Generating Questions

The main tools of solution-focused therapy are solution-generating questions. After getting a history of the problem, the clinician first asks, "when you have had this problem in the past, what did you do to try to solve it?" Also, "what's happening in your life when this is not a problem?" These queries are known as "exception questions." The idea behind them is that *every* problem has an exception; we just need to remind the client to find it. Here are a few other common, strength-building questions:

1   "What's different about the times when (the problem is not occurring)?"
2   "When you had this problem in the past, how did you solve it? How did you get that (the exception—previous success) to happen?"
    a   "It's difficult to end an abusive relationship? How did you manage to leave? You must be a strong woman."
    b   "You say your son is out of control, yet you managed to bring him in to see me. How did you make that happen?"
3   "What's going on right now that you would like to see continue?"
4   "How did you (do you) manage to survive (cope)?"

5 "When you resolve this problem, how will you know? How will you act differently?"
6 "How does (problematic behavior such as drinking excessively, neglecting children, staying with abusive partner etc.) help you?"
7 "What are you willing to change right now?"

Solution-focused therapists operationalize unconditional positive regard (described earlier in this chapter). For example, if a client procrastinates when faced with work tasks, the clinician presumes that the client believes they have at least some good reasons for their behavior and wants to know what they are. Then the clinician and the client can evaluate whether the costs of such behavior outweigh the benefits, leaving the decision to change in the hands of the client. Questions about how the client previously solved this problem, or similar situations in which the problem did not occur, offer clues as to what they can apply from the past to address their current problem.

> On a snowy day, Mack, a clinician in a nonprofit counseling center, received a call from the local police department. An officer was called to the home of the Smith family to break up a fist fight between Bob and his 16-year-old son Chad. Bob asked his son to shovel the driveway and Chad agreed to do so, but kept putting him off: "In a minute Dad; I am in the middle of a [video] game." Hours would go by with Bob getting increasingly angry. Finally, Bob, unplugged the television and ordered his son outside. In response, his son became furious and physically assaulted his father which led to the fist-to-cuffs. Bob and Chad came to the agency for a crisis visit.

During his assessment, Mack learned that Bob was a retired fire chief. This gave him an idea:

MACK: Tell me Bob, when you were head of the firehouse, I am guessing you had to get the people below you to do some tasks they did not want to do. Am I right?
BOB: Yes, absolutely. Everyone had a job to do around the firehouse. The newbies had the worst jobs, including scrubbing the bathrooms.
MACK: How did you get them to do these jobs?
BOB: Well, they had to! It was part of their job.
MACK: Yes, but I am guessing they could have refused if they wanted to. They were protected by a strong union, no?
BOB: Yes, that is right
MACK: So, what did you do to convince them?
BOB: Well, now that I think of it, I made sure the others saw that I was not above doing the work myself. For example, when it was time to clean up after a meal, I would get up and say, "C'mon guys, let's clean up this mess" and start picking up plates myself. The others would follow.

MACK: Hmmm ... sounds like good leadership to me, setting a good example for the others. So, what from this experience could you apply to your family?
BOB: (after a long pause) Well, I guess I could make tasks more collaborative. I could pick up a shovel or start with a chore and tell Chad, "Let's go."
MACK: Hmmm ... interesting. You willing to give it a try?
BOB: Yes.

At their subsequent session, Bob reported that he was employing this method very successfully. Both of his children were helping out more at home and the fighting over chores had ended. It is worth mentioning that this was not a solution Mack thought would work. However, he put his faith in Bob's solution which ultimately paid off.

Compliments are used profusely throughout solution-focused therapy to reinforce and build upon client strengths. However, as stated previously, they must be clearly hitched to a client behavior. Note how Mack compliments Bob's leadership skills in the example above. Drawing on another example, rather than, "You're such a good mother; that's great!", instead keep the compliment focused: "You really managed to get your kids to behave well during this session—not so easy." (Note the compliment contains an added dash of empathy.)

Another hallmark of solution-focused work is the miracle question:

Imagine that when you go to bed tonight, as you are sleeping a miracle happens, and the problem you have come to therapy for has been solved. What is the first thing you would notice when you woke up that would tell you that a miracle had occurred?

Here is how, Lakeisha, a 40-year-old African American woman in a troubled relationship responded when asked the miracle question:

LAKEISHA: My partner would lean across the bed and kiss me good morning.
CLINICIAN: What would you do in response?
LAKEISHA: I would kiss him back.
CLINICIAN: How might he respond?
LAKEISHA: Well (sheepishly), we might make love
CLINICIAN: How would you feel then?
LAKEISHA: Great!
CLINICIAN: What is the first thing your children would notice that would tell them some sort of miracle happened overnight? (Coworkers? Boss?)

As can be seen, solution-focused therapy is very much attuned to relationships and behavior between people, so the *relationship question* is central. For example, "What would your husband need to see to know there was a change in you?" "What would your troublesome boss think if you showed up to work and gave him a warm greeting instead of ignoring him?" "What would the judge and/or your child protective workers need to see different in you to know you are ready to have your children back?" Then the therapist can gently ask, "How ready are you to make those changes that your (husband, boss, judge) would see (or need to see)?" If your client is mandated, this question is particularly important.

Mandated Clients

If you are a social worker in a public or nonprofit agency, sooner or later, you will be assigned clients who have been ordered into therapy by someone in authority. For those who went into the field to help others and fantasized about working with grateful people, this can be a bit of a letdown, at least initially. Some of you may find yourselves working in jails, or child protective settings in which *all* of your clients are mandated. Further, children and adolescents are almost always "put" in therapy by someone else. No one likes to be told what to do, and people "sentenced" to therapy greet the occasion with the same enthusiasm as that of the condemned approaching the gallows. (Those assigned to help them might harbor similar feelings.) Involuntary clients can show up in our offices or present during our home visits with arms crossed, heads down, determined not to cooperate. It wouldn't be surprising if you found yourself anxiously wondering, how you are going to help them.

While there are many approaches to mandated clients, the following suggestions are heavily influenced by the solution-focused model (DeJong & Berg, 2012) and can be enormously helpful with this tricky client group.

1   First and most importantly, make sure the client fully understands the mandate. In line with the social work ethical value of self-determination, all clients, including those who are mandated, have the right to know what is expected of them. For example, how many sessions will there be and how will the sessions be paid for? They also need to know to whom the worker is required to report, in what format (a final written report? telephone or email communication?) and who will have access to this information. Trust is a big issue with these clients. You want to demonstrate that you will deal with them in ways that are honest, transparent, and fair. What complicates matters is that usually a mandated client has done something dangerous, illegal, or repulsive such as committing domestic violence or child abuse. As a result, various systems and professionals tend to dehumanize them, treating them with something less than respect. One all-to-common example of such treatment is when the mandator, who might be a judge, probation officer, or parent, neglects to fully inform these clients of the details of the mandate, making it even more important that the clinician finds out what they are and communicates them to the client.

2   A client's feelings of anger about the mandate are understandable and should be validated as "normal" under the circumstances. No one likes to be bossed around and that includes being forced to see a social worker. This goes double for people from ethnic groups that tend to stigmatize mental illness and its treatment. Let's face it; anger over being forced into therapy is normal and understandable. It is possible to empathize and validate client feelings without excusing behaviors, criminal or otherwise, that led to the mandate.

3   Everyone wants something to be better in their lives, even if they do not believe a therapist can help them achieve it. As someone working with a mandated client, you are seeking to find something that you can offer for which they might be a customer. For example, even if they deny having any therapeutic goals, virtually all mandated clients want to be released from the mandate. That is a good place to start: "Let's work on what it is that (the mandator) needs to see so that you no longer have to come in and see me."

4   The party doing the mandating, the client, and the therapist all need to have a clear understanding of the goals of treatment, and like all good goals, they need to be observable and measurable. I have seen goals for mandated clients written by judges, child protective workers, probation officers, and other mandators that read "client will deal with history of trauma" or "Beulah's parenting skills will improve" with no mention as to how progress will be assessed and by whom. Sometimes there is room for negotiation that could alter the goals, or the goals could change over time, which is understandable and to be expected. However, in order for the work to be fair, just, and effective, everyone must be on the same page and have a clear sense of what is expected of the client. As a matter of fact, having the goals written out somewhere so that all parties can refer to them at any time is a good idea.

5   All clients and all people have choices that they are making all of the time; never forget this. Remind the mandated client that they have *chosen* to be there. For sure, the consequences for not attending could be unpleasant, but nevertheless the client is choosing to avoid them by meeting with you. It is a good idea to reinforce and even gently compliment this: "I know you don't want to be here, but clearly you want to do the right thing to keep yourself out (or get yourself out of) trouble."

6   Finally, free yourself of the expectation that you have to change the client and somehow make them different. Psychotherapy may or may not work for a variety of reasons, and without client motivation, it is certainly no miracle cure. Your responsibility is to treat your mandated client fairly and humanely, and to advocate that others do the same, no matter what the outcome.

CLINICIAN: So, what is your understanding as to why you were sent here?

FRANK: I don't know but I don't need a therapist. This is ridiculous. I don't need any help.
CLINICIAN: I get it. I know you were sent to see me and it wasn't your choice. Do you know by whom?
FRANK: My probation officer said I had to come.
CLINICIAN: Yes, that is my understanding as well. You sound annoyed, and frankly, I don't blame you. Still, you showed up.
FRANK: I had no choice.
CLINICIAN: Well, Frank. I guess I am going to respectfully disagree with you there. I know it doesn't feel that way, but you always have a choice. You could have not come today.
FRANK: Well, if I had not, my probation officer might have violated me and then I'd have to go to jail.
CLINICIAN: For sure, not a great choice, but clearly you are making the one that is right for you and that keeps you out of trouble.
FRANK: (cool silence)
CLINICIAN: Though I get it. You don't want to be here.
FRANK: (cool silence; therapist notices a pattern here.)
CLINICIAN: Ok, everybody wants to change something in their lives. What is it you would like to change?
FRANK: Nothing, I don't need therapy and I don't want to be here.
CLINICIAN: OK, I can see that, and honestly, I agree with you. You shouldn't have to be here if you don't want to be. So, let's see if we can make it happen that you don't need to be here. What do you think your probation officer needs to see different from you to say, "Frank doesn't have to come to therapy anymore?"
FRANK: I don't know.
CLINICIAN: That must really stink, to be told you need to be here and not know what it will take to get you out of coming. Well, I think it's important that you know. From my understanding, he wants you to work on your anger. But that's pretty vague. You have a right to more specifics as to what he is hoping to see different in you, so let's call him to get an idea.

It is not unusual for mandators to be unclear with their clients about their expectations for therapy. Additionally, even if their goals for the client have been clearly communicated to them, the client has forgotten or is so angry that they don't want to acknowledge this. If it's the former, a call, email, or meeting with the mandator is indicated. If it's the latter, this must be approached with gentle understanding and empathy but also firmness. Never get into an argument with the client about their knowledge of the mandate, even if you suspect they are not telling the truth as this will not be helpful. Simply accept what they are saying at face value and proceed to get them clarification. As stated above, the mandator, the client, and the clinician need to be clear and in agreement about expectations.

FRANK: I think the PO (probation officer) wants me to find ways to control my temper to stay out of trouble.
CLINICIAN: So, what do you think of that? Are you ready to do that?
FRANK: Well, I can't get in trouble and go back to jail. If I do, I won't be able to see my kids and their mom.
CLINICIAN: Ok, like all good dads and husbands, your family is very important to you. How about if we work on your temper in ways that will get that PO off your back?
FRANK: (grudgingly) Ok.
CLINICIAN: In the meantime, let's contact your PO to find out what he would need to see that would convince him that you were successfully controlling your temper. You have a right to know this.

Once the therapist gets the answer from the PO, they and the client can develop objectives for treatment whose ultimate goal is to release the mandate and render the therapist unnecessary.

Adolescents and Children as Mandated Clients

It should also be remembered that more often than not, children and adolescents are mandated clients. For pre-teen and adolescent clients, the same techniques described above can be utilized. We can carefully empathize and align with these kids' desire to not be in therapy. As I do with other mandated clients, I like to tell kids that being in therapy is not really normal; instead they should be doing normal kid things like hanging with friends, playing video games, going to the mall, doing homework, and so on, and I want to get them back to that as soon as possible. As you say this, they may be somewhat surprised and understandably distrustful, but press on. Then switch the focus on what their parents and, if relevant, teachers want to see different and keep asking if they are willing to do anything to make that happen.

CLINICIAN: What is it your (parent/teacher) want to see different in order for them to say, "Jason does not have to come here anymore?"
JASON: Control my temper, I guess.
CLINICIAN: What would they need to see that would tell them you can control your temper?
JASON: Not get into any more fights
CLINICIAN: How could you do that? Avoid fights?
JASON: I don't know—especially when the other kids start them.
CLINICIAN: Well, it is important to stand up for yourself sometimes, I agree. However, there might be something you could do instead that doesn't get you into trouble and make it so you have to come to see me. Would you be willing to work with me on that?
JASON: Ok.

Sometimes, despite the wisdom on these pages, or that of your own discovered skills and techniques, mandated clients are just too angry to do anything during sessions but sulk. In these cases, continue to empathize, normalize their irritation, reinforce that they are doing what is good for them, and keep introducing and inviting the client to work on changes that would give them their "freedom" back.

More on Children

New clinicians might be initially surprised to learn that children generally do not respond to questions that typically work well with adults. For example, children usually cannot answer direct questions about their feelings (come to think of it, many adults are not so good at this either). However, children often lack the vocabulary to do so. Plus, the unfounded fear of saying the wrong thing and ruining the child forever might be an ever-present worry on the anxious beginner's mind.

The good news is that this worry is unfounded. First off, psychopathology is generally borne out of either sudden, powerful trauma, or repeated experiences of having one's emotional and developmental needs thwarted, all of which can be easily avoided in the therapy office or during the home visit. As with adults, there are very, very few individual and isolated clinician behaviors that can inflict long-term emotional damage on a child. If the intervention is not the right fit, it will be ignored or the child will let you know either directly or indirectly.

The very thing that makes psychotherapy challenging with children is what also protects them—that is, they are generally very strongly psychologically defended. Rather than acknowledging and expressing their feelings directly, they manifest them in their behaviors which serves to diminish potential psychic pain. Therefore, we must use indirect, projective methods. These are techniques that get at children's feelings, like drawing (Oster & Crone, 2004; Slayton, D'Archer, & Kaplan, 2010), storytelling (Gardner, 1986; Kottman, & Stiles, 2013), play therapy or even the use of comic book characters (Kendall, 2011). The idea is to use these tools to bypass defenses so that children can express unconscious or preconscious material symbolically and tell the truth about something potentially uncomfortable. These techniques can also be utilized in models of treatment such as cognitive behavioral (Kendall, 2011) and solution-focused therapy (Berg & Steiner, 2003) to help children describe situations that led them to behaviors that got them into trouble and then rehearse those that are more functional in cartoons, drawings, and storytelling (Kendall, 2011).

> Jay was a 12-year-old who was referred to me for an uncontrollable cough for which no physical cause could be found despite numerous examinations by medical professionals. He had been to several

> therapists before and there was no success. For better or worse, I had developed a reputation in the local mental health community as someone who was successful with difficult cases, so Jay was sent to me. When I received the referral, I thought, how bad could his cough be? Well, I received the answer when he entered the doorway of the clinic. His cough literally shook the timbers of the three-story Victorian structure that housed the clinic, to the extent that other clinicians including those on the third floor, interrupted their sessions to peek out of their doorways to see what the heck that earthshattering noise was.

Jay's parents were divorced and his mother and father shared joint custody. I tracked the origin of his problem by getting its history, and also tried to determine, from a family systems perspective (see Chapter 6), what might have caused this problem. Nothing significant emerged.

Despite early training which left me with a strong bias in favor of a family focus when working with children, a careful individual assessment with a child, using a projective technique such as drawing or storytelling can reveal an important direction for family work.

> I made arrangements to see Jay alone and had him draw me two pictures: 1) Free style meaning anything he wanted; and 2) A picture of himself and his family. The first picture revealed his love of sports cars, and yielded nothing useful. However, in the second picture, he drew a portrait of himself with his hand over his mouth. Generally, when someone puts one's hand over one's mouth, whether it be in a classroom, a group meeting or a therapy session, it is a universal sign that they are holding something back. I became intrigued and wondered aloud if there was something he wanted to say but felt stifled, which he denied. During the next session, he came in with a cut on his lip. When we were alone, I asked him what had happened. Nonchalantly, he relayed that his father hit him across the face and split his lip open after he backtalked to him. Of course, I needed to report this to the state child protective authorities and I brought the father into my office and told him so. Upon hearing this, the father broke down sobbing, admitted that he had hit his child and described his history of being abused by his own father. The father then asked for a referral for a therapist of his own. Interestingly, Jay refused to speak to me after that session. He claimed to be angry that I had betrayed his secret and got his father in trouble with the local child protective services. I interpreted this as Jay's way to save face; after "telling on" his father he needed to make me the enemy. The good news is that as soon as the abuse was uncovered and addressed, Jay's coughing ceased.

At Risk for Harm to Self or Others

More on Child Protection

An anxiety-provoking responsibility for most clinicians, particularly new ones, is that of mandated reporter. All clinicians and anyone who works with children including teachers, doctors, camp counselors, and daycare providers, are mandated reporters, meaning that by federal law, they *must* report any incidences of *suspected* child abuse to the hotline designated in their state. Reasons to suspect child abuse include but are not limited to bruises, burns, scratches, evidence of malnutrition, and a child telling you that they are being abused or neglected. Sometimes parents, or a child who is seeking to protect a parent, can devise an excuse that seems illogical, such as receiving a black eye due to a fall in the bathtub (an actual explanation I have heard more than once). Protecting children from abuse and neglect is a grave responsibility and can put the social worker in a difficult bind as they work to keep the child safe yet stay engaged with their parents. But an important responsibility it is. This is the law and there are no ifs ands and buts about it. Of course, the primary reason you must do this is to protect society's most vulnerable persons. A secondary reason is that you could lose your license or risk a jail sentence if you do not. Workers get into trouble when they follow directions from a superior not to report, and abdicate their responsibility for reporting to someone else. A fieldwork student who was placed in a school setting discussed a case in one of my classes where he had noticed suspicious bruises on a child's face. The class was in agreement that he needed to report this situation. However, the student's supervisor said she would do it herself. A week passed and she had yet to make the report, but the student thought he was covered because he had informed his supervisor. However, the law (and the ethical mandate) is quite clear that the person who knows about the incident must report it, no matter what their supervisor or administrator says. Neither a directive from a superior nor a promise from someone else to report absolves you of this important responsibility.

Here is a scary story that should serve as a cautionary tale. Early in my career, I worked at an agency in which many of the social workers did not get along with the executive director. We were each assigned a supervisor of record but some of my coworkers, in defiance of the director, sought supervision from a charismatic colleague, Jerome, who used to be the assistant director but was demoted due to conflicts with the administration. Mary was a young, new worker with less than six months of experience who was dedicated to working with stressed families but did not get along with her boss, so she instead consulted with the rogue supervisor. She told Jerome that during a home visit, one of her four-year-old clients reported that her stepfather had touched her genitals. Mary asked him if she should report it, and he replied, "Nah. If you reported everything we heard, we would be reporting all of the time." As it turns out, the client's neighbor overheard Mary's conversation during her home visit through the thin apartment walls and called the state child abuse hotline. When the case went in front of the judge, and he learned that the social worker knew about but failed to report this incident, he called Mary to his courtroom to reprimand her. He did not discipline her or initiate a process to have her license suspended, however word got around our small social work community and she was essentially blacklisted from other employment. Further, the agency's insurance would not cover her legal bills because she did not follow the chain of command and consult her supervisor of record. Take this story as a lesson. You are never absolved of your responsibility to report child abuse even if someone with more authority or experiences advises against it.

Another common reason workers get into trouble is that they often mistakenly believe they must get solid evidence that the child is being abused or neglected before reporting. This is not the case. The worker only needs to have *a reasonable suspicion*, however many clinicians are understandably uncomfortable with this ambiguity. Child abuse is a harrowing experience to witness or learn about. Further, workers who entered this field with the idea that they will be liked all of the time will be anxious about reporting on their clients. Thus, they will want clear, solid guidelines when sometimes, things will not be so clear. So, clinicians must use the criterion of *reasonable suspicion* which means that just about anyone who learned of the incident upon which the evidence is based would suspect abuse or neglect. For a child acting out sexually, the behavior in and of itself is not sufficient evidence that they are being sexually abused. However, a child's report of being touched inappropriately or sexually penetrated, reporting painful or injured genitals, the appearance of suspicious new bruises or any stories from clients that reveal possible abuse are all reportable. Any indication that parents are not properly feeding their children or are leaving them unsupervised at a very young age or in dangerous situations are reportable indications of neglect. Remember, it is the child protective department's responsibility to investigate the case, not that of the clinician. Also, when in doubt, it is perfectly acceptable to contact the local child protective hotline and run the case by them. If they deem the information reasonably suspicious, they will take the report and initiate an investigation. If not, they will let you know.

It is important to recognize that if the child in your treatment was abused by someone who is not responsible for the child's care, like a stranger or family friend, the issue needs to be reported to the police and *not* child protective services. If a parent refuses to make such a report, they are then to be hotlined for neglect. Further, if they refuse to procure necessary medical care for their children, that is considered child neglect. There have been several incidents during my career when a child was actively suicidal and the parents refused my order to take the child to a local emergency room until I threatened to report them.

Another issue to decide upon is whether to tell your clients beforehand that you are going to report them. Some child protective workers say never to tell parents as the element of surprise makes it difficult for parents to make up an excuse or cover up. I agree with this approach, particularly when it comes to sexual abuse. However, with regard to excessive corporal punishment, or even neglect committed by an ongoing client, I will let them know. I find, if we already have a good working alliance, then I can do this without irreversibly harming the relationship.

CLINICIAN: You've told me you hit your child with the wire from your iron. I'm afraid that I am obligated by law to report this.
MARIA: Really? Do you have to? I'm sorry; I just lost my temper. I won't let it happen again.
CLINICIAN: I will lose my job if I don't. Plus, we both want to make sure your child is safe.
MARIA: What is going to happen to my children? Will they be taken away from me?
CLINICIAN: I cannot promise anything, but in my experience that is highly unlikely. I am going to tell them that we are working together on ways to help you become a better parent so this type of incident never happens again. However, they will likely want to meet with you and ask you a few questions.
MARIA: OK, I guess I understand.
CLINICIAN: I know you are doing your best as a parent, and I will let them know that. Child protection might also have some ideas on resources that might help you.

In my experience, if the family already is working with a therapist, and the child is not in ongoing and imminent risk, child protective services tend to leave the child in the home and monitor the situation.

In my 40 years of practice, I can count on one hand the number of parents I have come across who really wanted to harm their children. Excessive corporal punishment is almost always based on good parental intentions, such as wanting their child to follow the rules, go to school, and be respectful to adults. However, adults who physically abuse their kids apply faulty and often dangerous methods to manifest these intentions. Parents who sexually abuse their children do not believe such treatment is harmful and, in a twisted way, think it is good for the child. Neglectful parents are often struggling with addiction or poverty. How to address these issues will be further discussed in Chapter 6.

Suicidal Clients

Besides being a mandated reporter, another anxiety-producing role for the clinical social worker is to prevent clients from harming themselves or others. Depending on the setting you are working in, suicidal behavior is fortunately, relatively rare. However, if you work in a mental health setting, including a private practice, you will eventually come across clients who are desperately unhappy and want to take their own lives.

Clients who are very depressed, anxious, or indicate they might be suicidal with statements such as: "I can't take this anymore," "What's the use of living?" and "I want to be with my (deceased relative)" are to be considered high risk for suicide. Clients who have a history of suicidal ideation and attempts are also at increased risk, as are those related to someone who has committed suicide, or has a friend or a classmate who has done so. A person who is giving away prized possessions should arouse suspicion. However, the biggest risk factor is if a client indicates that they have a plan that seems feasible and potentially effective.

CLINICIAN: You tell me you are feeling so badly that you want to die; tell me, have you done anything to hurt yourself? Do you have a plan, if so, what is it?
CLIENT: When I leave here, I am going to run my car off the road and crash into an overpass.
CLIENT: I have a stash of pills at home that I plan on taking.
CLIENT'S LOVED ONE: I noticed he bought a hose and found him trying to attach it to the exhaust pipe of his car.
CLIENT ON THE PHONE OR ZOOM: I have just slashed my wrists.

If the client has such a plan, the worker needs to arrange for an immediate assessment for hospitalization. This can be done at a local emergency room, preferably at a hospital that has a psychiatric unit. However, some local municipalities have special mental health crisis outreach teams that can come to the client's home or the clinician's office to do an assessment. It is best to check with your supervisor and your county's mental health department to determine what procedures and resources are in place to assist you in case of a suicidal emergency before one actually occurs. If the client is not deemed suicidal enough to warrant hospitalization, or if they are experiencing suicidal ideation but have no plan, you'll need to develop a safety plan that may consists of some or all of the following: 1) A contract with the client that they will not do anything to harm themselves between now and the next time you meet. This contract should include an agreement that if they get the urge to hurt themselves, they will call you (or the emergency number of your place of work); 2) A plan to ensure that the client is not alone. Request permission to contact a relative to ask to keep an eye on them; 3) The removal of all guns, knives or anything the client can use to harm themselves. If they cannot be removed from the home then they must be put away and locked up by whomever is keeping watch over the client; 4) a referral to a psychiatrist for medication evaluation. As a matter of fact, for anyone experiencing depression or anxiety that is resulting in oversleeping or insomnia, overeating or not eating enough, suicidal thoughts, or interfering with work or relationships, a psychiatric referral is indicated; 5) Between-session check-ins with the therapist to assess for suicidal thoughts, urges, and behaviors.

But Do This First

If the client who is sitting in front of you has yet to do something dangerous, you have time to explore what is making them so distressed. Further, it is reasonable to suspect that a client who comes to a therapist and reports suicidal thoughts or behaviors really wants to be talked out of the act. Therefore, as a clinician, you are afforded some time; use it to understand and empathize with what the client is experiencing.

CLIENT: I feel so awful. I really want to die; I can't see any point in going on.
CLINICIAN: Wow, you must be in a lot of pain. Tell me what is happening that is so terrible and painful that you no longer want to live?

This may be the most important question you ask a suicidal client. When a client reports suicidal thoughts to the therapist, they are communicating that they are in a great deal of anguish. *Initially* prioritizing the exploration of this pain over the safety plan often leads to a cathartic venting and problem-solving session that relieves client suffering and dissipates their suicidal feelings. I have seen many anxious workers focus on the suicide assessment at the expense of what the client is actually feeling. Ironically, this can come across as uncaring to clients who will perceive your only concern to be the risk of self-harm not the pain that generates it. Such a focus risks missing an important clinical opportunity. If the client is safely sitting across from you and is not injured, you have the time to address their anguish, so be sure to do that. Then, *before* that client leaves the session, check in with them about their suicidal feelings.

CLINICIAN: You told me earlier that you feel so bad you want to die. How are you feeling now?
CLIENT: Better, now that I have gotten things off my chest. I really do not want to kill myself. I just felt so awful, I did not know what to do.
CLINICIAN: Ok, good, I am glad you are feeling better—but I want us to establish a contract. Promise me that you will call me the next time you feel like you want to hurt yourself, can you do that?
CLIENT: Yes.
CLINICIAN: Also, I will call you to check in on you during the week to make sure you are ok.
CLIENT: Ok

If, at the end of the session, the client still reports feeling suicidal, has a plan, and cannot promise not to act on it, then an assessment for hospitalization at an emergency room or by a crisis outreach team (if available in your locality) is essential.

Duty to Warn

If a client tells you that they are planning to harm someone, as a clinician you must break confidentiality. You have a duty to not only contact the police but must also inform the person who is the target of such threats. It is a good idea for all clinicians to familiarize themselves with *Tarasoff vs. Regents of the University of California* (Gorshkalova & Munakomi, 2021). In summary, this is a case in which a man, Prosenjit Poddar, disclosed to his outpatient therapist at Cowell Memorial Hospital, UC Berkeley, that he was planning to kill a woman, named Tatiana Tarasoff, who was an unrequited love interest. The clinician contacted the police and requested that he be brought to the hospital for an involuntary inpatient psychiatric evaluation. The police interviewed and released him. Months later, when Ms. Tarasoff returned from a trip abroad, Mr. Poddar murdered her. Ms. Tarasoff's family successfully sued the University of California for failing to warn their daughter that she was in danger. As a result, clinicians are obligated to take action to protect anybody whom a client's behavior could endanger. This protective action includes alerting the target of a client threat as well as notifying the police and taking steps to hospitalize the client, if appropriate. It is important that clients understand the conditions under which you will not maintain confidentiality, and this includes if you reasonably suspect child abuse or neglect, or a client's propensity to harm themself or others. The Tarasoff decision means we must do everything in our power to keep safe whomever a client is planning to harm.

Case Management

As stated repeatedly, clinical social workers must be prepared to intervene and act on client environments. The more disadvantaged a client is based on income level, medical condition, age (children and the elderly), mandate, or disability, the more likely they will need advocacy and case management. When I worked with troubled children from poor neighborhoods, I was struck by how difficult it could be to schedule psychotherapy appointments with their parents. They would open their full appointment books and we would have to schedule around meetings with the probation officer, school counselor, pediatrician, child protective worker, case manager, and any provider of services the parent was receiving, such as counseling and parent education. Here are some insights. First, if you are connecting clients to services, more does not always mean better. I have heard mothers who were struggling with poverty complain that they could not maintain employment because their schedules were too booked up with appointments with helpers. I have also seen parents take children out of school so that they could keep these appointments. Most kids who are receiving mental health treatment are also having trouble in school, so pulling them out of class makes little sense and should be avoided or at least minimized whenever possible.

Second, the more cooks you have, the greater likelihood there will be disagreements, conflicts, and the pitting of one helper against another, particularly if there is no coordinated, overall plan. It is recommended that someone (preferably but not necessarily the social worker) take charge and work to coordinate the group as a team, scheduling regular meetings, perhaps once a month or so, and more often if the client is in crisis. The leader should evaluate what services are repetitive, and which people the parent or the child needs to meet with more frequently.

> Riva was referred to a private, not-for-profit child guidance agency when her children were removed from her custody upon being arrested and incarcerated for drug possession. Fortunately, she was not sentenced to jail but instead was ordered into treatment. After completing a week in detox and 30 days in rehab, she was in outpatient substance abuse therapy for six months along with individual psychotherapy at my agency. Early in therapy she clearly and consistently stated that she wanted her children back home. When she was asked what she was told she needed to do to make that happen, she claimed not to know. Like other mandated clients, it is not uncommon for those who are seeking to regain custody of their children to state that they do not know what needs to happen in order for their children to be returned. Thus, it is important to establish direct communication with the mandators and get the expectations as clear as possible.

Riva had a full-time job, an apartment, childcare, and seemed ready to parent again. So, the clinical social worker established a case conference with the child protective worker, the worker's supervisor (the decider), the substance abuse counselor, and the client. The client's progress was reviewed and people around the table agreed that Riva had made great strides in her recovery. Then the clinical social worker asked child protection what Riva needed to do to indicate that she was ready to get her kids back. There was some fumbling and eventually the child protective supervisor said she will know it when she sees it. The clinical social worker, who had training in goal setting and also a clear understanding of its importance, expressed surprise and concern, pointing out that this seemed unfair, as it set up an unclear target for the client. The child protective supervisor then turned to the substance abuse counselor and asked for her input. She responded that the client would be ready when she resolved her feelings about her history of being sexually abused. The clinical social worker exclaimed that this process could take years, even a lifetime. The substance abuse counselor agreed. So, this left the question as to what did this client need to be doing differently to indicate that she was, using Winnicott's language, a good enough mother (1988). At this point in the conference, everyone agreed that Ms. Riva deserved a "trial run" of having her children home for extended visits.

This client was involved in many different systems, because she was a mother in recovery, living in poverty, and with few resources. Though multiple services were necessary to assist her, they needed to be coordinated and the clinical social worker needed to be the one to do it. The situation is an important reminder that our work is *psychotherapy plus*, as it must extend beyond the psychotherapy we do with our clients, particularly those from oppressed groups like Riva, to ensure they are treated fairly and are empowered.

References

Beck, J. (2011). *Cognitive Therapy: Basics and Beyond* (2nd ed.). Guilford Press.
Berg, I. K., & Steiner, T. (2003). *Children's Solution Work*. WW. Norton.
Bowen, M., & Kerr, M. E. (2009). *Family Evaluation*. WW Norton & Company.
Bowlby, J. (2012). *A Secure Base*. Routledge.
Courtois, C. A., Ford, J. D., & Cloitre, M. (2009). *Best practices for psychotherapy for adults*. In C. A. Courtois, & J. D. Ford (Eds.). (2009). *Treating Complex Traumatic Stress Disorders: An Evidence-based Guide*. Guilford Press.
Danto, E. A. (2017). The psychoanalytic system of ideas. In F. J. Turner *(Ed.) Social Work Treatment: Interlocking Theoretical Approaches* (6th ed., pp. 398–410). Oxford University Press.
De Jong, P. & Berg, I.M. (2012). *Interviewing for Solutions* (4th ed.). Pearson.
Elliott, R., Bohart, A. C., Watson, J. C., & Murphy, D. (2018). Therapist empathy and client outcome: An updated meta-analysis. *Psychotherapy*, 55(4), 399–410. doi:10.1037/pst0000175.
Erickson, M. H. (1991). *My Voice Will Go with You: The Teaching Tales of Milton H. Erickson*. WW Norton & Company.
Farber, B. A., Suzuki, J. Y., & Lynch, D. A. (2018). Positive regard and psychotherapy outcome: A meta-analytic review. *Psychotherapy*, 55(4), 411–423. doi:10.1037%2Fpst0000171.
Franks, C. (Ed.) (1969). *Behavior Therapy: Appraisal and Status*. McGraw Hill.
Freud, S. (1939). *An Outline of Psychoanalysis*. Vol. 23, Hogarth.
Gardner, R. A. (1986). *Therapeutic Communication with Children: The Mutual Storytelling Technique*. Jason Aronson.
Gelso, C. I., & Hayes, J. A. (1998). *The Psychotherapy of Relationship: Theory, Research, and Practice*. Wiley.
Gorshkalova, O., & Munakomi, S. (2021). *Duty to Warn*. In: StatPearls [Internet], StatPearls Publishing. www.ncbi.nlm.nih.gov/books/NBK542236/
Hanna, E. A. (1993). The implications of shifting perspectives in countertransference on the therapeutic action of clinical social work part I. *Journal of Analytic Social Work*, 1(3), 25–52. doi:10.1300/J408v01n03_03.

Hollis, J. (2021). *Prisms: Reflections on this Journey We Call Life*. Chiron Publications.

Hendrix, H. (2007). *Getting the Love You Want: A Guide for Couples*. St. Martin's Griffin.

Hetherington, A. (2000). A psychodynamic profile of therapists who sexually exploit their clients. *British Journal of Psychotherapy*, 16(3), 274–286. doi:10.1111/j.1752-0118.2000.tb00519.x.

Jung, C. G. (2014). *The Archetypes and the Collective Unconscious*. Routledge.

Kendall, P. C. (Ed.). (2011). *Child and Adolescent Therapy: Cognitive-behavioral Procedures*. Guilford Press.

Kottman, T., & Stiles, K. (2013). The mutual storytelling technique: An Adlerian application in child therapy. *Techniques In Adlerian Psychology*, 46(2), 338.

Lambert, M. J. (2013). Outcome in psychotherapy: The past and important advances. *Psychotherapy*, 50(1), 42–51. doi:10.1037/a0030682

McKay, M., Davis, M., & Fanning, P. (2021). *Thoughts and Feelings: Taking Control of Your Moods and Your Life* (5th ed.). New Harbinger Publications.

Miller, A. (1990). *For Your Own Good: Hidden Cruelty in Child-rearing and the Roots of Violence*. Macmillan.

Mor, N., & Haran, D. (2009). Cognitive-behavioral therapy for depression. *Israel Journal of Psychiatry and Related Sciences*, 46(4), 269–273.

National Association of Social Workers (NASW) (2021). *Code of ethics of the National Association of Social Workers*. NASW Press. www.socialworkers.org/About/Ethics/Code-of-Ethics/Code-of-Ethics-English.

Norcross, J. C., & Lambert, M. J. (2019). *Psychotherapy relationships that work II* (Vol. 48, No. 1, p.4). Educational Publishing Foundation.

Oster, G. D., & Crone, P. G. (2004). *Using Drawings in Assessment and Therapy: A Guide for Mental Health Professionals* (2nd ed.). Brunner Routledge.

Renaud, J., Russell, J. J., & Myhr, G. (2014). Predicting who benefits most from cognitive-behavioral therapy for anxiety and depression. *Journal of Clinical Psychology*, 70(10), 924–932. doi:10.1002/jclp.22099.

Rogers, C. R. (1957). The necessary and sufficient conditions of therapeutic personality change. *Journal of Clinical Psychology*, 21(2), 95–103. doi:10.1080/1046171X.1989.12034347.

Rogers, C. R. (1961). *On Becoming a Person: A Therapist's View of Psychotherapy*. Houghton Mifflin Harcourt.

Rowe, W. S. (2017). Client centered theory and the person-centered approach: Value-based, empirically supported. In F. J. Turner (Ed.) *Social Work Treatment: Interlocking Theoretical Approaches* (6th ed., pp. 34–53). Oxford University Press.

Skinner, B. F. (1965). *Science and Human Behavior* (No. 92904). Simon and Schuster.

Slayton, S. C., D'Archer, J., & Kaplan, F. (2010). Outcome studies on the efficacy of art therapy: A review of findings. *Art Therapy*, 27(3), 108–118. doi:10.1080/07421656.2010.10129660.

Strean, H. S. (1986). Psychoanalytic theory. In F. J. Turner (Ed.) *Social Work Treatment: Interlocking Theoretical Approaches* (3rd ed., pp. 19–45) The Free Press.

Thomlison, R. J. (1986). Behavior therapy in social work practice. In F. J. Turner (Ed.) *Social Work Treatment: Interlocking Theoretical Approaches* (3rd ed., pp. 131–153). The Free Press.

Thyer, B. A. (2017). Social learning theory and social work treatment. In F. J. Turner (Ed.) *Social Work Treatment: Interlocking Theoretical Approaches* (6th ed., pp. 471–480). Oxford University Press.

Tolin, D. F. (2010). Is cognitive–behavioral therapy more effective than other therapies?: A meta-analytic review. *Clinical Psychology Review*, 30(6), 710–720. doi:10.1016/j.cpr.2010.05.003.

Tryon, G. S., Birch, S. E., & Verkuilen, J. (2018). Meta-analyses of the relation of goal consensus and collaboration to psychotherapy outcome. *Psychotherapy*, 55(4), 372–383. doi:10.1037/pst0000170.

Winnicott, D. W. (1988). *Human Nature*. Schocken Books.

Chapter 5

Healing Relationships with Each Other—Part I: Couples

Mary was finally able to get her husband Tom to agree to come to a couple's therapy session. However, it is clear that she sees *him* as the problem. Mary complains that Tom rarely shows her affection outside of sex, expects her to do all of the housework, and when she wants to talk about her dissatisfaction with their relationship, he shuts down. During the first session with the therapist, he remains silent and withdrawn: "See?! See what I mean? He's doing it NOW!" When the clinician tries to get the husband's point of view, "Tom, what do you think of Mary's complaints?" Mary interrupts and speaks for him: "Ugh, good luck! He never says anything!" enabling Tom to retreat back into his cave of unresponsive silence. When the clinician interrupts this pattern and finally draws him out, Tom will invalidate his wife's concerns by describing her as too emotional. What starts to become clear is that Mary's "let's talk about the relationship" is really "let's talk about what's wrong with you," and that her agenda is to enlist the therapist as an ally. Tom fights back using the most powerful weapons in his arsenal; silence peppered by occasional accusations that she is hysterical. In this way, like Mary, but using a different type of shield, Tom absolves himself of any responsibility for the couple problems which of course, enrages her. Like most couples who come to therapy, the problem is invariably and inevitably the other.

Family and couples therapy, treatment model notwithstanding, generally assesses and intervenes on relationship interactions. A basic premise is that there are mutually reciprocal, negative interaction patterns that must be uncovered, stopped, and replaced. Sounds simple, but is in fact, far easier said than done. All of us, veteran and neophytes alike, are tempted to step in and referee conflicts and this tendency is particularly apparent if that was our job in our family-of-origin. However, the referee role is a trap, and if you fall into it, you will be rendered clinically powerless. Your job is to get *them* to figure out how to stop reacting to each other, and to instead engage in constructive negotiation and problem-solving. More than ever, when working with relationships it is important to remember that the problems lie between the actors as do the solutions. The work of the clinician is to help the couple set up the right conditions for this to happen. The clinician must know their own biases about relationships, put them aside, and make front and center what the family or the couple's wishes are. In order for this to happen, the clinician needs to be comfortable occasionally existing in a state of not-knowing, coping with not being in control, and learning when to intervene and when to sit back and listen.

Couples come to us with various agendas, not all of which are conducive to actually improving their relationships. Basically, the therapist's job is to excavate and neutralize those agendas, get couple members to be less reactive to each other, and help them understand how their behaviors are interrelated; in other words when one partner does something, the other does something else in response and vice versa. Reactivity is when people are interacting with each other out of emotion, namely anger and sadness, without much thought about what they want different in their relationship and what they are willing to do to make that happen. This is one of the prime factors that must be addressed in virtually all couple and family therapy.

The Importance of Self-Awareness

The idea of working with multiple people at the same time such as couples, families, and groups understandably brings fresh anxieties to a clinician. The challenge of one client alone is daunting enough; the idea of a couple (or group or family) is frightening for a new clinician. What if they start to argue? What if they lose control? Or worse, what if *I* do? Well, that can and does happen. A clinician who sees families or couples must learn, on the one hand, to tolerate some chaos. They must, at times, decentralize themselves and let family members communicate with each other without their interference. As a result, there is more emotional charge in the room. On the other hand, the clinician must know when to step in, identify, and challenge the various unhelpful agendas and relationship behaviors clients bring into the session.

The anxiety inherent in treating relationships is magnified if the clinician is not forearmed with self-knowledge as well as an awareness of how they can get "caught" in couple and family dynamics. For example, if you were raised to be your mother's confidant when she had a conflict with your father, you might have a natural tendency to side with Mary. If you felt that your own mother was overpowering and too much of a nag, you might find yourself on Team Tom. Siding with either in this case is contraindicated and will not help the couple resolve their disputes. If conflict makes you in any way anxious because it got out of control when you were growing up or it was avoided altogether, you might consciously or unconsciously have a tendency to do whatever it takes to tamp down arguments, even if it means siding with the loudest voice if only to get it to quiet down.

It is surprisingly easy, even for the most experienced among us, to get caught up in relationship reactivity. However, the last thing members of a reactive couple or family needs is a reactive therapist. Thus, circling back to a central theme of this book, clinicians need to make sure their own psychological house is in order. Our parents' relationships with us and each other were our first classrooms. What was YOUR family like growing up? What were its strengths and where was it broken? What were the traumatic incidents in your family? How was conflict handled? What did you learn from the way they treated you? What were you taught about your worth in the world, your lovability? Were your parents controlling? Did they insist you take care of them? Were they immature and needy; did they need you to be an adult before you were ready? Finally, what were the *strengths* of your family? What were the positive things you learned from them?

Importantly, what is your own relationship history? What are your ideas about relationships? If you are single, have you been in a couple previously? Why or why not? (No judgment here. Lifelong singlehood does not mean one cannot work with couples, as long as this is a conscious choice.) If single and searching, what are your hopes and dreams for a union? Are they realistic? Have you hit upon obstacles? If in a relationship with a partner or spouse, what is it like? What are the strengths and weaknesses of the relationship? How about your relationship with your children, if you have any? What might be your negative relationship behaviors and biases? Based on your own experiences, what traps might you fall into? Referee? Rescue the nagger? Excuse the distancer? Conflict avoider?

As of this writing, I have been in a relationship for 40 years and am myself the product of a long-term marriage that ended when my mother died. I have a bias that people should stick things out and try to resolve conflicts as they emerge, which has led me to sometimes try to help couples stay together when they were better off apart. A seminal moment that brought this to my attention was when I had been working with a gay male couple who had been together 15 years. I had given them several homework assignments that they repeatedly failed to complete. Finally, out of exasperation, I exclaimed, "Guys! I think I am working harder than you both! I'm not even sure you should be together!" (The latter statement was admittedly uttered with some paradoxical intent). At that moment, the gentlemen looked at me and then each other and said, "I think he's right. Francis, I enjoyed our time together, and I will probably always love you, but I think it is time for us to part ways." "Ricky, I couldn't agree more. Should you move out, or should I?" The couple shook hands and then thanked me profusely for helping them. The lesson here is to be forearmed with self-knowledge ahead of time, to minimize your own issues from interfering in your work.

Couple and family therapy have a lot in common. However, there are important ways that they differ, so each deserves their own attention. The remainder of this chapter will be about working with couples. Clinical work with families will be described in Chapter 6.

Problematic Agendas

Many couples seeking our assistance have motivations that are not amenable to therapy. It is highly likely one or both members will be so angry, exasperated, or defeated that they will confront you with problematic agendas at the start of the session, so I want to address these common problematic frames and perspectives along with ways to neutralize them.

Couples therapy involves imparting the skills to handle conflict as well as helping couple members remember the bond between them. When first encountering a family or a couple, the therapist must engage each partner by getting their individual views of the problem and also demonstrating an understanding of each individual's pain. The clinician must also flesh out if their prime motive is to prove the other person is at fault. "He won't listen to me! Now YOU tell him he's wrong?" They believe that if they state their case, you will be judge, jury, and maybe even executioner. You will be tempted to at least partially meet their expectations (hopefully not the executioner role). However, this is a trap that will ensnare you into the couple or family's problems leaving you impotent as a therapist. Following are some ways this trap can show itself.

Refereeing

For a therapist, particularly a new therapist who is overly invested in proving how helpful they are (for fear they are not helpful at all), it is tempting to want to arbitrate conflict. Even I have occasionally fallen into this trap and sometimes still do, until I realize what is happening and extricate myself. I once heard of a case in which a couple was arguing about whether an electric toothbrush was more effective than its manual counterpart. The clinical social worker committed to evidence-based practice, consulted the scientific literature to explore this question and found, indeed, that the electric toothbrush worked better. She announced this news to the couple with great aplomb in the hope that this would resolve their argument. To her dismay, she found that rather than assuage their problems, this finding left the manual toothbrush proponent defeated and sulky; feelings that spurred further battle. Chastened, the loser was not about to admit defeat "Ok, you're right about *this* one, but what about ...?" This therapist made the common error of prioritizing content over process. Educators specialize in the former, therapists the latter. The real issue was not which toothbrush was more effective, but rather that the couple members were angry and frustrated about larger and deeper subjects than dental hygiene. Instead of a verdict, what this couple really needed was a model for how to discuss their feelings, and raise, negotiate, and resolve disagreements. Being summoned as a referee for couple difficulties is a dead end that will leave the clinician powerless and the issues unresolved. What they really need is a way to resolve conflict.

CLINICIAN: I can see you have a frustrating disagreement about this toothbrush issue. How is this conflict similar to others you have experienced? I am very interested in how you discuss these disagreements, how you try to resolve them, and what, if anything you do that is at least partially successful?

Social Agenda

CLINICIAN: You do realize that Mary shouldering the household duties is an example of sexism. Mary, you shouldn't have to put up with this. Tom, you should be doing more around the house.

Tom and Mary's clinician, a proud feminist, and an excellent advocate for women's rights initially sees this problem as a manifestation of the oppressive patriarchy that still tasks women with the lion's share of housework and childcare, leaving men off the hook. However, using this issue to side with Mary would trap her in the referee role. If she were to launch into a lecture about sex roles and unfairness at the start, it would replicate what Mary was already doing, and would continue to push Tom into stony silence leaving the conflict unresolved. Simply joining a side, even the *right* side, would do nothing to resolve the couple's problems and in fact would solidify them. Now, a beginner and, at times, even an experienced therapist might be tempted to interrupt and empathize and rescue Mary. Social workers are committed to social justice and are sensitive to how sexism rears its head in a family. One could interpret Tom's passive silence as sexism whereby he is not feeling responsible for what is happening in the home or in their relationship, and they would not be incorrect. So, it is easy to relate to Mary's pain and tempting to come to her defense. Nevertheless, remember, Mary is not your client, nor is Tom. It is Mary and Tom's *relationship* that is the patient and that is where the focus belongs. You are not married to either of these people and it is not your job to change them or to give either one of them a lesson in feminism, the patriarchy, or male privilege. A clinician can introduce these concepts and assist both members of the couple to find ways to deal with these issues that work for them while repairing and rebuilding their relationship. Your job is to push them in this direction. Shine a light on the role these issues might play in their problems and help *them* to figure out *their own way*.

CLINICIAN: We are all raised in a society that has different expectations for men and women's family roles. What role do you think this has in your conflict? Tom, you go first.

"You Always" "You Never"

Such statements suggest that the other person has done things the same way continuously and will never change. This thinking is an anathema to any type of psychotherapy and must be directly challenged. As a matter of fact, people divorce when they believe that their spouse or partner is incapable or unwilling to change—which is sometimes but not always true. The best way to get someone with whom you are in a relationship to change their behaviors is to first change your own. The clinician's job is to convince the clients of this.

Unflagging consistency, reflected in the statement "you always", is an illusion. Every problem, even the most repetitive and intractable, has exceptions or circumstances when the problem could occur but does not. When a spouse says, "you are always nagging me" or "you never talk to me" they are invariably wrong. There are indeed times the spouse is not nagging or is more communicative. However, in the heat of battle, these occasional exceptions are forgotten. Therapists can remind couples of these exceptions and mine them for potential solutions (DeJong & Berg, 2008). For example, I'm willing to bet that Mary is not nagging on those few occasions when she perceives Tom to be listening and communicating his caring. Mind you, when people are beginning to describe their problems or are in the throes of emotional distress, this is not the time to remind them of exceptions. However, after the problem is laid out and the clinician has an opportunity to empathize with the complainants, it is then time to push against this type of thinking. Remember the *instead* questions from the last chapter? These are occasions to get the clients to look forward to future goals instead of dwelling in the problematic past.

CLINICIAN: I can see you are frustrated with how difficult this problem is for the two of you. However, let's remember, you are here because you want to see your relationship change. People change all of the time and so can you and your (husband, wife, partner, child, parent). That's why you are here, right? So, let's focus on this and try to avoid "you always/never" for now. Instead, tell me what you would like to see different in the future?

More on Change

In 500 BC, the Greek philosopher Heraclitus of Ephesos asserted that the only thing constant is change. If Covid has taught us anything, it is that things can change in an instant. I hate to hear a social worker, of all people, say, "I hate change" when that is basically what we are called to help people do. We all need to be aware that changes are happening all of the time; we must applaud and seek out change in our clients and also ourselves. As therapists, our job is to steer the changes in the right direction. I know a teacher who describes herself as a "change junkie." We do not have to be addicted but let's face it, change is our stock-in-trade so we need to be among its strongest allies.

Specification Obsession

In troubled dyads, people will find themselves arguing over small details. When engaged in angry battle, they will try to discredit each other by proving that the other's memory of dates, times and specific aspects of an incident are inaccurate:

MARY: Last Monday when I asked you to help me move the sofa, you said you would help me later and never did.
TOM: That wasn't last Monday, that was Tuesday!
MARY: No, it wasn't, it was Monday.
TOM: I know it was Tuesday because that is the day the game was on TV.
MARY: No, you're wrong. You have a terrible memory. It was Monday.

The clinician needs to put a stop to this right away as it is distracting, unproductive, and can derail treatment. The belief that undergirds this behavior is that if the other is wrong about dates, then they are obviously obtuse enough to be wrong about the relationship.

CLINICIAN: Please! The exact dates and times *are not* important and are in fact, a distraction from the real problem at hand. What *is* important is you, Mary wanted help from Tom and felt frustrated that you didn't get it. Do I have that right?

It also could be that one or both members are so ready to fight they will look for any reason to do so. If you think this is the case, openly acknowledge and empathize, "Wow, I can see things are so difficult and painful and that you are so angry that it is hard to agree on *anything*," and then set a limit and redirect with interventions that are described later in this chapter.

I'm Leaving, So Take Care of Him

In this scenario, one partner is about to leave, so they use the therapy session to make the announcement, with the thought that the therapist will take care of the partner left behind. As long as that person is enrolled in therapy, the exiting partner believes they do not need to feel guilty about the trail of grief they leave behind; the therapist will clean up the mess.

Needless to say, this is a terrible idea; misinformed and even cowardly on the part of the leaving spouse. For sure, some couples experience irreconcilable differences and many decide to divorce. However, the ending of a relationship is rarely possible without emotional hardship and usually both parties become bereaved. Therapy is not a panacea for the grief that a break-up leaves in its wake. This is not to say people should not end unhappy relationships and seek support when they do. However, they must not overestimate the power of therapy as an analgesic. When relationships end, people are in pain. Therapy will not prevent that.

Fix Him!

In my experience, this is the most frequent problematic agenda of couples who seek therapy. The spouse or partner is certain that all of the problems are their crazy, sick, disturbed partner's fault, and by getting them into the clinician's office, the therapist will see this immediately and get to work on repairing him. Note, in this case I say *him* because, in my experience, in heterosexual couples, it is the woman who usually seeks out therapy to *fix* her male partner, though this can also happen if the pronouns are reversed, or are the same. The problem here is that for couples therapy to work, at least one member of the couple (but preferably both) are going to need to understand, that the problems lie not *within* individuals but *between* them; each partner plays a part in the couple's problems, and to fix the relationship, at least one member, but preferably both, will need to commit to changing their own behavior that contributes to the problematic relationship dynamics.

Systems Thinking

Virtually all models of couple and family therapy require an understanding of systems (Kerr & Bowen, 2009, Minuchin & Fishman, 1981, Nichols, 2016). From this perspective problems are seen as a symptom of dysfunction in the couple or family system as a whole as opposed to *within* an individual. You might find yourself thinking, the problem in this couple is the borderline wife (or angry husband), however this perspective will result in you joining a side. A clinician who takes sides simply replaces one member of the couple in the conflict, which does not lead to its resolution. This tendency is highlighted if you grew up in a family headed by parents like Mary and Tom. Instead, from a systems perspective we would be asking what interchanges are happening in this relationship that keeps the wife looking like a "borderline" or the husband angry? We then want to point out these problematic interactions in the hopes that they will choose to change them.

Even though individuals are of course important, the dyad of the couple operates as a unit in and of itself. Each individual part comes together to operate as a whole which is what needs to be considered as we help the system change. It also means that relationship behaviors are governed by mutually dependent, reciprocal interaction patterns, or *reciprocity*. For example, the more you pursue closeness in a relationship with me, the more I might distance. The more I distance, the more you might seek to pursue me. What comes first, the chicken or the egg, your pursuit or my distance, is not important; only that we are engaging in a dance where each of our steps is met by that of the other. Inevitably, the job of the clinician is to expand the definition of the problem away from the individual dancer and instead on the problematic dance they are doing together. There may be a dynamic in their relationship whereby the more she nags the more he pushes away, or the more he distances, the more she nags. Both members of the couple may have learned unhelpful problem-solving skills by the treatment they witnessed or received as children in their own families, and these histories can contribute to the problematic interaction pattern that must be resolved. From a systems point of view, Mary and Tom are locked in a mutually dependent, reciprocal interaction pattern—and if the clinician does not steer the couple away from mere content, it is unlikely that they will ever figure out how to stop the pattern. If Mary stops nagging, Tom will have an opportunity to move forward toward Mary. But if Tom stops distancing and reaches out to Mary for interaction, her nagging will likely cease. As a clinician, your job is to identify their dysfunctional patterns—and to help them find a solution that works for them.

The inconvenient truth for couples (and families) is that to be helped, at least one member must be willing to lay down their sword and to interact with the other in a different way, thus changing the system. As long as people stay locked in the idea that the other person is wrong without seeing their own contribution, nothing will change. They also need to understand that if one of them changes, the couple system will change around them. Convincing couples of this is the hard work. However, once they understand, it's smooth sailing. The challenge is to get them to accept these oranges when they were seeking apples.

MARY: Ugh, he never talks to me. When he comes home, he just gets on his computer right away and says nothing to me; I barely get a hello. He is so distant.

CLINICIAN: I can appreciate how frustrating and lonely this must be for you, Mary. However, in couples therapy we see that both partners have a role in problems. So as painful as this is, I am going to ask, do you have an idea of what you or the rest of the family is doing to help keep Tom distant?

TOM: Mary is such a nag! I can't handle it. That is why I often try to hide from her when I come home from work. There is always a problem or something I am not doing right.

CLINICIAN: Sounds awful, like you feel like you are always being picked on. However, do you have a sense that perhaps your distancing might contribute or even cause Mary to nag? Have you ever wondered if you did something different, this would have an impact on her nagging?

Challenging couple members in this way is confrontative. As stated before, no matter what the modality, clients will not be able to receive and benefit from interventions unless they feel heard and listened to. The hard part is that partners in a troubled couple are so angry at each other, it can be difficult to engage and empathize with both members at the same time in each other's presence. However, it is essential to do so. They must trust that the therapist means well before they are willing to lay down their arms and consider their own parts in the conflict.

Assessment and Treatment

Joining with the Couple

When starting out, of course it is a good idea to make an initial connection with each couple member:

CLINICIAN: Hello, my name is Michael LaSala. Before we get started, I'd like to get to know each of you a little bit. You must be Mary (extending my hand for a handshake).
MARY: Yes.
CLINICIAN: Are you ok to shake hands?

During this Covid pandemic era, when the bulk of this book was written, some clients did not want to shake hands, so a fist bump or a nod is acceptable. It is always good to ask the client about this as you extend your hand. Of course, if you are seeing clients online, this is moot.

CLINICIAN: Mary, I know you are a mother so you work a lot in the home, do you work outside the home as well?
MARY: Yes, I run a consulting business.
CLINICIAN: That sounds like a big job, you are a successful business woman I see.
MARY: Yes.
CLINICIAN: So, you are a leader and also an entrepreneur?
MARY: Yes, I guess you could say that.

It is always a good idea to find something complimentary to say when first engaging clients.

CLINICIAN: How about you Tom?
TOM: I do IT.
CLINICIAN: So, you're one of the heroes we tech-challenged people call when we get into trouble with our computers.
TOM: Yes, I guess so.
CLINICIAN: You folks have children?
MARY: Yes, Thomas who is 12, and Chiara who is 14.
CLINICIAN: So, the beginning of teenage years. Hmmm ...
MARY: Yes (softly chuckling).
CLINICIAN: Ok, people see me because they want to change something in their lives. What is it you folks are seeking to change?

As in individual therapy, begin the session asking each member of the couple, "What is it you would like to change?" and carefully note their answers. A tricky dilemma of couples therapy is how to stay engaged with both members without appearing as if you are taking sides or "flip flopping" in a hopeless effort to please them both. Some client couples are so angry and polarized, that joining with one will immediately engender reactive anger in another. What the clinician must continuously communicate is that they will not side with any individual, but instead will *always* be on the side of the *relationship*.

Scaling Questions

One way to get clients in a couple to move away from refereeing, "you never," "you always," and other unhelpful interaction patterns is to get them to articulate goals by asking scaling questions. Borrowing from solution-focused therapy (DeJong & Berg, 2008), this technique is designed to get each member of the couple to assess their level of motivation to improve their relationship and to share their assessments in the presence of their partner.

CLINICIAN: (to Tom) OK, now I have what might seem like a strange question. On a scale of 1–10, with one meaning you have no motivation and are ready to "throw in the towel," and 10 being you will do anything to improve and even save your relationship, where are you at on that scale in terms of motivation?
TOM: I would say between a 7 or an 8.
MARY: Really? I had no idea! I thought you were ready to check out of this marriage!

This reaction is not uncommon. Often when partners are angry, their commitment to the relationship is obscured for fear of appearing weak in the face of their partner's anger. In war, there is no benefit to appearing vulnerable.

CLINICIAN: Mary, where would you be on that scale?
MARY: Well, before hearing what Tom said, I would have said a 4 or a 5.
CLINICIAN: But now?
MARY: I would say a 6 or a 7.

No doubt, Mary interpreted Tom's inattentiveness as lack of caring. So, to learn the opposite melts Mary's reactivity.

CLINICIAN: Tom, you can see that your wife is surprised by your answer. What is it that tells you that you are at a 7 or 8?
TOM: She doesn't realize this, but I really do love her. She is a wonderful wife and a great mother. I would hate to lose her and that is why I am here. She just seems angry all of the time and I just don't know what to do to make her happy.
CLINICIAN: What would bring you up one level? To an 8 or 9?
TOM: If there was less arguing at home; more peace.
CLINICIAN: Well, the fact that you are so committed and appreciate her so much provides a good foundation for our work. We will work on ways you can understand what she needs so she can be less angry with you.

Scaling questions can also be used to articulate desired changes and set goals.

CLINICIAN: If therapy were to work out, where would you hope to be on that scale?
MARY: A 9.
CLINICIAN: OK good, so you are realistic—a 10 would be perfect, right? But you are wise enough to know that is not possible. So, what will you need to see to let you know that your relationship is at a 9?
MARY: We would be happier.
CLINICIAN: Ok, good start. What would be happening when you are happier?

Similar to individual therapy, it is not uncommon for people in couples therapy to initially give vague answers as to what they would like to see different. That is why it is important for the clinician to drill down.

MARY: We would be more in sync. He would be doing half of the housework; I would be less tired. Also, we would be spending time together like we used to, going for walks, to the movies, going out to eat; time with each other without the kids. Even have some romance, like we used to have.
CLINICIAN: That sounds nice. What about you Tom? What's your reaction to hearing this?

TOM: I think our relationship is good, but I want Mary to be happy, and I know she is not. I would like more time together when we are not fighting.
CLINICIAN: Is there anything on Mary's list that you are willing to commit to right now?
TOM: I get it, I need to do more around the house. I would like the romantic stuff to come back also.

It is not uncommon in a heterosexual relationship for the male spouse to deny having complaints about the relationship when his spouse does. When this occurs, the clinician needs to do some digging. I often say something softly challenging along the lines of:

CLINICIAN: Hmmm ... it is hard to believe, with your wife being so unhappy, that it is pleasant at home.
HUSBAND: Yes, I guess you are right, it isn't pleasant.
CLINICIAN: Isn't that where the expression, "happy wife, happy life" comes in?
HUSBAND: (slight chuckle) I guess, yeah.
CLINICIAN: So, on the other side of the coin, I'll bet it's hard to think things are going well if your wife is so upset, no?
HUSBAND: Yes, I guess you're right.

Additionally, when pushed, a heterosexual man in a troubled relationship might have complaints about the lack of sex. It is probably a good idea to ask almost all clients seeking couples counseling about sex. However, to do so, the clinician needs to overcome any squeamishness about the topic.

CLINICIAN: You folks mentioned romance several times, let me ask you both a question. How is your sex life?
MARY: Sex life?!?!? After working all day, and the cooking, laundry and cleaning, and putting my kids to bed, I am so tired I can't even think about that!
TOM: Well, I guess that is something I would like to see different, as in more of—that might bring my number up to a 9 or 10!
CLINICIAN: It's really amazing that despite your conflicts, you both want more romance and closeness. So, beneath the problems you have a strong bond. Romance and sex are things we can work on in here. I have a feeling that this might come naturally once we can get you both to talk about and resolve some of the problems in your relationship.

In general company, it is not considered appropriate to ask people about their sex lives. Such prying could be seen as voyeuristic and even inappropriately seductive. However, clinicians must bravely approach topics that are typically off limits in polite conversation, and if you are going to be doing couples therapy, you must become comfortable asking about sex. Doing so gives the couple the opportunity to break through the gates of this taboo, which not only prevents them from discussing their sex life with you but also each other.

Scaling questions can also be used to develop goals by getting the couple to be future oriented.

CLINICIAN: Ok, what is something you would like to see that would move your motivation up one point?
MARY: Well, my motivation has already increased after hearing Tom's number. But, if I saw him attempt to do more around the house, I would feel more motivated.
CLINICIAN: What do you think about that Tom?
TOM: I could do that.

As an aside, I like to tell married heterosexual (and some married gay) men or any couple fighting about household chores that housework is foreplay. There is actually a calendar entitled Porn for Women which shows various handsome, shirtless men ironing, vacuuming, and washing dishes. It gets a laugh out of the couple, but it also gets the point across, particularly to men.

Assessing the End of the Relationship

Scaling questions can be used to determine when one or both partners have decided to end the relationship and is just going through the motions. To ferret out this problematic agenda, it is important to find a way to gauge their motivation. One or both partners giving low scores (2 or 3) in response to a scaling question suggests that they do not really want to work on the relationship and it is worth clarifying whether what they really seek is separation. Again, the clinician needs to directly ask about this.

CLINICIAN: Hmmm ... you rated your motivation to work on this relationship as a 2. Tell me, and please be honest, does this mean you are ready to check out?

If the answer is yes, then it is time to change the agenda from couples therapy to helping the couple separate. This will save the couple (and you) a lot of work and aggravation.

Scaling Questions to Reassess

While scaling questions are a good way to offset nonproductive problem talk and establish goals, they can also be used during the course of therapy to assess where the couple is at with their original goals to see if any progress has been made. They can also be used to set new goals. As in individual therapy, if you feel lost or unsure where the work is going, it is time to reassess and possibly reestablish goals.

CLINICIAN: I am feeling a bit lost, so it might be a good idea to revisit and reassess where things are at. On a scale of 1–10, 10 being great, and one being awful and ready to quit, where are each of you in terms of how you think the relationship is going?
MARY: I say 6.
TOM: 7?
CLINICIAN: (asking each) What would bring it up, one point?

The couple's response to this question could lead to a reassessment of previous goals or the establishment of new ones.

Enactment: Assessing Interactions

A basic intervention designed to assess and alter interaction patterns is to have members engage in *enactments* (Nichols, 2016). In couples therapy, an enactment is when the therapist gets the couple to interact with each other in their presence. Initially, the enactment helps the clinician assess problematic interchanges. Subsequently, the therapist can then coach the family to interact in ways that are more productive.

Generally, when setting up an enactment, the therapist needs to first describe what they are instructing and why, and then assign a content topic for them to discuss.

CLINICIAN: In my work, I like to get couples to talk to each other in my presence, rather than having people just talk to me directly. It might seem a little strange at first, but I find that folks get used to it pretty quickly. So, I'd like you to move your chairs and face each other so you can talk directly to each other. Now, Mary, I notice you were talking about feeling overwhelmed by chores around the house. Right now, as you face each other, I want to see you, Mary, talk to your husband about this. That's right, just like that. Great! Now get started, and I'll be here listening.

The clinician must be prepared for some hesitation on the part of the couple. When people come to therapy, they anticipate more of a doctor-patient or teacher-student relationship. Thus, they expect the therapist to give a diagnosis, a treatment, or a lesson as they become passive recipients. At first it is jarring for couple members to talk to each other in the clinician's presence. So, a certain amount of explanation and prompting is frequently necessary.

In setting up the enactment, it is important that the clinician withdraw from the communication field by avoiding eye contact and turning away; the exact opposite of what you would do if you were trying to engage someone. This is done to discourage couple members from directing conversation to the therapist rather than each other. I encourage new therapists to cast their eyes downward, or fiddle with their clothing as they listen. Occasionally, they need to look up to make sure that the clients are talking to each other. A sign that the enactment is not happening is when they are referring to each other in the third person ("He does this" "She does that"). When this happens, the therapist is to look up, remind the clients of the directions, giving a prompt; "Don't talk to me, talk to [him/her] directly" and go back to the business of listening but looking away.

CLINICIAN: Now, be sure to face each other when you are talking, and talk to each other—not to me. I'm listening, don't worry; I'm hearing it all. I know it might feel strange, but make sure you are talking to each other.

MARY: I get so tired of trying to tell you how I'm feeling. When I talk to you, it's as if you don't really hear what I am saying. Do you really hear me, Tom?

TOM: Yes, I do.

MARY: Tom, you know I've asked you many times why you don't help me more around the house. You either promise to help more or you remain silent and do nothing. I'm tired, at the end of my rope and don't know what to do anymore. You know, when I leave work, I pick up the kids, help them with their homework, fix dinner, clean up, and do any other housework that needs to be done and all you do is come home and sit in front of the TV or your computer. When I try to talk to you about it, you remain silent or simply shrug. I don't know what to do anymore! How many times do I have to tell you that this is a problem before you do something about it?!?

TOM: (shrugs)

MARY: See (facing the therapist), that's what he does all the time and it gets me frustrated.

THERAPIST: Instead of telling me, tell Tom directly how you feel.

MARY: Tom, I am so frustrated, I'm at my wit's end.

TOM: I help sometimes.

MARY: Helping out *sometimes* is not enough!

TOM: (shrugs)

When first meeting a couple, I generally allow the enacted conversation to proceed without my interruption. I am assessing their interactions so I wait for it to come to a full stop. Usually, with a couple like Mary and Tom, we know we have hit the couple's interaction limit when there is silence.

(Tom's last shrug did it.) In exasperation, Mary stops and they both return their gaze to me, defeated.

CLINICIAN: Is this the place where you usually get stuck?
MARY: Yes.
CLINICIAN: Ok, now I know what needs to be worked on.

Coaching

Besides being a useful assessment tool, enactments can be used to help couples *change* problematic interaction patterns through coaching. The therapist observes the interchanges during the initial enactment, figures out what is going wrong, and gets the couple to change them. As a reminder, in a systemic and reciprocal pattern of interaction, if one person changes the way they interact in the system, the system will change around them. In a couple, sometimes the wisest choice is to start with the person who has the most motivation to change. Let's go back to the previous example with Mary.

CLINICIAN: Mary, I can certainly see your anger and frustration as you attempt to talk to your husband. However, do you think you are successful? Is he hearing you?
MARY: No.
CLINICIAN: That must be frustrating. Can you try a different way to talk to him to make sure he is hearing you?
MARY: I really have no idea how. I am lost.
CLINICIAN: Yes, I can see why. Tom, what do you think it will take to really hear and understand where Mary is coming from on this issue?
TOM: I hear her.
CLINICIAN: Yes, but she doesn't realize that you are in fact listening and are tuned in. Can you check it out and tell her what you think you hear her saying?

Note, in troubled couples, members typically feel they are not listened to, so through coaching I engage them in an exercise that will address this. The effectiveness of coaching enactments can be enhanced when partners are prompted to use "I" statements and include validation and empathy in their communications.

CLINICIAN: Ok Mary, I would like you to talk about your feelings and concerns using "I" statements such as, "I feel," "I wish," "I hope," and Tom, I just want you to listen. After Mary speaks, I want you to reflect back to her what you've heard to make sure you accurately understood what she was saying. OK, so go ahead Mary, tell Tom what your concerns are and how you have been feeling.

MARY: I feel overwhelmed by my job stress as well as all of the things I have to do at home (looking at the therapist).
CLINICIAN: No Mary, don't look at me and tell me. Face Tom and tell him directly.
MARY: Tom, you may not know this, but I have trouble sleeping at night even though I am so tired from all I have to do.
CLINICIAN: Tom, now replay back to Mary what you've heard.
TOM: I know you feel overwhelmed but you do not notice how much I do. Also, when I do try to lend a hand, you criticize what I am doing. So, I feel like I can never do anything right!
CLINICIAN: (redirecting) No Tom, don't respond or defend right now. I can hear your frustration, but Mary does not think you listen to her, so for now, just tell Mary what you have heard her say.

Tom's reaction is not uncommon, however at this moment, it is defeating the purpose of the exercise and must be stopped. Tom's defensive reaction could lead to a reactive defensiveness on Mary's part, which is the original, unhelpful pattern that must change.

TOM: OK, I hear that you are stressed out, that you have so much to do.
THERAPIST: Ok, good start Tom, now check it out with Mary to see if you've got it right.
MARY: Yes he ... whoops, *you* did.
TOM: But you've never really told me how much you have going on?

This needs to be redirected. What Tom says may or may not be true, and actually is not important. Couples therapy must be about the future, what will happen from now on. Certainly, the couple needs a chance to talk about past grievances, but eventually, the clinician needs to put limits on such discussion. If a couple gets stuck in the past, they will get nowhere.

CLINICIAN: But she is telling you now. How do you think Mary is feeling?
TOM: Stressed and angry.
CLINICIAN: Check it out with her.
TOM: Is that true?
MARY: Yes, that is correct.
CLINICIAN: Can you understand that at all?
TOM: Yes, I guess so.
MARY: That helps. It helps to know that Tom deep down really knows how I feel.
CLINICIAN: Mary, can you tell Tom what you need from him?
MARY: Yes, Tom, I need you to help out more around the house. I also need you to understand more when I am feeling stressed and worn out.
TOM: I can do that.

Then Tom and Mary, with the therapist's help, could devise a plan to address this issue.

Ongoing therapy is about continuing to get the couple to practice this. For sure, this behavioral, here-and-now model can be quite effective. However, when one or both couple members have problems doing this exercise, it might mean that the clinician needs to reach deeper and wider to get at some underlying emotional and relationship issues within each individual. (More on that later in this chapter.)

Process Questions

Process questions are designed to spread the responsibility for dyadic problems beyond the individual spouse and point out how two (or sometimes more) can share in the cause and also the solution of the conflicts. They are also a way to get at the reciprocity described earlier. An example of a process question is, when confronted by a partner who complains about an argumentative spouse, the clinician will ask: "What is it that you do that keeps the argument going?" This question redirects clients away from the idea that the problem lies within an individual and toward the concept that problems are embedded in the relationship.

Some additional examples of process questions include:

> Tom, what is it you think you do to keep Mary nagging?
> Mary, do you have any ideas about what you might be doing that pushes Tom away?
> Leonia, if you were to react differently when he shouts at you, what would you do? How might he respond?
> Fred, what would she say you could do to help her feel less lonely?
> Would you be willing to try it to see what would happen?

If Fred, Mary, Tom, or Leonia are unable to answer these questions, similar questions can be posed to their partners.

Mining for Strengths: What's Going Well?

As in initial individual therapy sessions (Chapter 4), strengths are important. Do not let the couple members leave until you ask what it is they would like to see *continue* in their relationship. What is going well? I also like to get a strength-based history of the couple. How did they meet? What attracted them to each other? It is important to recognize that more often than not, at one time the couples differing emotional or relating styles complemented each other, particularly in the beginning of the relationship. However, as time goes on, differences that were once charming, can become sources of unhappiness, and couple members can find themselves in polarized positions. For example, the strong silent type can, over time, appear as a cold fish. The fiery, passionate partner, who might attract the strong silent type can begin to seem shrewish and volatile. One can admire an ambitious, upwardly mobile professional until it feels as if their workaholic tendencies are getting in the way of couple and family time. I remind the couple that their personality differences remain compatible once they are less extreme.

After the initial meeting, I start each subsequent session with the question, "What, if anything is going better since our last session?" I then ask a series of follow up questions to determine why the improvements occurred and what behaviors and experiences the couple has hit upon that they could repeat.

Other Coaching Techniques

If you grew up with siblings, chances are you fought with them when you were both children. A technique adopted by many parents is to put the two siblings together and, rather than referee, order them to work things out. Sometimes, and under the right circumstances, when put together and pressured to solve a conflict with little or no advice, people can find their own ways to do so without suggestions from an outsider. This directive can be used as an assessment method, whereby the clinician can observe and evaluate the client's problem-solving skills, and carefully note what goes right, what goes wrong, and where to intervene. Don't be surprised if the simple pressure of the moment pushes people to change their positions. While this might not always be the case, I have found that most people who come to therapy already know the solutions to their problems, even if they do not realize that they do. As a result, therapy is about helping them uncover and apply them and this technique can help them do that.

This method can also work with dyads after they have been meeting with the therapist for a while. Couples can get socialized into doing enactments to the extent that when they start talking directly to the therapist, they stop themselves and say, "Oh yeah" and start talking to each other without any prompts. Once the couple gets into the habit of enactment, the clinician can then put people together and direct them to find a solution, and/or even a compromise without the therapist intervening.

CLINICIAN: Let me see how the two of you try to resolve this. Keep talking until you get to a solution. Go ahead and try and I will listen.

This prompt alone could expedite how the couple gets to a resolution.

TOM: I know I could do a better job helping out at home. I didn't realize you were so upset about this. I will try to do better.
MARY: Thanks, I would appreciate that.

The clinician is there to help the clients if they lose focus and get stuck in the weeds. For example, in the midst of such a discussion, the couple could regress to asking for a referee or to the assertions of "you always" or "you never." This is an opportunity for the clinician to cut the problematic communication and get them back on track.

Between-Session Homework

It is always advisable to try to give some kind of between-session homework to couples. A good idea is to assign at least one day per week during which couples are to practice enactments, namely talking and listening to each other in ways demonstrated earlier with Tom and Mary. This way people can transfer what they are learning beyond the session. Between-session assignments can also be given to build positive feelings in the couple. Clinicians can ask couples to take time before the next session to notice what is lovable about the partner and/or what is positive about the relationship. Another assignment is to ask them to note when their partner is doing something "right." You can also ask them to experiment with new ways of interacting that they discover in the session. Hendrix asks spouses to make a list of caring behaviors that please their partners and to choose to enact one or more from the list as between-session homework (Hendrix, 2007). Insoo Kim Berg (De Jong & Berg, 2008) assigns spouses to pick a day without telling their partner and act as if the changes that they want to see in their relationship already have happened. As part of the homework assignment, couple members are to come back to therapy and report on what happened. As a rule, if the couple completes the homework assignment, definitely keep giving them. If the clients do not do their homework, then stop assigning it. If you get a sense that they are not completing assignments because they are unmotivated to work on their relationship, challenge that directly, perhaps with a revisiting of scaling questions.

Going Deeper

The two-headed beast of blame and defensiveness is so salient in troubled couples that almost anything that can break this pattern is useful. Quite often, what underlies one's reactivity is a fear, consciously acknowledged or not, that there is something wrong with *they themselves* and therefore, *they* are the ones truly at fault. Sometimes, realizing that one's partner's behavior stems from their troubled family history can be enough to garner patience and understanding that in turn can heal the couple and even the individual partners.

When seeking a mate, we often unconsciously choose people who represent or resemble our parents and who seem to compensate for parts of ourselves that our childhood experiences forced us to repress. In effect, we set up a type of transference with our partners that flows out of our childhood histories, and it is important to understand that they are doing the same thing. Problems emerge when we project our unmet needs onto each other and respond with anger, withdrawal, judgment, acting out, or any number of unhelpful ways when these needs are not met.

According to attachment theory, we are all born wired to seek emotional and physical closeness (Bowlby, 2012). Such closeness has positive effects on one's central nervous system and, in turn, one's overall physical and psychological health. If childhood caregivers supply this closeness in a consistently responsive, dependable way, the child develops a secure attachment which leads to a grounded, integrated, positive sense of self in adulthood. Securely attached people can acknowledge and regulate their own emotions and develop stable and meaningful relationships with others.

If the caretaker is inconsistent, inaccessible, unresponsive, or threatening, the child develops what is known as an insecure attachment (Bowlby, 2012; Page, 2017). Anxiously attached individuals fear abandonment which compels them to interpret all negative, and even some neutral messages from partners as threats to leave. This fear compels them to seek closeness and reassurance in ways that seem clingy, manipulative, or controlling, and are ultimately wildly unsuccessful. Sadly, such behaviors could result in the very distancing and abandonment the anxiously attached individual fears. People with an avoidant attachment see others as a source of either pain, abuse, or deprivation and, as a result, withdraw in silent retreat, giving up on ever getting what they need. Several models of couples' work are based on some form of attachment theory, whether directly or indirectly acknowledged. For example, Hendrix (2007) defines *imago* as a composite of all of the people who influenced you as a child, and particularly your caretakers, and we bring these imagos into our adult relationships. Murray Bowen (Bowen & Kerr, 2012) describes how relationship dysfunction gets passed down through generations via parent-child relationships. Emotionally focused therapy (EFT) seeks to repair these attachment problems in the context of adult relationships (Johnson, 2019). Whatever model of couples therapy draws you, it is important to recognize that in your session there are always more than two other people in the room; there's the couple and also members of their families-of-origin directly impacting their relating behavior. For example, Mary might be demonstrating an anxious attachment style while Tom may be avoidant. Seeing one's partner's troublesome relating behavior as the result of childhood wounds can quell defensiveness and even engender sympathy on the part of the other ("Oh, so this really is not my fault, and in many ways, not really his"). This opens the door to less reactive interrelating (always the goal) that clears the way for relationship repair. Early attachment problems can be healed in subsequent adult relationships (Johnson, 2019), and couples therapy holds the potential to build the type of couple that can be a source of healing for both partners.

Clinicians can get at these family-of-origin issues by first taking a thorough family history of each member of the couple. It is not uncommon for therapists to meet individually with each person early in the therapy in order to do this, though exploring one partner's family history while in the presence of the other can increase couple empathy. Here are some questions to ask that can assist you in understanding the family background of a couple member.

1 Tell me about your family growing up. In general, what was it like?
2 How well did you get along with your peers? Did you have friends? A lot? Were you bullied or mistreated?
3 If you were hurt or upset, whom would you go to for help?
4 How would your parents respond if you were hurt? How did they comfort you, if at all?
5 Did you feel loved by your parents?

   a Did they make you feel special? How?
   b Did they help you feel independent and competent? How?

6 How did your parents get along with each other? As you grew up, what role models did you have for healthy relating?
7 How aware are you of your partner's (spouse's, wife's, husband's) relationships during (his, her, their) childhood?
8 In your extended family, what were marriages like?

As a result of these questions, partners learn about their own and each other's leftover wounds and unmet needs from their childhoods, setting the stage for understanding how they project them onto each other. Tom might have had a father who modeled stoicism in the face of his mother's repeated angry outbursts, influencing Tom to do the same in the face of Mary's complaints.

CLINICIAN: Tom, after hearing about your mother's relationship with your father, I am wondering if, when Mary angrily asks you to help out more or be more communicative, it reminds you of your mother's way of approaching your father, which sounds like it overwhelmed him. Your feelings about your parents' relationship may be coloring your current relationship with Mary. You shield yourself behind a wall of distance in the same way your dad did, but this leaves Mary feeling angry and both of you feeling lonely. Now that you are an adult and know this, I am wondering whether you are now ready to do things differently in your current generation in order to save your marriage.

Once Tom understands this and realizes the loneliness and isolation he and his father experienced, as well as Mary's emotional wounds, he may feel freer to choose to relate to Mary differently. As a result of the family-of-origin questions, Mary also gains insight. She realizes that she pursues Tom so strongly because as a middle child in a large family headed by two emotionally distant and overwhelmed parents, she felt lonely and emotionally neglected by her own family. Growing up, the only way to get attention was to be loud or misbehave in some big way. By exploring her family-of-origin, she came to realize that Tom's silence activated these old emotional memories of neglect, leaving her feeling sad and also rageful.

TOM: (upon hearing this) Wow, I never knew that.
CLINICIAN: How might this information affect how you interact with Mary, particularly when she is upset? Tell her.
TOM: I am going to try to have more patience with you.
MARY: And I am going to try to find better ways to approach you when I am feeling lonely or angry. You're not my neglectful parents (chuckle); I realize that now.
TOM: And you are not my mother, thank God (also chuckling).

Biology?

There may be a biological predisposition that might influence how men and women differentially handle conflict. It has been hypothesized that due to sex differences in their autonomic nervous systems, men have less ability than women to tolerate emotional stress, so they get overloaded quickly and then, tend to emotionally shut down during confrontation to decrease the stimulation, which a woman might perceive as uncaring (Gottman, 1994). I have framed male detachment and distance during an argument in this way, and have called for the couples to time out when this happens and resume the discussion later, or to save it for the therapy session. This frame has provided relief to the couples I have worked with, enough so they can depersonalize the cause of their difficulties. Again, anything that can get people not to personalize and become reactive to the behavior of their partners can be helpful to the therapeutic process.

Couples and Context

On June 26, 2015, the Supreme Court of the United States ruled to recognize and in effect legalize same-sex marriage thus granting all federal benefits to same-sex couples (*Obergefell v. Hodges*, 2015); irrefutable proof of progress in the advancement of lesbian, gay, and bisexual rights. However, there is still a ways to go. For example, there is no federal law that prohibits discrimination in housing or employment (NeJaime, 2015). Additionally, these couples are still stigmatized and many people and religious institutions do not recognize these marriages. Often, gay men and lesbian women face disapproval from their families of origin. Overall, there is no evidence that same-sex relationships are any less satisfying than their heterosexual counterparts. In fact, such couples are known to be more flexible when it comes to tasks and behaviors usually assigned or adopted by gender (Barrett, 2015a; Moskowitz & Hart, 2011). However, stigma and discrimination can impact relationship quality. A not uncommon area of disagreement is how to interact with each other's families-of-origin, particularly if they disapprove of the union. Same-sex couples that face intergenerational disapproval have been found to be less satisfying and, according to some findings, more troubled than couples who enjoy family support (LaSala, 2001; Reczek, 2016).

Same-sex couples can also fall victim to the same socialization pressures as their heterosexual counterparts. For example, during conflict, if two men emotionally distance through silence, neither is confronting, acknowledging, or raising the problematic issues in the couple. Many gay male couples allow sexual encounters outside their relationships (Gomez et al., 2012), and while this might not be a problem in and of itself, it could be a way of distancing, particularly if the couple is conflicted. It is a good idea to ask such couples about their extradyadic agreements and be prepared to help them develop mutually agreed upon arrangements that ensure that outside sex is not used as a distancing or deflecting maneuver. Women couples have been seen as vulnerable to a type of over-closeness, which could stifle each partner's individual autonomy and leave them feeling isolated from others (Gold, 2003). Enactment and coaching can still be utilized, even if the content that is addressed is somewhat different than for heterosexual couples.

Slavery and the oppression of Black men and women have affected both, albeit in distinctive ways, which impacts their marriages (Etienne, 2019). While there is not enough space here to identify all of the differences among various types of couples, it is imperative that as clinical social workers, we are lifetime students of culture as well as the impacts of oppression and discrimination on the clients we see (for example, see Boyd-Franklin, 2013; Kelly, 2017; LaSala, 2010; Mallon, 2017; McGoldrick, et al., 2005; Nealy, 2017).

Power

Many relating behaviors are rooted in societal expectations and power differentials (McGoldrick, 1999). Financially and socially, women have more to lose if the marriage fails, which could explain their tendency to emotionally pursue their spouses and to be the ones to raise problems so they can be addressed.

The systemic thinking that undergirds process questions such as "Mary, what do you do to keep Tom so distant?" can obscure power inequities. If Mary is working outside of the home, she likely earns significantly less money than Tom. Women who get divorced often experience a drop in income and socioeconomic class. How much freedom does Mary have (or feel she has) in challenging her husband and potentially risking the economic stability of her home and children? Thus, we might consider putting a bit more pressure on Tom to find ways to improve communication with Mary (rather than vice versa) as was done during the enactment described in this chapter. Years ago at a conference, I once heard Betty Carter, a renowned social worker and family therapist who worked with wealthy couples in Westchester NY, talk about confronting financial power head on, asking male high-wage earners to put half of their assets in their wives' names. When men balked, she replied, "You don't want your wives to stay married to you *only* because of your money, do you?" She also advised women with wealthy husbands to pursue jobs and professions so that they had something to fall back on in case the marriage failed. While many (most?) social workers will not have a caseload of wealthy clients, it is important to recognize and understand how financial and earning differentials at all socioeconomic levels may lead to an imbalance of power that plays a role in relationship problems, and to keep that in mind as you assist the couples in their care.

Domestic Violence

Recognizing power differentials is even more essential for couples in which there is domestic or interpersonal violence. The physically stronger, more aggressive partner, typically the male in heterosexual dyads, wields more physical and financial power, and of course, we cannot expect, nor is it safe for someone who is continuously beaten, threatened, or victimized, to challenge and confront their partner in ways that are typical in couples therapy. Instead, the clinical social worker must help partners get into safe environments away from the abuser. Domestic violence is a crime, not a mental health disorder, so the abuser needs to be reported to the criminal justice system. Additionally, anger management treatment might also be called for if the perpetrator is willing to accept it.

For years it was believed that one should never do couples or family work when there has been violence. The concern was that couples therapy was not possible if someone was beating their partner. There was also a fear that the object of the violence (usually the female partner) could pay a price later at home for what she had said during the session. These are all important concerns and good reasons NOT to do couples work with dyads experiencing persistent and ongoing violence.

However, one agency I worked at developed a family violence program in response to requests from the local United Way, regional family court judges, and victims themselves. Initially, we started out with anger management groups. What we quickly found was that the men along with their partners wanted couples therapy. Some partners struggled with anxious attachment styles including fears of abandonment, while others loved their partners, and believed that outside of the violence, they had a good relationship worth saving. Thus, they sought couples counseling because they wanted the violence to stop and to stay together. We had such a repetitive demand at my agency from these couples, that in keeping with the social work commitment to self-determination, we believed we had to give it a try. It is important to note that not all domestic violence looks the same. The classic way to think about this problem is monstrously abusive men bullying cowering powerless women. This model does fit some situations. However, there are couples where there is only a singular incident of violence or the violence is episodic, happening once or twice a year. There are also incidents where the woman initiates violence or is the sole perpetrator.

Here is what we found that worked with these couples.

1 Careful screening. In order to qualify for couples therapy, the violence must not be more than infrequent, no more than once in a six-month period. We learned that people who committed violence infrequently did have the capability to control their impulses. Further, the perpetrator needed to take full responsibility for their actions. If these conditions were not met, couples work was ruled out and we referred the perpetrator to individual and group therapy. We saw it as a good sign (but not a requirement) if the perpetrating partner was being followed by a probation officer or judge, so that there were clear repercussions if there was another incident of abuse. We also preferred that if the couple was physically separated that they remain that way as this helped keep the victim safe and kept the abusive spouse's motivation high as he was invariably anxious to reunite. We met individually with the victim in order to help them develop safety plans and urge them not to take the partner back until they saw clear signs of improvement.

2 If they met the criteria, a couples safety contract was developed, discussed, and signed by both partners. The contract contained the following stipulations:

   a Periodic individual sessions were to be held with the victim so she could talk about her level of safety without the presence of her partner.
   b The perpetrator needed to be engaged in an anger management group. We had one on our premises that was research-informed and based on cognitive behavioral and solution-focused principles.
   c *Both* partners needed to develop a safety plan, which was what they would do in case the perpetrator felt the urge to be violent. The woman would need to have a bag packed and a safe place to flee, while the perpetrator was to temporarily leave the premises in order to cool off. We brainstormed with these men as to what their

coping mechanisms were on the occasions when they controlled their anger (exceptions) and we incorporated them into the plan. Others in the family needed to agree to and support this safety plan.
d   We were always clear that violence was a crime, not a mental health problem nor a result of an unhappy relationship. There was to be no more violence *in the family* which included a woman hitting a man or parents hitting children or children assaulting each other. We set up this rule when we found that all too frequently, there was a family narrative that some violence was acceptable. The family needed to commit to a culture of nonviolence by signing a separate no-violence contract.

In our experience, some couples reported that when the man wanted to leave the home for a break during an argument, as agreed to in the safety contract, women blocked the door. Of course, we told women never to do that. However, what we found was that when men went to leave, these women felt abandoned and worried that the issues they were arguing about would not get addressed. Thus, as part of the plan, men needed to reassure their partners that when they left it was not permanent and that whatever issue they were arguing about would be addressed at a later time, either at home or in the therapist's office.

Same-sex couples are not immune from the problems of domestic violence (Barrett, 2015b) which has been estimated to affect one-quarter to one-half of all same-sex relationships (Alexander, 2002; McClennen, 2005), and these prevalence estimates are comparable to those of heterosexual relationships. It is important to recognize that same-sex couples also experience problems related to power differentials, including domestic violence, even though at first glance, they might be more difficult to identify. Money, attractiveness, physical size, emotional dependence even racial, ethnic identities, and immigration status are all factors that could account for power differentials. The job of the therapist when working with couples is to carefully assess for these differences, point them out to their clients and ask them to find ways to address them as they resolve their difficulties.

Recognizing problematic agendas, joining and harnessing motivation and using enactments to assess and help the couples heal their relationships by changing their interaction patterns also applies to work with families. However, when working with families, we are dealing with a larger and in many ways more complicated system, as will be described in the next chapter.

References

Alexander, C.J. (2002). Violence in gay and lesbian relationships. *Journal of Gay and Lesbian Social Services*, 14(1), 95–98. doi:10.1300/J041v14n01_06.

Barrett, C. (2015a). Queering the home: The domestic labor of lesbian and gay couples in contemporary England. *Home Cultures*, 12(2), 193–211. doi:10.1080/17406315.2015.1046298.

Barrett, B. J. (2015b). Domestic violence in the LGBT community. In *Encyclopedia of Social Work*. doi:10.1093/acrefore/9780199975839.013.1133.

Bowen, M., & Kerr, M. E. (2009). *Family Evaluation*. WW Norton & Company.

Bowlby, J. (2012). *A Secure Base*. Routledge.

Boyd-Franklin, N. (2013). *Black Families in Therapy: Understanding the African American experience*. Guilford Press.

DeJong, P., & Berg, I. M. (2008). *Interviewing for Solutions* (4th ed.). Pearson.

Etienne, V. (2019). Saving Black marriages. www.savingblackmarriages.com/.

Frost, D. M., Lehavot, K., & Meyer, I. H. (2015). Minority stress and physical health among sexual minority individuals. *Journal of Behavioral Medicine*, 38(1), 1–8. doi:10.1007/s10865-013-9523-8.

Gold, L. (2003). A critical analysis of fusion in lesbian relationships. *Canadian Social Work Review/Revue Canadienne de Service Social*, 20(2), 259–271.

Gomez, A. M., Beougher, S. C., Chakravarty, D., Neilands, T. B., Mandic, C. G., Darbes, L. A., & Hoff, C. C. (2012). Relationship dynamics as predictors of broken agreements about outside sexual partners: Implications for HIV prevention among gay couples. *AIDS and Behavior*, 16(6), 1584–1588. doi:10.1007/s10461-011-0074-0.

Gottman, J. M. (1994). *What Predicts Divorce: The Relationship between Marital Processes and Marital Outcomes*. Lawrence Erlbaum Associates Publishers.

Hendrix, H. (2007). *Getting the Love You Want: A Guide for Couples*. Owl Books.

Johnson, S. M. (2019). *Attachment Theory in Practice: Emotionally Focused Therapy (EFT) with Individuals, Couples, and Families*. Guilford Press.

Kelly, S. (Ed.). (2017). *Diversity in Couple and Family Therapy: Ethnicities, Sexualities, and Socioeconomics*. ABC-CLIO.

Kerr, M. E., & Bowen, M. (2009). *Family Evaluation*. W.W. Norton & Company.

LaSala, M. C. (2001). The importance of partners to lesbians' intergenerational relationships. *Social Work Research*, 25(1), 27–35. doi:10.1093/swr/25.1.27.

LaSala, M.C. (2010). *Coming Out, Coming Home: Helping Families Adjust to a Gay or Lesbian Child*. Columbia University Press.

Mallon, G.P. (Ed.). (2017). *Social Work Practice with Lesbian, Gay, Bisexual, and Transgender People* (3rd ed.). Routledge.

McClennen, J. C. (2005). Domestic violence between same-gender partners: Recent findings and future research. *Journal of Interpersonal Violence*, 20(2), 149–154. doi:10.1177/0886260504268762.

McGoldrick, M., (1999). Women through the family life cycle. In B. Carter & M. McGoldrick (Eds.) *The Expanded Family Life Cycle: Individual, Family, and Social Perspectives* (3rd ed., pp. 106–123). Allyn and Bacon.

McGoldrick, M., Giordano, J., & Garcia-Preto, N. (Eds.). (2005). *Ethnicity and Family Therapy* (3rd ed.). Guilford Press.

Minuchin, S. & Fishman, H. C. (1981). *Family Therapy Techniques*. Harvard.

Moskowitz, D. A., & Hart, T. A. (2011). The influence of physical body traits and masculinity on anal sex roles in gay and bisexual men. *Archives of Sexual Behavior*, 40(4), 835–841. doi:10.1007/s10508-011-9754-0.

Nealy, E. C. (2017). *Trans Kids and Teens: Pride, Joy, and Families in Transition.* WW Norton & Company.

NeJaime, D. (2015, June 26). With ruling on marriage equality, fight for gay families is next. *Los Angeles Times.* www.latimes.com/nation/la-oe-nejaime-gay-marriage-decision-does-not-solve-everything-20150628-story.html

Nichols, M. P. (2016). *Family Therapy: Concepts and Methods* (11th ed.). Pearson.

Obergefell vs. Hodges, 576 U.S. (2015) (no. 14–556), 2015 WL 2473451.

Page, T. (2017). Attachment theory and social work treatment. In F. J. Turner (Ed.) *Social Work Treatment: Interlocking Theoretical Approaches* (6th ed., pp. 1–22). Oxford University Press.

Reczek, C. (2016). Parental disapproval and gay and lesbian relationship quality. *Journal of Family Issues*, 37(15), 2189–2122. doi:10.1177/0192513X14566638.

Chapter 6

Healing Relationships with Each Other—Part II: Families

Families have a powerful force field around them. When they are in conflict, they can suck the clinician into their problematic dynamics, even more so than couples. When you are in the room with conflicted parents and children, it is all too easy to unknowingly freefall into your own family issues and become reactive. As asserted in previous chapters, it is imperative that you find ways to recognize, acknowledge, and overcome (or at least work to overcome) your own current and family issues, even more so as you approach the potential minefield of work with families and couples. Murray Bowen, one of the early pioneers of family therapy, believed it was contraindicated to work with families without examining one's own family-of-origin issues and has developed a model for how to do so (Bowen, 1993). Whatever method of family treatment you choose, it is essential to work on yourself so you are less vulnerable to being subsumed by the troubled families with whom you will work.

When considering how to heal families, we must continue to think systemically, using enactments, coaching, and strength building, albeit more broadly than when working with couples. At times, workers can feel powerless and overwhelmed; the more people in the room, the greater likelihood that things can feel out of the worker's control, sometimes quickly and suddenly. As in couples work, it is important to remember, if family arguments escalate in your presence, they are to be welcomed as assessment opportunities. There are times when the worker must put their hands on the reins, step in and be more directive; the trick is knowing when.

In my experience, children's mental or emotional difficulties inevitably revolve around family problems and can either obscure, or illuminate family dysfunction. Problematic systemic dynamics are what creates symptoms among individuals in the family. Once we can decipher the code of children's misbehavior, we can find the family dysfunction in its translation. Again, what is most important are the relationships *between* family members and these are the targets of intervention.

DOI: 10.4324/9781003011712-6

Systems

In working with families, it is necessary to take a more comprehensive view of systems that includes assessing and intervening with system and subsystem boundaries (Minuchin & Fishman, 1981; Nichols, 2017). What we look for are boundaries that are firm enough to protect the family and maintain cohesiveness. These boundaries also need to be sufficiently flexible to allow for an exchange of energy between the family system and the environment. Boundaries between parent and child subsystems need to enable the well-being, development, connectiveness, and autonomy of its members. When working with families, we can encounter boundaries surrounding them that are too loose and permeable.

> During a session with the Jones family, the therapist noticed that people had trouble staying off of their phones. The two adolescent children were frequently texting, and at one point during the session, Mr. Jones left the room to take "an important work-related call." The therapist started to suspect that this family system might have weak external boundaries. When he asked about their home life, he found that the family was rarely together in one room; they never experienced outings as a family or even ate dinner together. Without a substantive boundary enclosing the family, people drifted apart and seemed isolated from one another. Could that be why the teenagers were acting out? To bring the family together?

Boundaries can also be too rigid, creating a wall when a permeable membrane is what is needed. Sometimes, family boundary issues can be detected even in the physical environment where families live.

> Sophia, who was employed at a nonprofit agency contracted to provide home-based therapy to families involved in the child welfare system, was meeting this family for the first time. When she pulled up to the family home, she noticed tall hedges around the property. There was a large, snarling pitbull tied up in the front yard, and Sophia wasn't sure the leash was short enough to allow her to enter the house out of its reach. When she finally got to the door, the doorbell was broken and she had to loudly knock several times before someone eventually let her in. When she met with the mother, father, and daughter, she found them wary, cool, and reluctant to disclose much information about themselves. Sophia surmised that this family had a strong boundary around itself, which is not uncommon for families that are hiding something, like abusive or criminal behavior. Further assessment revealed that this indeed was the case. The family led a neighborhood drug dealing operation.

It is important to recognize that our individual ideas and tolerance for system boundaries might be directly related to the boundaries of our own families. That is why it is important to take into consideration one's own family system when assessing and intervening on those of others.

Subsystems

Each family has a parental subsystem and a child subsystem. Boundaries around each of these subsystems must be strong enough to maintain parental authority yet sufficiently porous to allow love and support to flow back and forth. For the family to function properly, the parental subsystem must maintain a hierarchal position that puts them in charge and maintains leadership. Without this, there can be chaos in the family. It is important to note that this subsystem can consist of a single parent, grandparents, aunts, foster parents; this subsystem is more about who is in charge and has responsibility for the children, with the understanding that this could be culturally based. For example, African American families might have a powerful grandmother who has significant childrearing responsibilities and therefore must be included in any family therapy (Boyd-Franklin, 2013). What is vital is that the parental subsystem be in charge, setting limits and boundaries and also providing nurturance and support. Children need a balance of nurturance and discipline, and it is the job of the clinician to assess for this in the family. Families in which children constantly interrupt and do not attend to parental directives are systems in which the hierarchies are not functioning, and the boundaries between subsystems, namely parents and children, are too loose. As a result, the parental subsystem is not maintaining its executive function. In the following example, we see evidence that the family hierarchy is not fully intact nor functional:

> Ramona, a 30-year-old mother of Tyrell, aged 4, brought her son to see the clinical social worker because she was worried that her son was "out of control." During their first session, Tyrell would not stop running around the room and throwing toys, and when his mother tried to get him to stop and sit down for a few minutes, he slapped her.

If children believe they can assault a parent, it is a clear sign that the hierarchy of the system is not sufficiently intact and must be strengthened. When they see this, clinicians need to immediately send a clear message that this is inappropriate:

CLINICIAN: Wow, I can see that things are out of control here if Tyrell thinks it is ok to hit you.
RAMONA: Yes (looking downward).

It is easy to see how Ramona might feel some shame, so the clinician must recognize this by giving a message of empathy and support along with communicating that Tyrell's behavior is a problem.

CLINICIAN: (gently) I am guessing this is not only frustrating but embarrassing as well.
RAMONA: (softly) Yes, that is true.
CLINICIAN: Ok, well, no one said kids are easy to raise. They don't come with instruction manuals, do they? However, it is a testament to your commitment as a mother that you knew enough to seek help, and you have come to the right place. I suspect that you know you really need to nip this in the bud now as this behavior will not be cute at age 16. Let's start by brainstorming some actions you can take to let Tyrone know that hitting you is never acceptable.

Here, the clinician empathizes with the mother, but also makes it clear that this behavior must change and Ramona must reestablish boundaries around the parental system as well as a stronger hierarchy. As a result, with the therapist's help, she developed a series of clear consequences to be applied when Tyrone smacked her, such as loudly and firmly stating "NO" along with putting Tyrone in brief time outs in a corner of her home where there is no television, computers, or phones. These actions were ultimately effective.

Conversely, if these subsystem boundaries are excessively rigid, parental controls can be too strong and overly strict, resulting in children who are either rebellious and acting out or who become overly dependent on parents because they have not been permitted to sufficiently develop their own autonomy.

> Mohammed and Reina kept a tight rein on their teenaged daughters as dictated by the culture of the country they emigrated from in the Middle East. There were strict rules around bedtime and extensive chores around the house. As dictated by their home culture (but in conflict with that of the U.S.), the girls needed to come straight home from school and were not to socialize with boys, and infractions were met with severe consequences such as long exiles to their rooms. There were no real problems for the family until the oldest girl, Jasmine, entered adolescence and wanted more freedom to socialize like her U.S. born classmates. At 15, she wanted to attend dances at her school and also meet her friends at the mall. Her parents, who worried that she would be socializing with boys without a chaperone, forbade this. She complied with her parents' wishes until she turned 15, when she started secretly dating a boy who was 18, and began to sneak out of the house to see him. In response, her parents started to lock her in her bedroom

at night. She disclosed this to a school counselor who contacted child protective services, as this is a form of child abuse. Child welfare referred the family for treatment.

Early in the first meeting with this family, the clinician, indirectly approached the need for the parents to loosen the potentially culturally based family boundaries:

> I see how, like all good parents, you want your daughter to be protected and safe. I can also appreciate how difficult it is to adjust to a new culture where girls have more freedom. Let's talk about how your family and Jasmine can negotiate the clash between your own and U.S. culture in ways that keep her safe and also help her grow into the young woman you can be proud of.

See the exercise at the end of Chapter 8 that demonstrates how to assist families with rigid boundaries that are culturally based.

It is important to recognize that, in effect, each individual in the family represents a system of sorts. Thus, boundaries can be weak and diffuse *between* people as well. This can result in a type of pseudo-over-closeness in which people cannot really see each other for who they really are because of their need to control others due to their fears of abandonment, or of being overwhelmed. When people interrupt each other, it is a sign that this pseudo-closeness called *enmeshment* by family therapists, is at play (Minuchin & Fishman, 1981; Nichols, 2017). Alternatively, disengagement is when boundaries are too firm and impermeable between people. When family members seem distant, both physically and emotionally, and unresponsive to each other, they are likely struggling with disengagement.

Appropriate boundaries and hierarchies can look differently depending on the developmental phase of the child (McGoldrick & Carter, 1999). Infants and toddlers require more closeness and guidance from their parents, which would be inappropriate for older children. As a child goes from early adolescence, to adolescence, to late adolescence, to young adulthood, they need to grow increasingly autonomous from their parents while maintaining family connections. These boundaries might also vary, depending on the cultural background of the family. It is interesting to note that in the U.S. and other western cultures, the mark of successful parenting is when a child moves out of the home and becomes an independent adult. In almost all other cultures, proof of successful childrearing is indicated by an adult child who takes care of their extended family (McGoldrick, Giordano, & Garcia-Preto, 2005). External boundaries around the family can also vary, especially for cultures in which the importance of the nuclear family is deemphasized in favor of connections to the extended family. Thus, it is important to modify one's ideas about boundaries when working cross culturally.

Abuse: Misguided Attempts at Setting Boundaries

Child abuse and neglect represent boundary problems in the extreme. Children remain the most oppressed and powerless people in our society, and we must do all we can to ensure their safety from abuse and neglect. Very few parents actually want to harm their children. I have found that the intention behind spanking, hitting (or worse) is not necessarily to harm the child but to get them to behave or attend to important responsibilities such as following rules either in school, the community, or in the home. Families in which there is physical child abuse, tend to have overly rigid hierarchal boundaries. I worked with a family that harshly punished their children for minor transgressions. For not completing a chore correctly, a teenager's cell phone was taken away for one month. After they left therapy, I learned that the child was being tied to a chair and beaten for missing his curfew; an extreme case of rigid boundaries and hierarchies for sure. This was a middle class, upwardly mobile Black family. They understood that as a young Black man, their son was a potential target for police and also poor peer influences, so they believed they needed to work extra hard to teach their son to be obedient and thus stay out of trouble. The problem was not in their motives but in their execution. Nevertheless, their child was eventually placed in foster care after a particularly violent incident. If I had continued to work with them, I would have validated their good intentions but also stated: "Let's find a way that you can teach your child how to behave that is safer, more effective, and keeps you out of trouble; I have some ideas about this and I would like to hear yours as well ..."

Parents who are neglectful frequently experience difficulties of their own, namely substance abuse or mental health problems that overwhelm their parenting abilities. I once worked with a mother who was in recovery and was seeking to regain custody of her children. During the height of her addiction, she had left her four-year-old child in the company of two Doberman Pinschers to watch over him as she searched for a fix. However, once she was in active recovery and her addictions were no longer interfering with her judgment, her good parenting instincts and skills reemerged.

Systems and Symptoms

Learning about working with families might cause a new clinician to worry that they have made some mistakes that might have ruined *their own* children. First off, the advice given repeatedly throughout this book, that social workers realizing, acknowledging, and seeking to address their own wounds in preparation for their professional role, is relevant for the parental role as well. The better handle you can get on your own parents' mistakes, the less likely you are to repeat them with your own children. Second, it is important to recognize that all parents occasionally slip up. Sometimes, the same parent can be too lenient and at other times too hard on their children. There is no such thing as a perfect parent. However, Winnicott's (1988) concept of a "good enough mother" applies here, whereby parenting does not have to be flawless but sufficiently, consistently appropriate to raise a healthy child. People in family systems develop symptoms when the problems in relationships *are pervasive and repetitive enough* to get in the way of a person's well-being or development. If children see their parents argue occasionally, it should not be emotionally harmful—it might even be helpful in that it teaches that conflicts in couples are to be expected. It is especially advantageous if children see their parents resolve them. However, if for example, parents' arguments get loud, abusive, or they threaten divorce (abandonment), this could interfere with children feeling safe and secure as parent and child subsystems break down. As a result, they could develop symptoms of anxiety which (not uncommonly) play themselves out in behavioral problems such as school refusal, defiance, or some kind of self-harming behavior.

The trick for parenting is how to treat the child in a way that communicates that they are special and loved but also maintains limits and boundaries that prepare them for the future. A family needs to support a child's need to grow and become increasingly autonomous yet stay connected to the family, and in a reciprocal fashion, the child needs to take on more and more responsibility for themselves while maintaining family relationships.

Assessment

Assessment begins as soon as the family walks through the door. Sometimes, a family provides assessment clues when they first sit down with the clinician. As the family enters your office and assembles themselves, I take careful note of where people sit. If someone "accidentally" sits in my chair, I hypothesize that person as having an explicit or implicit leadership role. Also, I pay close attention to how and what the family is discussing, if anything, on the way into the office. Are they bickering? Tense? Are they friendly to one another? This is a good sign that despite the problems in the family, some connection remains. A good rule is to ignore nothing when meeting with the family, including how they initially greet you and how they interact with you and each other.

Engagement

CLINICIAN: Before we get to the meat of the matter or the problems, I would like to start out by getting to know each of you. First, I would like to start with you, Tania.

As in all models of clinical social work, engagement is crucial. As I have asserted earlier, no intervention will work until each client feels heard and understood. You are going to challenge and at times confront family members, so they will first need to trust you.

To start out, the clinician should introduce themselves to each family member. There are no consistent rules as to who gets greeted and introduced first. As with couples, what is of utmost importance is that the clinician communicates that they are interested in each person and the family as a whole, beyond the problems that they bring into sessions. I have seen some clinicians who always start with parents in order to reinforce the hierarchies right from the start, while others begin by first getting to know the child. In my experience, there is no wrong choice here. Since I have utilized family therapy predominantly in settings for children, the child is usually considered "the problem" or in family therapy vernacular, *the identified patient* (Nichols, 2017). Because they are going to be the likely focus of negative attention in the session, I often try to positively engage them first:

CLINICIAN: Hello there. What's your name?
CHILD: Frankie.
CLINICIAN: Nice name, Frankie, how old are you?
CHILD: 6.
CLINICIAN: What grade are you in school?
CHILD: First.
CLINICIAN: What is your favorite subject in school?
CHILD: Science, also gym.
CLINICIAN: What do you like about science?
CHILD: (shrugs). I like numbers, I guess.
CLINICIAN: Generally, people who are good at subjects like them. Are you good at science?
CHILD: Yes, I am. I get A's in it.
CLINICIAN: Wow, that's great. Science isn't an easy subject. Who do you get your science ability from?
CHILD: (shrugs)
CLINICIAN: You Mom? Or Dad?
MOM: Not me—maybe my husband.
DAD: Possibly, I'm a biologist.
CLINICIAN: So, Frankie, you get your science ability from Dad, huh?

The therapist starts with low intensity questions that focus on a child's interests and strengths, and positively connects the child to their parents. However, the clinician can use any number of topics around which to engage the child. Such areas to explore could be what the child likes to do when they are not in school, what music they like, and you can also ask about any interesting articles of clothing they are wearing.

Next move to the parents. Start out with low intensity questions and ask them what they do for a living. As they answer, keep an ear open for a strength or occupational skill they have that is potentially relevant to the family and the presenting problem.

CLINICIAN: In addition to the work you do as a mother, which I'm sure is a lot, do you work outside of the home as well?

Note, *never* ask a mother *if* she works. Anyone who is a mother or who knows one, understands that the burden of childrearing and housekeeping (still) falls disproportionately on the mother and as a result, they work all of the time, especially if they have an additional job outside of the home. What you are seeking is information about any *paid* job a woman has in order to understand her overall work burden:

MOTHER: I am a nurse's aide. I take care of sick and elderly people in their homes.
CLINICIAN: Ok, so in addition to being a caretaker as a mother, you are also one at your job. So, you are taking care of and nurturing people all of the time. I wonder if that is rewarding or tiring or both?
MOTHER: Ha! It can be both, but lately, it's just tiring!

You might later draw on her caretaking experiences and skills as you suggest changes in her mothering behavior that might help address the family's difficulties.

CLINICIAN: How about you, Dad?
FATHER: I am a foreman at the GE plant.
CLINICIAN: So, you are a leader; you know how to get others to follow you.

Store this information in your metaphorical back pocket, as father's leadership abilities might also come in handy as you address boundary and hierarchy problems in the family.

Goal Setting

Once I have engaged each family member, I ask my usual question:

> "People come to see me because they want to change something in their lives. What is it that you as a family want to work on changing?"

Typically, the response is that they want the identified patient's behavior to change:

> "We want Rob to listen."
> "We want Anna to do better in school."

"I want Darell to stay away from bad influences in the neighborhood."

As a reminder, agencies and funders want goals to be as measurable and observable as possible:

CLINICIAN: When Rob is listening better, what will you see that is different? What will you notice him doing differently?
MOM: He will be doing his chores without being reminded, doing his homework, and not out drinking and doing God-knows-what with his friends.
DAD: Alice will be doing her homework and passing all of her classes.
MOM: Charles will not be associating with those bad elements in the neighborhood.
CLINICIAN: What will Charles be doing *instead*?
MOM: He will be helping me more around the house, getting good grades in school, and making plans for his future.

Instead questions, as described in the previous chapter, can be used to convert a complaint or negative goal into a positive one (DeJong & Berg, 2008) "What would you be seeing different" even, "if I saw Robert *listening* what would I see differently?" are all questions that can lead to the development of goals that are observable, measurable, and thus within reach of achievement.

Tracking

One method for understanding what a symptom says about family boundaries is *tracking*. When we track, we are interrogating a symptom, asking questions about it until we discover its purpose in the family. Following are questions designed to track a symptom:

1 Tell me about Johnny's misbehavior
2 When did it start?
3 How often does it occur?
4 Who notices it first? Who next?
5 How does Mom react? Dad? The other siblings?
6 What if anything works in correcting the behavior? Does anything help, even just a little? What doesn't?
7 What does Johnny do afterwards? What do you do?
8 Where else does this behavior show itself? When? How?

Max was a 13-year-old boy referred to mental health services for encopresis which is a fancy word for soiling his pants. Through tracking, the clinician discovered that his soiling started about six months ago and took place only in school. After each incident, he went to the school nurse, who would call his mother who would then take him home. Through tracking, it became clear that Max's behavior was reinforced by the "rewards" of his mother's attention and getting to leave school. This suggests a loose parent-child boundary. As it turns out, Max's father was home ill, in the late stages of terminal cancer and about six months prior, his health worsened and he moved to a hospital bed in the living room. It is not uncommon for parent-child boundaries to break down when they are in crises, whether that be domestic violence, family illness, impending divorce, or death. Children in such families often want to be home to "keep an eye on things."

The following plan was developed for Max's family: 1) Max's mother equipped the school nurse with a set of clean clothes that he could change into following an encopresis incident, without the reinforcement of his mom coming to school to pick him up; 2) It was also arranged that he be homeschooled in the final weeks of his father's life; 3) Max underwent a full physical including gastrointestinal examination (always recommended for encopresis) that revealed an impacted bowel brought on by stress; 4) finally, family sessions took place at home where members could openly discuss their feelings about father's impeding death and how they could work as a family in loving and supportive ways to get through this difficult time. Ultimately, Max's encopresis was resolved through family therapy, medication, and a change in diet.

Enactments in the Family

As with couples, enactments can be used in the family system to assess family boundaries. We want to see the family's "dance" in our presence so we can get a sense of how they function, what their strengths are and also what needs to change. Once the family is settled, the beginning of the first session, might go something like this.

CLINICIAN: So, what is it you like to do for fun?
FRANKIE: I like to play video games and …
MOTHER: Tell him how you like soccer!
DAD: Jeez, Martha, let the boy talk for himself!

From this early spontaneous interaction, we are learning how the boundaries might be off in this family. While we never base our assessment on such a short interchange, we can begin to develop a working hypothesis about this family. There might be a poor boundary between mother and son, leading to an intrusive closeness. In response, Dad might feel disengaged, resulting in a parental conflict as indicated in this interaction.

Conversely, conflict with Dad might be pushing Frankie and his mother closer together. As stated in the last chapter, when it comes to systemic thinking, what comes first does not matter as long as the interaction pattern is altered.

When there is distance or disengagement in a couple, it is not unusual for one member (usually the mother) to become overclose with the child. Sooner or later, this enmeshment becomes conflictual, particularly during adolescence, when children are seeking to emotionally separate from their parents and discover their own identities. I cannot tell you how many times I have heard, "She was always my little girl, until she turned 13 and then became someone else."

A child's acting out can become fodder for a couple's problems. Consider Mary and Tom; they might not be able to agree about how to handle their conflict, which might have created distance in the couple. Mary might be fighting with their 14-year-old daughter Chiara while Tom sets up an inappropriate alliance with her. A sign of this might be that Tom remains silent when Mary is trying to speak/argue with Chiara or that he defends Chiara in her arguments with her mother. The important thing is that the parental subsystem needs to be united. If they are not together, things won't change for Chiara. From a systems point of view, Chiara's behavior could be seen as a way to call attention to the marital problems.

Between sessions, Chiara missed her curfew and came home intoxicated. Mary has been bickering with her daughter ever since and is threatening to ground her, while Tom has remained silent:

CHIARA: Mom, why do you have to be such a bitch?
MARY: I can't believe you are talking to me that way. Especially after the way you came home last night.
CHIARA: C'mon, what's the big deal? I made one small mistake and you are losing your s–t over nothing.
TOM: (remains silent, appears distracted and checked out. Note, by not participating in this argument, he is tacitly aligning with his daughter.)

The therapist notices the pattern:

CLINICIAN: I notice that you Mary, and you Chiara are doing all of the talking about this and you, Tom, are pretty quiet. I am wondering what that's about.
MARY: (jumps in) He never says anything.
CLINICIAN: Hmmmm … Mary, let me see you ask him for help.
MARY: Tom, don't you have anything to say?
TOM: I am sick of hearing the two of you bicker. I wish you would do it in another room when I'm home.
CHIARA: See Mom, even Dad agrees with me that you are a bitch.

MARY: Chiara, you are a spoiled ungrateful child.
CHIARA: Mom you are ridiculous.
MARY: YOU'RE the ridiculous one!

Mary and Chiara argue like siblings while Tom remains silent. This further suggests that the parent-child boundaries and hierarchies are weak.

Is the real problem at hand Chiara's misbehavior, or that Tom and Mary's marital problems are so acute that they are unable to come together to address it? The child's acting-out behavior may serve to bring the family to therapy, so that the couple can ultimately repair their marriage. The important thing is that through this enactment, we are getting a taste of the family's dysfunctional patterns.

Triangles

A triangle is when a conflicted relationship, instead of being resolved, is stabilized by a third person because the tension gets diverted (Bowen & Kerr, 2009). Perhaps all of us have had a conflict with someone and have sought allies in order to get validation or support. Triangles become problematic if we never resolve things with the original person with whom we are in conflict. By triangulating, we may feel better; however, the original problem never gets resolved. If triangles persist, symptoms can develop, such as Chiara's problem behavior. For Tom and Mary, there is a possibility of a diffuse parental subsystem boundary and a misalliance between father and daughter. By remaining quiet when his daughter calls his wife a nasty name, is he setting up Chiara to be *his* ally in his war against Mary? Are Chiara's words really those of Tom? A triangle becomes apparent as Tom's silence or support of Chiara drags her into what is really the couple's conflict, as Chiara deflects the tension away from Tom and Mary. When Tom joins in with Chiara to complain about her mother, this is additional evidence of a triangle. Inevitably, a triangle is resolved when the two in the original conflict, in this case Tom and Mary, talk to each other, leaving Chiara out of any couples' conflict, and in effect, closing the triangle.

Coaching

CLINICIAN: Tom, you're always so quiet when things come up about Chiara, however, as her dad, I'll bet you have some strong opinions. What do you think about what is going on here?
TOM: Well, kids will be kids, right? When we're young we're always doing something like this, breaking the rules, etc.
CHIARA: See Mom, THAT is what I have been trying to tell you!

The clinician notices that Tom undercuts what Mary is trying to do, weakening any hope of executive function in the family system. Tom gives tacit permission to Chiara to keep acting the way she does, setting up a triangle by indirectly empowering her to fight his battles with his wife. If the family is going to improve, the parents must become more united and in charge.

CLINICIAN: Hold on Chiara. Let me just deal with this with your mother and father for right now, and you sit back and take a break. It seems that you two (gesturing to Tom and Mary) are not in agreement about how to deal with Chiara. Mary, you seem like you want to take the active approach of applying consequences, while Tom, you see the situation as normal and therefore no action is needed. However, I am concerned that Chiara is getting mixed messages. Chiara, how about if you take a break and wait in the waiting room while I work with your folks?

Working with the Parental Subsystem

Sometimes, when treating a family with a troubled child, it is necessary to work alone with the parental subsystem. If the therapist and the family agree that the problems in the child's behavior stem from difficulties between the parents (or difficulties of one parent if it is a single parent household) then separate sessions might be indicated. For example, if a parent was beaten by their own parents as a child, it might be difficult for them to discipline their own children without repeating the pattern. Alternatively, they might go in the extreme opposite direction by not setting limits at all. Such a topic is ideal for individual or couples therapy outside of the child's earshot.

Getting back to Tom and Mary, Chiara does not and should not have to see her parents hammer out an agreement about her discipline. That should be done in private and then both parents should present the plan to Chiara in a united manner, showing they are a team. In this situation, the clinician is demonstrating how to do this via coaching them during an enactment. After Chiara leaves, the clinician continues:

CLINICIAN: Chiara needs some strong parenting right now, and I know it might not seem like it, but she wants it as well. I would like to see the two of you face each other and come up with a joint plan as to how to deal with this situation with Chiara.

This often works. When people calm down and are pushed in the direction of negotiation, it is amazing how they can come up with solutions to their problems. In this case, Tom and Mary might come together to decide to negotiate a firm curfew for Chiara as well as consequences when it is not adhered to. In doing so, they may also discover ways to resolve marital conflicts that do not involve Chiara. However, if they prove unable to come up with an agreement about Chiara, it might mean that Tom and Mary's couple issues, as described earlier, are getting in the way of their parenting roles, indicating the need for couples work.

Sometimes, weak boundaries can manifest themselves in children getting actively involved and openly taking sides in parental marital problems:

MARY: Tom, I am so sick of asking you for help. It's as if you don't care for your family!
CHIARA: See Mom, all you ever do is nag. You nag Dad like you nag me, and I'm sure he is sick of it. Ugh!

Here the therapist can assist the family in repairing or even establishing good boundaries.

CLINICIAN: Tom, it seems as if your daughter believes you need her help in dealing with your wife. Is that true? Do you need her to help you argue?
TOM: No, not at all.
CLINICIAN: Well, can you let her know that?
TOM: Chiara, honey, I do not need you to help me when I am talking to your mom.
CLINICIAN: Good (to Chiara). Take a break, Chiara and let the adults handle this.

What is essential to note here is that it is not the clinician who is trying to correct Chiara but getting the parents to do so. Families only get one hour a week, at most, with the therapist who cannot be (and should not be) parenting the child in any way. Instead, the focus needs to be on organizing the family so that they can find ways to resolve their issues. Tom and Mary (and not the clinician) need to work out their disagreements and come up with ways to consistently, and conjointly parent Chiara and also resolve their couple issues.

More on Coaching

Linda was a single parent of Jack, aged 10, whom she brought into a children's mental health clinic for firesetting. For sure, this is dangerous behavior and any clinician who takes on this case *would* and *should* be understandably nervous. Of course, it is always a good idea to get consultation and more information when approaching a new and scary symptom, particularly as a beginner. However, it is also invariably useful to *track* the behavior to get a sense of its cause, what keeps it going, and how it highlights problems in the family system. After tracking this behavior, I discovered that Jack would set fires when Linda's abusive boyfriend, who sometimes lived with the family, struck her. It was also important to find out what Jack set on fire and interestingly, it was his mother's bed that he ignited on two such occasions. In Jack's presence, I proffered the frame of his behavior as a way to protect his mother, sending up smoke signals as it were, in her own bedroom. In an effort to help strengthen boundaries and more specifically the hierarchy in the family, I challenged his mother: "Linda, I know this is a very tough situation, but do you really want Jack to feel he needs to protect you?" At that point, Jack became angry, stood in front of his mother and said, "Leave her alone, asshole" and held up his fists, threatening to strike me. I responded by identifying that he was angry, assuring him that I would not harm his mother like other men have. I added that it was understandable that he felt he needed to protect his mother, but that I would help her so he could relinquish his protective responsibilities. He wasn't buying it, so I asked his mother again, "Do you need Jack to protect you?" She replied, "No, of course not." I responded, "Ok, then let me see you convince him." What is important to understand is that I did not take it upon myself to convince Jack, but instead coached Linda to do it. After all, Jack is *her* child, not mine, and she will need to do this outside of the session when I am not present. During the process, Linda realized she needed a safety plan which I helped her develop. (Linda and her boyfriend were not appropriate candidates for couples treatment due to the level and repetitiveness of the violence and his refusal to participate.) She also knew she had to end her relationship with her boyfriend, and reassure Jack that they would be safe. Within days of that session, Jack lit another fire and was temporarily placed in a special shelter, which I interpreted as a way to make sure she was serious. During that period, Linda broke off her abusive relationship and quickly regained custody of her son. Jack never set another fire.

David, Debra, their 16-year-old son Robert, and 12-year-old-daughter Melissa had been in family therapy for several weeks. During that time, David and Debra worked at setting better limits with both of their children, resolving many of their parenting disagreements. Four weeks prior to the session described below, Robert, snuck out of his home in the middle of the night and then had come home drunk. His mother had also caught him with marijuana in his jacket pocket. He had claimed he was holding it for a friend; an excuse which is as common as it is unbelievable. His parents had grounded him for six weeks and were reluctant to once again allow him to go out with his friends. Robert believed his parents did not give him enough freedom and thought that after a month, he had served his time and should be released. However, his previous behavior suggested to his parents that he was unable to handle such freedom.

CLINICIAN: OK, so I can see that you, Robert, think your parents do not give you enough freedom and treat you like a child, and Mom and Dad, think you can't handle being out of close supervision. I generally like to see people interact with each other in front of me when I work with families. I know that may seem strange and a bit uncomfortable at first but people get used to it. Plus, it gives me an opportunity to see how people talk to each other. So Robert, right here, right now, I would like to see you try to convince your parents to give you more freedom. Go ahead and talk to them directly, and I will sit here and watch.

ROBERT: You are so f-----g unfair. All my friends get to stay out until midnight on a weekend, but I have to be back early, like I'm a little kid.

DAD: Well after the last incident, we are not sure whether to trust you.

ROBERT: What? I have done nothing wrong since that time I got into trouble, have I?

MOM: Robert, that was less than a month ago.

CLINICIAN: Hmmm ... Robert, I can sense your frustration, but is this working? Are you convincing your parents that they should ease up on you?

("Is this working?" is one of my favorite interventions when people are having trouble getting their points across to each other.)

ROBERT: It's because they are assholes (parents gasp).

CLINICIAN: Maybe, but they are YOUR assholes. So, you need to figure out how you are going to work with them and convince them to give you back your freedom. But I have an idea. They seem to have trouble with trusting you. Find out what it will take to get them to trust you. Go ahead and ask them, and I will help if you need it.

ROBERT: Mom, Dad, tell me what I need to do.

It is worth noting that as an older adolescent, it is developmentally appropriate for him to begin to learn how to negotiate with his parents. With the clinician's help, he worked out a deal with his parents whereby he checks in with them by text when he is out and he submits to having his backpack checked when he leaves and returns. Again, notice that the clinician did not take sides nor tell Robert or his parents what to do. Through coaching, the clinician can help family members build new relationships that provide better, developmentally appropriate boundaries and support for the child.

The boundaries and thus the coaching may change based on the race, ethnicity, or sexual orientation of the family members. Tyra was a 40-year-old single parent of Dante, a 16-year-old African American young man. Recently, Dante's grades were slipping in school plus he was staying out late at night past curfew and not regularly informing his mother where he was at night. She was worried and harbored plenty of fears.

CLINICIAN: People come to see me because they want something in their lives to change. What is it you would like to change?

TYRA: I am very worried about my son. He comes home late at night, doesn't call me when he is out, and I am not sure what he is doing.
DANTE: Oh c'mon Ma! I am 16 and you treat me like a baby and worry too much.
TYRA: Well, what are you doing out at 11:00 pm at night? You must be up to no good.
DANTE: Mom, I'm just over Raffi's house, hanging out playing video games, that's all.
TYRA: You think I was born yesterday young man? I know you must be getting into some trouble out there. Plus, not letting me know where you are is disrespectful.
DANTE: (sits back, crosses his arms, and looks down).
CLINICIAN: Is this how things go at home?
TYRA: Yes, I just can't talk to him.
CLINICIAN: OK, it sounds like, under your anger, you are worried about Dante, that if he is out late he must be getting into trouble.
TYRA: Yes, that is true.
CLINICIAN: Can you say why?
TYRA: Why?!! Do you see what is going on in the streets? Do you see how many Black boys and men are getting shot and killed? George Floyd is only the latest example.

Clearly, Tyra was trying to set tighter boundaries around her family to protect her son, who is, in many ways, at more risk than Robert.

CLINICIAN: Wow, yes of course. I could see why you would be incredibly anxious. Now, I would like to try something. Turn and face Dante and talk to him about how you feel. Use "I" statements as in "I feel ..." and let him know your concerns.
TYRA: Dante, you might not realize this, but every time you leave the house, I worry that you are not going to come back—that something will happen to you.
DANTE: Mom! I've told you; I am not a baby and I can take care of myself!
CLINICIAN: Hold on, Dante. I can see you are frustrated, but for right now, I would like you to tell your mother what you just heard her say. Go on.
DANTE: You said that you are worried and afraid for me when I go out.
CLINICIAN: Ask her if you got that right?
DANTE: Ma, did you?
TYRA: Yes.
CLINICIAN: Ok good. Mom, so you think Dante understands where you are coming from? Ask him.
TYRA: No, I don't think so.
DANTE: Yes, Mom, I do but you need to trust me that I will be ok.

CLINICIAN: As you can see, Dante, she might not be buying it. So, for right now, I would like to see you try to reassure your mother about how you keep yourself safe.
DANTE: Mom, I am going to be ok. I'm not stupid, I watch the news too. Raffi and TeShawn and the others are all good guys from the football team. We are just at each other's house playing video games or shooting hoops.
TYRA: (jumps in) OK, I will try to be less nervous, but I would like you to check in with me, even if it is text, every couple of hours when you are out, so I know you are ok.
DANTE: Ok, I would be willing to do that.
CLINICIAN: Your mom is a tough customer. Ask her if there is anything else you can do to reassure her that you are keeping yourself safe.

Again, note that the clinician is not telling Dante what he should do to stay safe nor is he trying to convince Tyra not to be so worried. Instead, the therapist is helping this dyad resolve these issues themselves in their own way. The clinician might fill the sails with wind, but does not steer the boat; that is the family's job.

Of course, in real life, families usually take much longer to resolve their conflicts than Tyra and Dante do in this hypothetical first session. Helping families change their interaction patterns is hard work usually involving repeated coaching on the part of the clinician.

Enactments and Intensity

One thing to keep in mind is that making family members talk to each other will almost certainly raise the tension in the room as it pushes families to face their difficulties head on. For some families, the tension and intensity of the arguments could rise to the level that people are shouting and threatening, which is not helpful and in fact can hamper the therapists' efforts. Occasionally but rarely, people become so agitated that they threaten to commit violence. It is during these incidents that the therapist needs to take charge and STOP the enactment. This basically means getting the family members to cease speaking to each other and to talk directly to you as the clinician. If necessary, position the chairs so that family members can no longer fully see each other. This breaks the tension and lowers the emotional tone in the family.

CLINICIAN: I see things are getting heated. Cindy, instead of talking to your husband, tell ME what your issues are with him. Everyone else, just listen for now. Cindy, look at me and tell me what is making you so angry?

Sometimes, I might position myself in between family members who cannot stop shouting at each other. Blocking members from seeing each other, also lowers the reactivity and intensity. However, I never put myself at risk of physical harm, and you shouldn't either. If people cannot calm down, or if there is a threat of violence, stop the session and separate family members at least for a brief interlude.

CLINICIAN: Wow, anger and other emotions are running high. Let's take a break for a few minutes. Dad, why don't you go outside and get some air.

I might also reschedule the session for another time. I have always been able to stop a session before things got violent. I then have assessed for safety, and sent families home with a safety plan, even it if was instructions to not discuss the charged topic for the next 24 hours. A student of mine reported in supervision that during a session, a mother and teenaged daughter started to slap each other. In supervision, I told her to put a stop to this right away and to let them know that any violence is prohibited in your session and also outside of it. During the next session, she warned the family that if there was any more violence during their meetings, she would no longer see them. She then worked with them to develop a no-violence contract (see Chapter 5). Fortunately, these interventions calmed them down, but if they did not, she would have stopped seeing them as a dyad and referred them to anger management treatment.

The Art of the Reframe

Overall, the secret of any type of family or couple therapy is to get people to be less reactive to each other. When family members get in their minds that they have no control over what is happening in their relationships with their children and spouses, they develop hypotheses about problems that are characterological such as "he takes after his no-good father" or "my spouse is crazy/an idiot/a bitch/a cold bastard." These purported causes of family problems have no solution, or at least none that any clinician can effectuate. Frankly, I have never known anyone who responded to being called, crazy, idiot, bitch, or cold bastard by saying, "Yes, you're right; I'll work on changing myself right away" or a therapist who could de-bitch anyone or warm up a cold bastard. Further, sometimes asking a partner "What is your contribution to his cold-bastard behavior?" simply escalates defensiveness. In these cases, the therapist can reframe a family problem that offers a way out.

The key to a reframe is that it depathologizes behaviors which cuts down on reactivity. A good reframe offers the couple an understanding of their problems that go beyond their angry and hurt reactions. Reframing is about understanding that there is a positive intent behind a behavior and as the therapist, it is your job to help clients find it. Table 6.1 offers possible reframes.

Table 6.1 Client Complaints and Positive Reframes

Client Behavior	Therapist Reframe
Excessive corporal punishment	Parent with good intentions who needs safer ways to instruct their child
Nagging and criticizing	Parent/spouse knows child/partner can do better
Distant parent	Parent is special, bonded with others who want more of them. Ask "What is so special about (Mom, Dad) that you want to spend more time with them?"
Acting-out child	Independent, strong-willed (potentially a good thing if child is a woman or a member of an oppressed community)
Argumentative partner *	Fiery
Under-reactive distant partner*	Strong, silent type

*I have often framed this type of couple as "fire and ice." I have also used this frame to join with the couple, by reporting that I am in a similar type of couple. The ice partner needs to turn up the volume and the fire needs to tone it down leaving room for ice to talk and be heard (without melting!).

Importantly, reframing suggests that a solution might be about fine tuning or redirecting so that the intention behind the behavior is more clearly communicated. When people have a less negative view of their partners, children, or parents, they are more likely to become less reactive, consider abandoning their polarized positions, and be willing to entertain some changes. In the previous examples, Chiara and Dante could be seen as independent, strong-willed, and willing to assert themselves; such qualities would no doubt come in handy for a woman or a Black man living in today's world. Tyra, Mary, and Tom clearly love their children and want to keep them safe, and this love underlies their arguments with them.

I have done extensive research with families that have a gay, lesbian, or transgender youth (LaSala, 2010). My research assistant, herself the mother of a lesbian daughter, always reminded me that parents want their children to be happy, healthy, and safe. I would add that children want their parents to be proud of them. Often, in families with a coming out LGBT child, parents say things to their children like: "Do you know you are choosing a difficult lifestyle?" "You are making yourself a target" "Gay men get AIDS, is that what you want?" "You are going to hell when you die." All of these statements can be reframed as love (yes love) and thus profound worry for their children. I am clear that when a parent says things like this, they are coming from a place of great anguish—and I label it as such. Children who lose patience with these parents, "You are so backwards," "You don't understand, I have no choice" are seeking love, understanding, and acceptance. Many parents who reject their children, do so in the hopes they can get them to "give up" their identities so they can be, in their parent's view, safe and happy. However, like child abuse, rejecting children to pressure them is completely misguided and an example of good intentions badly executed. How do we convince such parents to behave otherwise? We first must empathize with the shock, guilt, and fear they feel when their child comes out; and then reach for the love and worry for their children that these feelings obscure.

Child as Co-Therapist

A child's acting-out behavior that brings the family to therapy can call attention to changes necessary in the marital relationship. Ask the acting-out child what they think needs to change in their family and pay close attention to the answer. Through tracking, find out what happens as a result of the problematic behavior. In the example with Jack, his firesetting helped convince his mother to leave an abusive relationship. Children's misbehavior, like Chiara's could be interpreted as her effort to get her parents to be more united and work out their own marital problems. It is not uncommon for the acting-out child to be spot on with what needs to change in the family: "Mom needs to stop letting Dad boss her around." There have been times when, during a session, I have verbally anointed an acting-out child as my co-family therapist. Again, thinking systemically, we always look at the meanings and purposes of individual behaviors in the overall system.

Intergenerational Influences

As in individual and couples therapy, history is important. When behaviorally oriented interventions like enactment, coaching, process questions, and reframing fail, it once again might be an indication to go deeper and wider, and one way to do that is to search for clues and solutions in family histories. The first place we learn how to be parents is from our own parents. I have worked with many families in which the parent was severely abused as a child, and as a result, was overly lenient with their own children, setting up poor hierarchical boundaries. These kids grew up feeling they could do whatever they wanted with no limitations and did not respond well to limits when they were all-too-rarely applied. Much to their chagrin, these children grew up to be bullies, treating their parents in the same way the parents' parents treated them.

Murray Bowen coined the term *multigenerational transmission process* to describe how, like heirlooms, family problems get passed down from generation to generation (Bowen & Kerr, 2009). In questioning the family about a particular problem such as alcoholism, it can be a good idea to ask where else in the extended family, or in previous generations, has this problem shown up, asking not only about grandparents but also great grandparents, aunts, uncles. and cousins? The therapist can also help the family trace relationship patterns across generations, such as women who pursue and men who distance; women who are strong, and men who are unreliable. Strengths can be assessed across generations as well. McGoldrick and her colleagues offer a diagrammatic map which can be constructed with the help of the family in order to get a visual sense of the historic influences on their current problems (see McGoldrick, Gerson, & Petry, 2008). The understanding gained can result in family members being less reactive and more understanding with each other. For example, if Chiara is showing signs of alcohol abuse by coming home intoxicated after outings with friends, this might reflect a propensity for alcohol problems that go back several generations. It is neither Tom nor Mary's fault alone, or even that of their ancestors; biology might even be playing a role. This understanding could free the couple up to become less defensive and blaming, and to constructively address this pattern in the current generation.

It is important to recognize that sometimes the intergenerational influence is a person who is alive and living in the home. Thus, when meeting a family for the first time, it is important to know who lives in the home, with the understanding that each person who resides there has a role and an influence, and thus, should be included in some way in the therapy. Nancy Boyd-Franklin (2013) describes how, in African American families, biological parents might not be the ones who actually parent the children or they might share these duties with a grandmother, aunt, or uncle, or someone who is considered family but is not a blood relative. Thus, it is a major gaff (and waste of time) to only work with a single parent mother when her own mother is heavily involved in child rearing.

Family Therapy with One Person

In the beginning of family therapy's emergence (80s and 90s), many practitioners insisted that every member of the household attend every session, or else they would not see them. In my family therapy classes, students worried that they were in settings where they did not or could not see families, thus they believed family therapy was impossible. What undergirds these ideas is the belief that one cannot do family therapy without the entire family present. This is wrong. First off, as social workers, we do not always have the option of not seeing or not trying to help whomever shows up at our offices (or during our home visits). We commit to working with people at low-income socioeconomic groups who are paid by the hour or otherwise in jobs where they cannot take time off. Families in which people can leave work to attend psychotherapy sessions are likely economically privileged. Second, as social workers we cannot, in good conscience, turn people away who don't fully comply with what could be seen as a difficult demand. Third, the number of people in the room does not family therapy make. Family therapy is about the *target* of the therapy, not the number of people present. If you are helping/coaching a person to have better relationships with their family members, you are doing family therapy, even if you are working with only one person. From a systems perspective, if one part of the system (or person) changes, the rest of the system must change with it. Think of a mobile, if you gently pull down on one dangling piece, the rest of the mobile will readjust to a new position. This is what can happen when one person is in therapy to work on family relationships and begins to change their relating behaviors. Interventions consist largely of process questions that get at the reciprocity or the interrelationship of behaviors. Thus, a lot of the therapy is responding to a person's complaints with "and what is *your* role in that problem?" As stated repeatedly in this book, clients will not accept interventions without feeling understood by the clinician. Asking a person who is complaining about their spouse, partner, or child what *their* role is in the problem can feel like a stiff drink, so the therapist has to carefully prepare the client.

CLINICIAN: So, what is it you want to change?

GLADYS: My marriage is a mess. My husband works all of the time and then comes home late at night and sits in front of the television. Our children are 5 and 7. They are good kids but can be quite a handful and I could use more help from him.

CLINICIAN: Sounds very lonely, Gladys, and also tiring.

GLADYS: Yes, very much so. It seems I am always by myself, doing things by myself, and I don't have a companion to talk to.

CLINICIAN: So, are you thinking things can be better with your husband and also your family? Or are you looking for help leaving your husband?

GLADYS: No, I don't want to leave my husband and I really want my marriage to work. Plus, I can see how it would help my kids if we got along better.

CLINICIAN: Where is he? How come he did not come with you today?

GLADYS: He is against the idea. When I asked him, he said, "I don't believe in therapy, but you can go if you want to."

CLINICIAN: Gee, it must be disappointing to have problems in your marriage and a spouse who does not want to seek help when you do. However, we can work together to figure out ways to improve things at home. It won't be easy because our work will put the onus on you to change.

GLADYS: I see.

CLINICIAN: Good. I am going to help you look at how *your own* behaviors might be contributing to the problem with your husband and children, and that might be difficult to hear, especially if you are angry at them, which is understandable. However, in reality, the only thing we can change is our own behavior and I can hopefully help you do that even though it might not feel so good. Are you willing to give it a try?

GLADYS: Yes, I guess so.

CLINICIAN: I understand from what you have been saying that your husband is not really working with you on the family and actually seems pretty distant. Tough question here, but what might you be doing that could be pushing him away?

GLADYS: Hmmm ... nothing that I can think of.

CLINICIAN: Ok, let's try this another way. Tell me about the last time your husband came home and talked to you more. Let's look at what's happening when things go differently.

For a classic, seminal article on doing family therapy with one person, see McGoldrick and Carter (2001), and also see Szapocznik's work (Szapocznik et al., 1986). Remember, even if a person is in what is labeled individual therapy, the changes they make will impact those around them—so technically, all psychotherapy could be seen as family therapy.

In couples and family work, the clinician establishes a healing relationship with clients so that they can repair their relationships with each other. Keep in mind that the impacts of healing a family are far reaching whereby improved family relationships impact not only people alive now but also future generations. In the next chapter, I continue with the theme of healing relationships among clients to describe working with groups and group therapy.

References

Bowen, M. (1993). *Family Therapy in Clinical Practice*. Jason Aronson.

Bowen, M., & Kerr, M. E. (2009). *Family Evaluation*. WW Norton & Company.

Boyd-Franklin, N. (2013). *Black Families in Therapy: Understanding the African American Experience* (2nd ed.). Guilford Press.

DeJong, P., & Berg, I. M. (2008). *Interviewing for Solutions* (4th ed.). Pearson.

LaSala, M. C. (2010). *Coming Out, Coming Home: Helping Families Adjust to a Gay or Lesbian Child*. Columbia University Press.

McGoldrick, M. (1999). Self in context: The individual life cycle in systemic perspective. In B. Carter & M. McGoldrick (eds.) *The Expanded Family Life Cycle: Individual, Family, and Social Perspectives* (3rd ed., pp. 27–46). Allyn and Bacon.

McGoldrick, M., & Carter, B. (2001). Advances in coaching: Family therapy with one person. *Journal of Marital and Family Therapy*, 27(3), 281–300.

McGoldrick, M., Gerson, R., & Petry, S. S. (2008). *Genograms: Assessment and Intervention*. WW Norton & Company.

McGoldrick, M., Giordano, J., & Garcia-Preto, N. (Eds.). (2005). *Ethnicity and Family Therapy* (2nd ed.). Guilford Press.

Minuchin, S., & Fishman, H. C. (1981). *Family Therapy Techniques*. Harvard University Press.

Nichols, M. (2017). *Family Therapy: Concepts and Methods* (11th ed.). Pearson.

Szapocznik, J., Kurtines, W., Foote, F., Perez-Vidal, A., & Hervis, O. (1986). Conjoint versus one person family therapy: Further evidence for the effectiveness of conducting family therapy through one person. *Journal of Consulting and Clinical Psychology*, 54(3), 395–397. doi:10.1037/0022-006X.54.3.395.

Chapter 7

Healing Relationship with Each Other—Part III: Groups

Groups and Their Purpose

As a clinical social worker, it is likely you will be called upon to do some type of group practice in your career for lots of good reasons. Research findings suggest that groups can be highly effective for helping people improve their social skills, reduce social isolation, cope with stigma, and can provide a supportive community (Yalom & Leszcz, 2020), as well as companionship, and assistance with problems such as substance abuse (Weiss et al., 2004; Wendt & Gone, 2017), trauma (Gross & Wattenberg, 2021), or grieving (Bryant et al., 2017). Groups are a way to educate a number of people at the same time; such as a class of students. Further, groups can be used as a means to provide supervision for several people at once, which draws upon not only the group leader but also the input of peers. A minimal requirement is that the group is based on a certain commonality shared by all of its members, drawing on the idea that they are all "in the same boat."

In therapy groups, the leader establishes a healing relationship with the group and facilitates such among its members. As can be seen by the example below, a core component of group practice is to draw upon member participation in the treatment process.

RACHEL: My boyfriend and I got into one of our many fights last night. He ended up yelling at me again because he thought I didn't cook his steak properly. I do everything I can to please him but he never seems to be happy with me. Plus, I suspect he is having an affair with one of his coworkers. I've seen some flirty texts on his phone.
CLINICIAN: Sounds like a very difficult situation, Rachel. Does anyone have any reactions to what Rachel has just shared?
STEVE: (to Rachel) Well, you know what you need to do. You just need to leave that guy. He doesn't treat you right. He thinks you are a doormat. You are a pretty girl with so much potential. Why are you wasting your time with a jerk like that? You could do much better. You know that, don't you? Just get over him.

DOI: 10.4324/9781003011712-7

RACHEL: (silence, looking downward)
CLINICIAN: (to group) What is going on here? What are people seeing?
MARIA: Steve is trying to be helpful to Rachel.
CLINICIAN: For sure. Is it working?
DAVID: Hmmm ... I don't know, maybe?
CLINICIAN: Who here would be willing to ask Rachel?
DAVID: Well, does it Rachel? Does it help?
RACHEL: I think Steve means well and I get he is trying to help. However, I have tried to leave and I cannot.
STEVE: It is true, I was just trying to help.
DAVID: Yes, but it was like a lecture. Sort of "Father knows best."
CLINICIAN: I guess I would have to agree. Steve, your heart is definitely in the right place. But I am wondering, have you ever had experiences before when you tried to be helpful, but somehow it just wasn't landing right?
STEVE: I guess so, yes.
CLINICIAN: Does anyone in the group have any ideas as to what Steve can do or say to be more helpful?
MELISSA: I have an idea. Steve, how about if you ask Rachel right now what would help her?
STEVE: Ok (turning to Rachel). What could I do that would be helpful to you?
RACHEL: I think to just listen would be helpful. It is good to know that people are on my side. They don't need to fix the problem; they just need to listen and hear me as I try to figure it out. I'm open to advice, but I don't like feeling like it is being pushed on me.
CLINICIAN: Who here in the group has had experiences like Steve? Where they wanted to help but found themselves not helpful?
LEROY: (raising his hand)
CLINICIAN: Ok, you Leroy? Great; can you share your experience, perhaps with an example?

When run properly, there is less pressure on the leader to be the "all knowing expert." As you can see by the case example, the therapist is not the one doing all of the intervening, but instead shares this responsibility with group members. Decentralizing oneself as therapist and positioning group members to share information and feedback with each other is the thrust of this work.

Yalom and Leszcz (2020) describe how one of the most beneficial aspects of groups is for clients to see others get better and healthier. Another benefit is the sharing of practical knowledge among group members. I have sat through many group sessions where members exchange important information about resources, medications, and treatment providers, most of which I had been previously unaware.

For certain difficulties, group practice has a long legacy. Substance abuse treatment has a substantial history of group treatment, including self-help and professionally led groups. Support groups provide safe spaces for people to discuss experiences of trauma and to give and receive what Shulman (2015) would call mutual aid. It is vital to understand the difference between the three types of groups; namely support, educational, and therapeutic. Groups may start out one way and then morph into something else without the specific intention of the leader or the informed consent of the participants. Thus, it is important to understand the different types of groups and to make a conscious decision as to the kind of group you will be leading.

Types of Groups

Support Groups

In support groups, members with a similar problem or characteristic meet and assist each other without the leadership or assistance of a professional counselor or therapist. Members share and exchange information, resources, and provide emotional support to each other. I have sent people to support groups for parents of LGBT youth, and also groups for transgender persons, and in both cases, people get information and find compatriots who are negotiating similar circumstances. In many (most?) support groups there is a conscious decision *not* to include a mental health professional as people want to discuss various topics without feeling as if they are being assessed, diagnosed, or professionally treated. For groups like the Depression Bipolar Support Alliance (DBSA) (www.dbsalliance.org), people desire a space to compare notes and even criticize services they are receiving. In some instances, they believe that a clinician who has not "walked the walk" would not be helpful.

Alcoholics Anonymous (AA) (www.aa.org) as well as other 12-step programs have a rather extensive history successfully assisting people who are struggling with addiction. Nowadays, there are numerous 12-step groups for people trying to break free from a variety of compulsive behaviors including addiction to substances (Narcotics Anonymous) (www.na.org), sex (Sexual Addicts Anonymous) (https://saa-recovery.org/), overeating (Overeaters Anonymous) (https://oa.org/), and gambling (Gamblers Anonymous) www.gamblersanonymous.org/ga/), to name a few. It is important to recognize that the early developers of AA framed alcoholism as a disease that the mental health field had failed to ameliorate (Edwards, 2002). Try as they might, mental health professionals could not counsel people out of their addiction. So, it is perhaps no surprise that 12-step groups do not include mental health professionals as facilitators. To this day, there can be a tension between mental health and addiction providers. The prevailing wisdom is when a person is struggling with addiction, attending meetings usually comprises a large component of their treatment and some providers make it a requirement. Most 12-step groups have a strong spiritual component, "Let go, let God" that many find useful. However, for those who are agnostic or nonbelievers, there are 12-step meetings that are atheistic in view https://aasecular.org/online-meetings/. A set of principles and steps undergird these groups which can be found in what is known as the Big Book www.aa.org/pages/en_US/alcoholics-anonymous.

Support groups can provide a sense of community, an opportunity to share experiences and coping, and make new like-minded friends. Though many profess to be leaderless, these groups have a designee who organizes the space for the group, the schedule and the refreshments, and keeps things running smoothly.

Professionally Facilitated Support Groups

Groups that focus on a particular topic or population that are run by professionals provide a helpful way for members to get important information from leaders along with other members. The primary purpose of these groups is to help people recover and cope more effectively with whatever problem that is the group's focus. It is not uncommon for the professional to be an expert in the group's substantive area and thus be able to provide clients with sought after information.

In a parents-of-transgender-youth group I ran, parents offered each other support, information, and processed their confusion, feelings of fear, loss, pride, and guilt. The group included "senior" members whose children had come out to them years earlier, who knew the state anti-discrimination laws, were able to negotiate with local school districts to allow their children to present as their affirmed gender and use the corresponding bathrooms and locker rooms. The group also included parents who had just discovered their child's gender identity and were struggling; it was not uncommon for newcomers to quickly dissolve into tears in the beginning of the group session. My job as facilitator was to share my expertise in the area of trans identity. I also made sure that everyone who wanted to talk had an opportunity to do so, but more on that later.

Supervision Groups

In virtually all states, to qualify for your clinical social work license, you need to have your practice supervised by an experienced clinician for the first 2–3 years of your career. Group supervision has the advantage of being lower cost for the participants in that the supervisor charges less per person in the group setting than they would for individual supervision sessions. This is a big plus for participants early in their social work careers and who, due to low beginner salaries and student loans, cannot afford much. Further, as in a classroom, supervisees could benefit from learning about how peers handle their cases.

Therapeutic Groups

Therapeutic groups are run by professionals and focus on changes in a client's emotional state and social skills via interactions and feedback from the group members. Such groups are laboratories in which people's social behaviors can be observed, targeted, and participants can experiment with new, more functional ways of interacting. This is a distinct advantage over individual sessions, where people demonstrate their relating behavior in a more limited sense in their interactions with the therapist. In a group, the clinician can observe, assess, intervene, and encourage group members to provide helpful feedback on behaviors that are in response to a variety of personalities.

As in couple and family therapy, a major focus is on the relationships *between* people within the group in the hopes that clients will gain insight, both from the therapist and each other, into their relating behaviors. However, unlike family therapy, people are interacting with strangers, at least initially. Under the guidance of the therapist and with the help of group members, participants can learn how their interacting behaviors are sabotaging their efforts to form satisfying relationships. As in professionally led support groups, people share information and are encouraged to process their feelings. Reciprocity, as discussed in the couple and family therapy chapters, is addressed in terms of helping clients figure out what they might be doing that is inadvertently scaring others off, or making them uncomfortable or angry. Such groups assist people in correcting their misperceptions about their social interactions and the role they play in their behavioral problems. For such a group to function effectively, members need to be free to express their emotions and vulnerabilities and accept very personal feedback without fear of judgment or rejection, similar to the holding environment discussed in Chapter 4. Yalom and Leszcz (2020) describe how in these groups, members hopefully provide a corrective emotional experience for each other that can resolve symptoms of depression and anxiety. It is the clinician's job to lead in the creation of such an environment.

General Guidelines

A few things need to be kept in mind when deciding to run a group. The clinical social worker has two clients: the group and the individual in the group, and must attend to both. In addition, perhaps more than other models of clinical practice, the clinician has to act in ways that go against social norms, punching a hole in the membrane of social politeness which we are all socialized to observe. These actions include, quieting overactive members, challenging those who remain silent and withdrawn, and reaching for feelings and thoughts that people are hesitant to discuss, especially in front of a group. Thus, it is essential that the therapist create a safe environment while also demonstrating the courage to raise difficult, uncomfortable issues.

What is of utmost importance is to make sure everyone is onboard with the group's purpose. I have heard of social work classes about group practice that have been turned into group therapy sessions without the students' tacit agreement beforehand and much to their consternation. Social workers and social work students often pursue opportunities for self-discovery and insight, and as I have stated previously, it is always a good idea for a clinical social worker to participate in therapy themselves to gain insight and work through their issues, and also to experience what it is like to be a client. However, without the students' agreement, the instructor is violating the social work ethical standards of informed consent and self-determination (NASW, 2021). Additionally, it is questionable whether the power imbalance between the social work student and instructor leaves the student to feel free to object. I currently run a clinical supervision group of paraprofessional healthcare providers. It started out as a group to explore clinical issues but morphed into a place to discuss and strategize how to effectively interact with agency administrators. It was important to query members to make sure everyone was in agreement with this new direction.

That said, almost every group, including a social work class, shares certain characteristics. They are gathered for a common purpose, whether that is for therapy, supervision, support, or education, and at times the purposes might overlap. For example, a clinician facilitating a supervision group might make some comments about interactions among people in the group. People's relating behaviors tend to emerge, for better or worse, in virtually all group settings. By now, you have been sitting in classrooms for many years, so you already know this.

Decisions

If you are starting a group in a setting that typically does not have them, great! Your clients and your agency will benefit from your creativity and initiative. As you proceed, use these questions to guide the group's development.

1   Why start or run this group? What tells you a group is a good idea? Sometimes groups have problematic agendas. Agency administrators often see groups as a lower cost alternative to individual therapy in that several clients are served at the same time by one clinician, which saves on resources—not a bad thing, especially for poorly resourced nonprofit agencies. Seeing several clients at once is also a way to reduce extensive waiting lists. Enrolling these clients into groups, provided they agree with this option, might be better than keeping distressed people in an

indefinite holding pattern. Nevertheless, cutting down on waiting lists or lowering costs are not adequate reasons to run groups. Acceptable rationales include building community among a group of people who share a certain problem, exchanging information, and, if it is a therapeutic group, getting feedback to improve communication and interactive behaviors. Saving on resources is a nice side effect but should not be the primary purpose of group practice.

2 What kind of group do you want to create? As stated previously, different types of groups have distinct objectives. If the primary purposes of the group are information exchange and community building, a support group is best. If you want to help people go deeper into their relating dynamics, a therapeutic group is the way to go. A combination of the two types of groups is possible, as long as the objectives are clearly stated to the clients from the onset.

3 Carefully and thoroughly consider occasions or circumstances when groups might be considered counterproductive or contraindicated. For many, therapy has a stigma; people worry that they are "crazy" or that others will think they are. Thus, once they finally get the nerve to open up to a therapist about their problems, they might not cotton to the idea of sharing their vulnerabilities with a group of strangers. People who have experienced trauma such as sexual assault might be struggling with a (misplaced) sense of shame and therefore are highly reluctant to discuss their thoughts and feelings in a group. Pushing them to do so might be seen as a symbolic recapitulation of the assault. Further, hearing other people's stories about a trauma you also have experienced could be triggering. For example, in a cancer survivors' support group, some members' health can worsen and people might die, which could traumatize the surviving members. If you have been sexually abused, it could be too difficult, even traumatic, to hear about another person's abusive experience.

4 What support do you have from your superiors and peers? Drawing on a timeworn cliché, it takes a village to start and run a group. If you are starting one in an outpatient mental health clinic or any setting where there is not a tradition of running groups, you are going to need resources including a space that is large enough to seat people comfortably and that is also confidential and private. If you want a coleader, that's an extra cost, and therefore you will need administrative approval.

5 If, unlike a psychiatric inpatient unit or a substance abuse treatment center, you are in a setting that does not require clients to engage in groups, the heavy lifting will be in recruiting clients. You will need the support of your colleagues who will really need to see the necessity for such a group in order to urge their already busy clients to join. Will your colleagues support you in this endeavor by sending referrals?

6   Are there enough interested clients to form a group? I have seen many clinicians try to start a group but were foiled by insufficient interest. Rosa worked in a public children's mental health clinic and wanted to start a group for parents of children on the autism spectrum. It seemed a good idea as these parents could benefit from exchanging information and support, but what she hadn't counted on was how busy these parents were. They were already bringing their children to psychiatrists, individual therapists, attending family therapy, and school meetings, and simply did not have the emotional bandwidth, time, or energy to attend yet another appointment. Thus, it is important to develop a group based on member motivation as participants need to believe this will be a good reason to give up their free time. For example, in my geographic area there was what appeared to be the emergence of a rather sizeable cohort of trans and gender fluid children coming out to their parents. The youth felt isolated and longed to connect to a community of like others, so they were enthusiastic customers for a group. Concomitantly, there was a large group of parents who were struggling with their own distressing emotional reactions and who were eager to learn how to cope with the challenges inherent in raising these children. Thus, it was easy to attract a roomful of youth and two roomfuls of such parents seeking help.

It is important to make note of the ethnicity of your target population. People of color may be less willing to join groups, particularly those largely populated by White people. I have spoken at many PFLAG group meetings (Parents, Family, and Friends of Gay (LGBT)) people, however the only groups I have seen who have a significant proportion of persons of color, were specifically targeted toward this population (https://pflag.org/pflag-academy-demand/family-acceptance-within-families-color-recording-training-toolkit). Such parents need a place to talk about their experiences of the intersections of racism and homophobia/transphobia, and the presence of a large proportion of White people could inhibit such a discussion. Further, people who come from cultures historically forced into group settings or collectives, such as those from communist and post-Soviet countries, may be particularly resistant to groups.

7   Should the group be open or closed? In other words, should you start the group with a set number of people and keep it to that number, not allowing others to enter? Or, should the group remain open so that others can join at any time? The advantage of a closed group is that a sense of intimacy and community can be created if the same members meet continuously. The advantage of the open group is that people can enter at any time and it helps keep the numbers up in case there is significant drop out. Sometimes in open groups people assume the role of

mentor to the newer members, sharing what they have learned, which is of therapeutic value not only to the object of their ministrations, but to the self-appointed mentors themselves.

8   In addition to determining whether this is to be a closed or open group, the leader must decide whether the group will be time-limited or open-ended. Time-limited groups tend to be closed groups, admitting a certain number of people at first and then closing itself off. This is understandable whereby it is potentially disruptive to keep letting members into a group that is limited to, for example, six sessions. What is essential in running a closed group is that everyone understands when it is going to end. In doing short-term, time-limited work, termination starts at the first session whereby the leader reminds the group before each session what number session it is and how many are left. (This goes for time-limited, individual, family, and couples therapy as well.)

9   Will the group be educational, support-based, or therapeutic? More importantly, do the potential clients understand the difference and can they fully consent to what the group will be? I have supervised a clinician who ran a therapeutic group for male perpetrators of domestic violence. The men approached the group as if it were a completely educational endeavor, arriving with a court mandate, and calling the agency asking about the "violence class." Major components of the group were educational in nature whereby clients were taught the wheel of violence (https://domesticviolence.org/violence-wheel/) (Domestic Abuse Intervention Project, nd) and precepts from cognitive behavioral therapy. However, when called upon for anything beyond passive participation, the men were reluctant. They were accustomed to the instructor-student model of education, and as a result, became stuck in this way of interacting when actually, these men needed feedback and insight into their interactions. In supervision, the supervisee and I realized that he was more comfortable with the educational approach, thus he was not sufficiently pushing the members for participation. Following our consultation, he began to gently confront the men to speak up about their own experiences and directed them to respond and help each other.

10 It is important to be mindful of the group's purpose as well as its goals and objectives. What skills do you hope participants will have once they leave the group? For the men's domestic violence group, participants were to adopt cognitive behavioral methods of coping with anger and anxiety so that these emotions could be controlled and would not lead to violence. They were also to learn appropriate conflict reduction that would offset angry and dangerous escalations.

In virtually all clinical social work, the strong desire to help (and the fear that one won't be able to) can lead a clinician to find themselves taking a central position as an educator rather than a therapist or facilitator. A complementary pattern can develop in that the more the therapist works the less the clients will. The good news is that if the clinician can manage their fears and stay decentralized, a kind of magic takes over when other members of the group take on the healing responsibilities for each other. For example, in the men's anger management group, when members were asked to discuss incidents during which they resisted the impulse to act violently when angry, they began to brainstorm and exchange ways they controlled their tempers in difficult circumstances (such as road rage or annoyances at work). They traded helpful self-talk phrases such as, "breathe deeply," "don't let this get to you," "this is no big deal, not worth getting angry and in trouble over" to calm themselves down. However, this does not mean the therapist gets to nap or do online shopping during the session. The effort to avoid overfunctioning does not excuse the clinician from remaining vigilant and ready to act if needed. As a therapist, you are there to redirect if the conversation goes off course or to challenge inappropriate suggestions such as drinking, taking drugs, or any form of violence.

Getting Started

Now that you've gotten the group situated and everyone is in the room, how do you begin? For sure, you want to introduce yourself. Many social workers, particularly beginners, are shy about discussing their qualifications. However, it is important that your clients know your credentials and that they are trusting themselves to a competent professional. Then, quite quickly, you need to describe the groups' purpose and how your credentials relate to it.

It is always a nice touch to begin with a compliment. Here is an example that demonstrates how I began with that group of paraprofessionals who did HIV prevention work with African American and Latinx gay communities:

> My name is Michael LaSala, I am Professor of Social Work at Rutgers, and I have been asked to lead this group. I have been a psychotherapist for close to 40 years working with LGBT people and I also do HIV prevention research within this community. People who do the work you do have my utmost respect and admiration. I believe this work is more than a job, but a calling. You folks are heroes to want to go back and assist your community. You are also storehouses of information and expertise. When I work with groups, I encourage people to share their information and ideas with each other. After all, you are the experts in this work and in your communities, more so than I, so I will be pushing you all to exchange ideas with each other, rather than providing solutions myself. This might feel weird at first, but as we go forward, I believe you will not only get used to it, but find it to be helpful.

There are a couple of ways to proceed from here. First, it is of course always a good idea to have participants introduce themselves and talk about why they are in the group; what is it about the group's purpose that they personally relate to along with what do they hope to get out of the group? Yalom talks about how this is a time when people are silently evaluating each other, and also wondering whether they themselves belong (Yalom & Leszcz, 2020). It is important for the group leader to understand and silently acknowledge this as the group begins, reassuring members as needed.

Next, it is advisable to negotiate rules and guidelines. The leader should have some ideas about basic rules but a good move is to, at least initially, turn this task over to the group. "So, before we get started on the meat of the matter, what do you think the rules of the group should be?" Giving the group this task is a way to begin to socialize members as to how the group will run; specifically, that the leader will not be directing and controlling how the group goes but that members will share these responsibilities.

It is essential that there are ground rules around confidentiality. The leader must keep information confidential and is ethically bound to do so. However, group members may not share the same understanding and must be educated about the importance of confidentiality. This is particularly important if you are running a group with workers from the same agency. If people believe that what they say will be broadcast throughout the workplace, they would not be as open. To help offset this, explain the importance of confidentiality ("What happens in the group stays in the group") and exact a pledge from each member to commit to this.

Then it is time to get group members to start to talk about problems. I like to start out as broadly as possible, but still within the confines of the group's purpose. "Who is willing to get us started by bringing up some of the issues you deal with on the job. Who would like to start?" Often, this introduction is followed by a period of silence that might seem eternal, depending on your anxiety level. If people do not jump in right away, the new clinician needs to fight off thoughts that something is going wrong, at least initially. I recommend the 20 second rule. If after your introduction, no one jumps in to speak, stay quiet and silently count to 20 before saying anything. Keep in mind that if you are anxious there might be a tendency to quickly run through the numbers, so try "one alligator, two alligator, three …" This silence, which is an intervention in and of itself, will put pressure on the group until someone speaks. If the silence continues for much longer than 20 seconds, the members' hesitance or distrust should be addressed. In the beginning of a group, this is normal and to be expected to some extent, so I recommend that the clinician normalize this as much as possible:

> I notice you folks are pretty quiet, and hesitant to jump in. I don't blame you. I am a stranger as are many people in the group. Perhaps we need to spend some time discussing what would help you feel safe enough to discuss these sensitive issues.

Everyone has a right to know what they are getting into. When leading an open group, where participants can join at any time, it is important that new members understand its purpose and its rules. In keeping with the idea of a decentralized leader, it is advised that the leader get ongoing group members to take the lead in discussing these items with newcomers, perhaps with some prompting: "Who here would like to give Jake the lowdown on the group, its purpose, and the rules?" If the group is closed, you might only have to do this once with periodic reminders, especially when the group strays from its original purpose or members violate the rules. This helps set the expectation that the leader does not shoulder the full responsibility for leading the group but that this is shared among members.

Sometimes in agencies, things come up in groups that need to be addressed by administration. At one point, while running the HIV prevention worker's group, I found that several of the gay male outreach workers were being sexually harassed by their clients and occasionally by their coworkers. One man was even sexually assaulted by a client. However, the agency offered no sexual harassment training and workers rarely engaged the reporting procedures, resulting in colleagues and administrators blaming workers for being "flirtatious" with their clients. I urged the group to advocate for themselves to their administration. I also asked permission to make a recommendation to the executive director, which the group granted. Sadly, the agency did not act on my recommendation to train the staff to recognize and address sexual harassment and other related inappropriate behaviors. However, the group members are now more aware of agency reporting procedures around sexual harassment and assault, and have learned to set boundaries around this behavior.

Problematic Group Behavior

In any group, the behavior that prevents these clients from engaging in meaningful relationships will rear their head. As a matter of fact, you hope for this as a clinician as they present opportunities for intervention and growth. Here are some (but not all) of the troublesome roles that will likely emerge in your groups.

The Dominator

This is a person who seems to take over right from the start. At first, this can bring relief to the leader who fears that after introductions, things will go silent. It is also a relief for shy people in the group, who feel initially off-the-hook for participating as long as the dominator is talking. However, if the dominator continues, there will be little space for anyone else to participate even when they want to. This will frustrate some group members, and silence others. It is important to recognize that the leader's job is to make sure everyone has a chance to participate, so you must turn the volume down on the dominator, so that others have the space to talk.

CLINICIAN: (to dominator) Yes, you make several important points, but let's slow things down a bit and hear what other people think of what you are saying. Charlie, you've been pretty quiet while Max is speaking. What are your reactions? Is there anything he says that rings true for you?

In this way, as in couple and family work, the clinician is establishing a culture where people are talking to each other rather than solely to the clinician. If a participant keeps taking over the group by responding to each and every person's comments with advice, this likely reflects a tendency to try to dominate in their relationships outside of the group. So challenging Max on this behavior is vital.

CLINICIAN: Max, I notice that you seem to really try to take over the group. You have a lot of helpful experiences to share, that's for sure. However, I am wondering what the other group members might be thinking. Would you be open to getting feedback from the group?
MAX: Ummm, yes, ok.
CLINICIAN: Do you think you could ask for it?
MAX: (to the group) Sure, I would be open to feedback, if you are willing to give it.
AUDREY: Well, now that we're talking about it, you do talk a lot. A lot of what you say is helpful; I for one have benefitted from the advice you gave me about my husband. However, I sometimes feel like I cannot get a word in edgewise when I want to talk. Plus, I worry what would happen if I disagreed with your advice and did not follow it.
PHIL: You talk so much and give advice all of the time. I know you mean well, but it's as if you think you know better than anyone else. I could understand why people might start to get sick of it.
CLINICIAN: How is that for you to hear, Max?
MAX: Ouch, it is really hard. Am I really like this? I had no idea. I need to really think about this.

Note that Max indicated that this confrontation was somewhat painful. Some pain or discomfort when confronted is an unavoidable part of the growth process. However, if it is too much the client can shut down, become overly defensive, or even attack. If this happens, the clinician can intervene to help soften the blow sufficiently so the client can hear and benefit from the feedback.

CLINICIAN: Yes Max, this type of feedback can be difficult to hear. I, and I suspect some others in the group know you mean well; your advice is often on-target, and your heart is in the right place, but I know you want to learn how to be closer to others by being helpful. If you want to help people, perhaps this group is a place to find ways to help that are more helpful and, like the rest of the group, to figure out how you might be getting in your own way in your personal relationships.

Note how the clinician applies empathy, mentions a strength, and also links the confrontation to Max's goals for treatment. Executing a confrontation in this way makes the sting more bearable. If Max's behavior was repetitive, a possible intervention might be:

CLINICIAN: Max, do you ever get a sense that the very people you care about might be backing away from you when you wish they were closer?
MAX: Yes, all of the time. I have mentioned this in my individual therapy.
CLINICIAN: I am wondering, based on what is happening in the group, if that happens because people you care about feel silenced by you, or shut down. Are you willing to give that some thought; perhaps chew on it for a while?
MAX: Wow, yes, I guess so. I've never thought of myself in that way.
CLINICIAN: Who else here has dealt with this issue, either as an advice giver or being the one getting a lot of advice?

The clinician has temporarily taken charge of the group to deal with this issue, but then turns the reins back over to the group members.

The Silent One

Lula is what is known in groups as the silent one. She says little or nothing in the group, letting the extroverts and dominators take over as she hides in their shadows.

CLINICIAN: Lula, I noticed you are quiet during the group. Anyone else notice how quiet Lula has been?
CYNTHIA: Yes, I have noticed it. I am wondering what she is thinking when others speak; what is going through her mind?
WALLY: Me too. I always worry she is judging what people are saying. Without her saying anything, it is impossible to know what she is thinking or feeling.
CLINICIAN: Who would be willing to go ahead and ask her?
WALLY: Lula, what is happening, what are you thinking about what Max just said?
LULA: I am thinking he and I don't really have a lot in common with how we interact. He is really good about speaking up, but I am very shy.
CLINICIAN: Lula, I am wondering if speaking up and speaking your mind is an issue for you in your relationships outside of group?

LULA: Hmmm ... I really have to think about that. My husband always says, "a penny for your thoughts" and I usually ignore him. I don't know if that bothers him or not.
CLINICIAN: Lula, I wonder if there is something that we can do in the group to help you with this? I know from the few times you have spoken up that you have a lot of wisdom to share with us. Is there something we could do to help you feel more comfortable to participate?

(Note the compliment embedded in the confrontation.)

LULA: I think just by bringing it up is helpful.
CLINICIAN: What ideas do other members of the group have that can help Lula?
LATRICE: I am shy but I make sure to push myself to speak up when I need to. It's not easy but I'm learning how to do it!

In group therapy, we see Lula's behavior as reflective of her interactions and behaviors outside of the group, thus it is justifiable to wonder if Lula has trouble asserting herself in her relationships with family members, colleagues, and authority figures. Is it harder for her to speak up to men or women? All of this can be asked about and assessed through the group, where Lula can gain insight into her behaviors and experiment with new ones. It is the group members' responsibility to give each other feedback on these behaviors, and it is the clinician's job to suggest how these interactions might generalize outside of the group. The group setting allows these dominating and self-silencing behaviors to emerge *in vivo* and thus be addressed as they are happening.

The Distractor

Inevitably, things can occasionally get tense. There can be disagreements, even arguments in the group. Or alternatively, the group can shut down and go silent in the face of an emotionally difficult situation. Sometimes, one or more members might find ways to distract the group, leading them away from the heat of potential conflict.

FRANK: Hey Max, maybe you should quiet down and let others speak for a change, for God's sake!
LEE: Hey, did anyone see the Yankee game last night?
WALLY: Yeah, it was great, but they took a risk by not relieving the pitcher earlier.
LEE: You know, I was thinking the exact same thing. I ...
CLINICIAN: Hold on a sec Lee, let's get back to what Frank was saying. Frank, please continue.

Again, what we are looking for are patterns. If this was a one-off distraction, we might overlook it. However, if Lee keeps repeating his distracting behavior, either by changing the topic, telling a joke, or trying to shift the conversation away from a difficult topic, it would be important to explore it further. Because distractors can be so effective at, well, distracting group members, I find that the clinician needs to confront this head on, at least initially.

CLINICIAN: I notice that when things get a bit hot in here, Lee says something to distract us. Am I the only one noticing this?
WALLY: Now that you mention it …
LATRICE: Yes, as I think back, I think you are right.
CLINICIAN: I am wondering if we could stop for a moment, Lee and get you to tell us what it feels like for you when you see a conflict.
LEE: Well, I never thought about it, but now that you mention it, it makes me uncomfortable. I become worried something bad will happen and someone will get hurt.
CLINICIAN: Does anyone else feel this way in the group and would like to share?
DIANE: Yes, I do. But I wind up retreating and becoming silent when this happens.
DIRK: (after a pause) Yes, when I was a kid, I watched my parents fight. Sometimes it got violent. So, seeing people argue and raise their voices makes me nervous.
LEE: Yes, that happens to me too and I feel the same way.
CLINICIAN: Lee and Diane, thank you for sharing that with us. It is natural to be uncomfortable in conflict, even more so if you experienced it a lot as a child (turning to the group); I am wondering who else in the group can identify with what Lee and Diane has just said, in that they are very uncomfortable to witness conflict.

Note that the leader oscillates between dealing with individuals and also using individual's behaviors to springboard discussions among the group at large.

People Pleaser

The people pleaser is similar to the distractor in that they are terribly uncomfortable with conflict and avoid it by only making statements that they perceive will get others to like them. These people have a terrible time with disagreement and tend to swallow their own needs and feelings to attend to those of others. The people pleaser's desire for other members' approval, including the leader, could interfere with expressing their own feelings, needs, and vulnerabilities in the group.

CLINICIAN: Wally, I notice you are always agreeing with what people are saying, which leads me to wonder, what are you really thinking?

People pleasers can also be rescuers in the group, which is unhelpful. In response to Max being confronted, a people pleaser might chime in, "Hey Max, I don't think what you do is so bad. I really like you." Such a statement insinuates that those who are trying to help Max, do not like him and this could have a stifling effect on group member's willingness to confront him.

What is important to recognize is that all of these behaviors provide clues as to the individual member's difficulties outside of the group. Once these interaction patterns are identified, the group leader and members can start to point them out as they emerge ("There you go again Max"). As members become more socialized to the group process and learn about confrontation through the leader's modeling, they become adept at confronting each other in ways that ultimately help their relationships outside of the group. Let's face it, being able to effectively confront someone is an important relationship skill.

Fleeing Pain

Lee's, Diane's, Max's, Wally's, Latrice's, and Lula's issues are not surprising or unusual. A common group behavior is when participants seem to spend a good deal of effort avoiding problems and fleeing pain. As Yalom states, if an elephant in the room is being avoided in a group, nothing else can be accomplished (Yalom & Leszcz, 2020). Recently, I held a remote (Zoom) session with the paraprofessional public health workers I refer to earlier in this chapter. The purpose of this group was to provide clinical guidance as well as advice and mutual support to each other as they coped with the stresses of their jobs. During this one session, they relayed that their supervisor of record, Jamie, had quit rather suddenly. As people spoke about his leaving, several were angry, particularly about how he quit without notice. Others seemed sad. When I tried to reach for these feelings, there was defensiveness along with some silliness among the group members; one member even put on a blond wig and modeled it for the camera, of course distracting the other members. Another talked about the supervisor's leaving with much angry emotion yet denied feeling angry. Others spoke of wanting to move on, and did not see the value in churning up such feelings. For sure, these behaviors were designed to distract from discomfort and deny feelings, so as leader it was my job to identify that they were fleeing the work: "You guys are acting silly but I think there are some powerful emotions that you are experiencing that are making you uncomfortable." After letting this go on for a few moments, I reflected to the group:

> I notice when I talk about anger or sadness people might feel about Jamie, you start joking and fooling around. I know there were a lot of

mixed and complicated feelings about his leaving. I wonder if all of this funny stuff is a way to avoid the topic and feelings associated with it. What do you all think about that?

This initiated a group discussion about how their feelings about Jamie were a mixed bag. On the one hand, he could be personally engaging, inspiring to his staff, giving pep talks that bolstered their commitment to their work. On the other hand, group members believed he micromanaged, constantly checking and badgering staff to get their work done, while at the same time failing to advocate for resources they needed. Some members of the group reported maintaining a personal relationship with this supervisor despite his failings, while others felt that he maintained poor boundaries and provoked subordinates to do the same. By pushing group members to talk about this to each other when they did not want to, I was encouraging them to violate a norm *not* to talk about painful feelings. This was also an opportunity for people to learn (through a negative example) of what NOT to do when leaving a job; how to leave a position in a professional manner, and the damage people do when they suddenly up and walk out and badmouth the agency as they exit.

Other Problematic Group Behaviors: Ignore Nothing

As a reminder, all behaviors in therapy are grist for the mill and must not be overlooked. It is up to the therapist and other members to determine what they mean. For example, is coming late to the group session motivated by unconscious (or not so unconscious) anxiety and avoidance? Is it a sign that the person is unaware and insensitive as to how disruptive coming late to the group is to other members? Early in my career, I was told by a supervisor that coming early to a session indicates anxiety about the work, while coming consistently late is a sign of resistance. Perhaps, but for sure, something like consistent lateness needs to be acknowledged, interpreted, and confronted.

CLINICIAN: Shauna, I notice that you come late a lot to the group sessions and I am wondering what the group thinks about this.
WALLY: Well, it seems disruptive, like we have to stop the action while she settles in.

(Clearly, Wally is making progress in terms of his people pleasing.)

LEE: Yes, it really stops the flow. You know I love you Shauna, but I gotta tell the truth.
SHAUNA: Hey, I'm really sorry, it's just the traffic.

CLINICIAN: I am wondering if it *is* really the traffic, or that there is something about the group that makes you uncomfortable that you perhaps want to avoid.

SHAUNA: Wow, you really look for hidden meaning in everything, don't you?

CLINICIAN: Yes, I do; guilty as charged (slight laugh). In many ways, that is my job. Let's just keep an eye on this issue as we go forward, and let me know if or when what we are doing makes you feel uncomfortable so we can fully examine it.

In this interchange, you can see how the group member in conjunction with the clinician works to confront this issue. As can be seen, the clinician can provide an interpretation which elaborates on the group feedback. By raising the issue, the clinician is setting the stage for examining underlying motivations for behaviors and planting a seed for future understandings. What is also important to recognize here is that the client does not have to agree with the clinician. In fact, sometimes the clinician is wrong; "A cigar is just a cigar" and Shauna's issue just might be the traffic. Therefore, it is always a good idea to back off if a client disagrees and consider the interpretation might be either inaccurate or premature. Heed the words of the innovative and pioneering psychotherapist, Carl Whitaker, who wisely advised, "Learn to advance and retreat from every position that you take ... and remember, zealots are the first to be eaten by cannibals."

While it is almost always preferable to let the group members do the work, sometimes the leader needs to jump in and educate group members on issues for which they may lack information. Consider these interchanges from the support group for parents of transgender youth I refer to earlier.

JONI: I bought my son-now daughter [client's words] a blouse. However, she refuses to wear it. As a matter of fact, her clothes still look more like a man's. I don't understand why.

LYDIA: Yes, it was the same thing with my child. She rarely put on women's clothes.

CLINICIAN: What do you make of this?

JONI: I really don't know. It's so strange.

CLINICIAN: Does anyone have any experiences or ideas about what Joni is talking about?

LYDIA: Yeah, my child did the same thing. Now she occasionally wears a blouse, but I am still confused. If you are really a woman like you say, why won't you do this?

CLINICIAN: If your child won't wear a blouse or a skirt, are you wondering whether they are really transgender?

JONI: Yes—if she is not sure, why put herself and her parents through all of this?

In this case, because group members were not coming up with anything helpful, the clinician needed to probe a bit and reach for the underlying issue, which is the fear that children were not "sure" about their gender identities and might be putting themselves and their family members through a difficult time for something that was not real. This led to a redirected discussion in the group led by some of the more senior members.

RALPH: My kid went through that as well in the beginning. Turns out, wearing the clothes made her feel strange at first; she had to ease into it. Maybe that is what your daughter is going through.
PHYLLIS: You know, things are changing. More kids are identifying as "gender queer" or "gender fluid" rather than transgender. It's confusing for old fogeys like me to understand, but it's happening.
JONI: Wow, this is all a strange new world to me and my husband.
RALPH: For sure; we've all been there and we're still learning.
PHYLLIS: Maybe you could find a way to ask your daughter about these things.
JONI: Hmmm … I guess I need to think about that.
CLINICIAN: Wow, we are really fortunate enough to have experienced parents in the room who can lend their expertise. Phyllis raises a good question. Have any of you spoken to your children about this topic? What have you found helpful? What not so much? Can you share these things with each other?

Not only is the clinician probing for underlying feelings, he is getting group members to help each other out and is once again decentering himself. Now, if the group goes off the rails, the clinician is there to provide a safety net and correct any misinformation.

JONI: I am starting to think this might just be a phase. Maybe my son isn't really trans and is spending too much time on the internet being influenced and convinced that he is something he is not.
SHARON: Yeah, you could be right. Kids are very gullible these days.

(Silence)

CLINICIAN: Does anyone have any opposing ideas to what Joni and Sharon are saying?

(Silence)

Here the clinician gives the group a chance to weigh in and provide correct information. However, as this doesn't (and didn't) happen, the therapist needed to jump in.

CLINICIAN: Ok then. I can understand that it is confusing to have a child come out to you as transgender and then not seem to follow through with certain expected behaviors. However, there is no real evidence that such kids are overly influenced by social media to be trans. Instead, we find that they look toward it for verification. There could be a number of explanations for your daughter's behavior. Let's go back to seeing if the group here could help you figure out a way to talk to her about this.

Though the worker has grabbed the steering wheel, this again is temporary. As soon as he can, he returns control back to the group.

Another Example

One must continue to remind oneself that whatever happens, even if (or especially if) it is unpleasant, it is always an opportunity for growth, albeit initially concealed. The following incident occurred during the second session of a group for transgender youth run by two facilitators, one a trans-identified woman (Maria) and the other a cisgender woman (Cindy). The group was rather large. At one point, Cindy left to go the bathroom. Once she left the room, one of the client members said, "Oh good, now the *cis* woman has left, so it is finally just us trans folks." When Cindy returned, there was an uncomfortable silence which she noted. Then a member relayed what had been said. Cindy became very upset that the group had been talking behind her back and she believed Maria failed to support or protect her. As a result, she stormed out of the session in tears. Cindy was a bright, sensitive clinician, and extremely dedicated to the well-being of trans people. However, as what happens to all of us, she found herself having a very strong countertransference reaction that she needed to explore.

During supervision, she courageously processed her feelings and discovered that she often *did* feel like an outsider and occasionally doubted her abilities to work with a demographic so different from her own. Of course, this feeling is not unusual. As social workers, we frequently need to empathize and work with people from different walks of life. Thus, it is essential that we be lifelong learners and that we are humble but also curious about populations we know little about. In supervision, Cindy and her supervisor developed the hypothesis that what had happened had possibly tapped into themes that needed discussion in the group, namely insider/outsider issues as well as the relationships between trans and cis people. For sure, this was indeed fertile ground to explore on a lot of levels.

Following supervision, Cindy talked with Maria and expressed how she felt unsupported. Maria relayed that she found the entire situation overwhelming when it first occurred and apologized for not jumping on it right away. She described how her identification with folks in the group led her to hesitate. Fortunately, thanks to a long-term, solid foundation of professional partnership, Maria and Cindy were able to repair their professional relationship and proceed.

During the next group session, Cindy discussed her hurt over what was said when she left the room. She told the group that she realized she became highly emotional after the incident and needed to explore her own feelings (which, by the way, was good role modeling for the group members). After reflection and supervision, she realized this comment might have pointed to important issues such as the concern among group members that a cisgender woman could not understand their problems and therefore could not assist them. She plunged into this topic by asking the group what it felt like to have a cis woman as a coleader. What were the pros (if any) as well as the cons? Group members, in an effort to placate and protect, immediately asserted that they liked her and valued her as a cofacilitator. Cindy wisely pushed back. "Please be honest and do not feel you have to protect me from your feelings. Although I felt hurt before, I have processed this and now want to know what this issue is like *for you*." Very timidly, two group members then stated that they felt as if they could not say *everything* they wanted to in front of her—that she might not understand or even worse, that they might feel judged by her. Group members shared sad and at times horrific stories about being judged, stigmatized, and abused by cisgender peers, family members, and teachers. This started a discussion around fear of being judged as well as what Cindy could do to help the group feel more comfortable sharing with her. It also segued into a talk about helpful and self-protective ways to interact with cis people in general.

Additionally, there was a fruitful discussion of insider outsider dynamics. How much of an outsider is a cisgender woman? Can she talk about how she can understand what the group members are going through with any credibility? How about Maria? Though she is trans identified, are her experiences the same as others in the group? How are the leaders similar and different from group members and what does this mean for the group? The point of this case is to show that everything—even things that are upsetting to the clinician provide important information that should be mined. The clinician must remain open and non-defensive, and see such incidents as opportunities for healing.

Groups for Children

Early in my career, I was asked to run a socialization group for middle school children who had problems with their behavior and social interactions. There were 6–8 kids in this group and for the second session, I decided to bring a bag of candy corn to celebrate Halloween. I learned the hard way that introducing a jolt of sugar to a bunch of already anxious, hyperactive kids was a recipe for disaster. During that session, I discovered where the expression "climbing the walls" came from as I watched youngsters stand on chairs and literally try to scale to the ceiling.

Chances are, if you have been asked to run a group with kids, they are experiencing some type of behavioral or emotional problems. Thus, the more structure, the better. I like to assign some kind of activity for each group session, like having them draw a picture of a problem they recently experienced or a picture of their family. When children are involved in a project, they can at times let their guards down and begin to disclose issues that bother them. It is important to remember from a previous chapter that children are so emotionally defended that they often cannot answer direct questions about their feelings. So projective techniques, such as picture drawing and telling stories about the pictures, can work well in a group setting. I have also used the Talking, Thinking, Feeling, Doing, Game (www.therapeuticresources.com/TalkingFeelingDoingGameDrRichardAGardner.html) with some success. A joint exercise that all of the members can participate in, while providing some structure, will maximize success.

Termination

Sometimes, at the end of a time-limited class or a group, leaders have celebrations to mark the ending as well as the "graduation" of its members. I'm all for parties, and I would agree that it is nice to send off members in a celebratory way. However, the danger is that such parties can conceal feelings about terminations and endings in ways that are in conflict with the overall clinical aim of the group. In other words, pizza and cake can be a way to cover over the difficult-to-talk about feelings of sadness, anger, and any other feelings. I am not saying not to have going-away parties; go ahead and have the celebration. But be sure to leave time and space for the complicated issues and feelings that termination brings up. Before the party, spend some time reaching for feelings such as sadness, pride, anxiety, and others. Process them as fully as you can before reaching for the pizza and cake.

References

Bryant, R. A., Kenny, L., Joscelyne, A., Rawson, N., Maccallum, F., Cahill, C., ... & Nickerson, A. (2017). Treating prolonged grief disorder: A 2-year follow-up of a randomized controlled trial. *The Journal of Clinical Psychiatry*, 78(9), 1363–1368. doi:10.4088/JCP.16m10729.

Domestic Abuse Intervention Project (n.d.) Power and control wheel. National Center on Domestic and Sexual Violence. https://domesticviolence.org/violence-wheel/

Edwards, G. (2002). *Alcohol: The World's Favorite Drug*. Thomas Dunne Books.

Gross, D. L., & Wattenberg, M. S. (2021). Group psychotherapy and treatment of trauma: A history. In M. S. Wattenberg, D. L. Gross, B. L. Niles, W. S. Unger, & M. T. Shea (Eds.). *Present-Centered Group Therapy for PTSD* (pp. 205–224). Routledge.

National Association of Social Workers (NASW) (2021). *Code of Ethics of the National Association of Social Workers*. NASW Press. www.socialworkers.org/About/Ethics/Code-of-Ethics/Code-of-Ethics-English

Shulman, L. (2015). *The Skills of Helping Individuals, Families, Groups, and Communities* (11th ed.), F.E. Peacock.

Weiss, R. D., Jaffee, W. B., de Menil, V. P., & Cogley, C. B. (2004). Group therapy for substance use disorders: What do we know? *Harvard Review of Psychiatry*, 12(6), 339–350. doi:10.1080/10673220490905723.

Wendt, D. C., & Gone, J. P. (2017). Group therapy for substance use disorders: a survey of clinician practices. *Journal of Groups in Addiction & Recovery*, 12(4), 243–259. doi:10.1080/1556035X.2017.1348280.

Yalom, I. D., & Leszcz, M. (2020). *The Theory and Practice of Group Psychotherapy* (6th ed.). Basic Books.

Chapter 8

Healing Relationships with Clients from Diverse and Oppressed Groups

Social work pioneer Joan Laird (1996) cautions social workers not to employ theories about various groups and cultures to make cookie-cutter assumptions based on what we think we know, but instead to use this knowledge to *listen* to our clients from diverse and oppressed groups with a trained ear. I liken a clinician's cultural knowledge to being an outfielder on a baseball team; they cannot predict the exact trajectory of the ball that might be coming their way, but they are prepared with the knowledge and skills to catch it if it does. Too often, well-meaning, beginner social workers approach clients whose race, ethnicity, sexual orientation, or gender identity is different from their own with a clumsiness that is tone deaf to their client's needs. Communicating our understanding of the intersecting oppressions our clients face is not to be done as if we are checking off a box. Instead, we must approach our clients with not only an understanding and willingness to understand culture and social injustice, but also how our clients perceive its role in their perspectives and problems.

First a word about the term *diversity*. In our increasingly multicultural world, being knowledgeable about the experiences of our clients from various racial, ethnic, religious, ableness, sexual orientation, or gender identity groups is essential. We must develop and maintain an ever-expanding storehouse of knowledge about the different customs, foods, practices, and histories of our client groups. However, we must also be aware of the experiences and impacts of power and oppression on our clients. For example, a White therapist might enjoy soul food and know the role it plays in some African American's diets. However, would they know that it originates from the need for slaves to make do with discarded food scraps considered undesirable by their owners (Miller, 2013)? It is important to recognize the emphasis on food for people of Italian and Chinese heritage, but to also understand that the types of food and the rituals around them have very specific social and historical meanings, some of which are based on legacies of poverty. A clinical social worker must attend to not only the traditions and practices of different cultures but also their relevance to power, oppression, and privilege in our society, and for that reason, I will use the terms *diversity* and *oppression* throughout this chapter.

DOI: 10.4324/9781003011712-8

The Impacts of Oppression in the Lives of Our Clients

Not surprisingly, being in an oppressed group can put people at higher risk for physical and mental health problems. Ilan Meyer has applied minority stress theory to frame how stigma and oppression of lesbian, gay, bisexual, transgender, and queer (LGBTQ) persons leads to higher rates of suicide, substance abuse, and HIV-risk behaviors among segments of this population (Kosciw et al., 2020; O'Brien et al., 2016; Pachankis et al., 2015). Proujansky and Pachankis (2014) theorize that gay men abuse substances and deploy other unhealthy behaviors in an effort to regulate their feelings resulting from their own societally-based, internal homophobia. Gay men grow up in a society that privileges traditional masculine roles that include being sexual with women. When men transgress this norm by having sex with other men, it is seen as an abdication of the privileges associated with gender. Many, but not all gay men grew up demonstrating cross-gender behavioral expressions and being physically and verbally harassed for it. For women, "tomboy" behaviors are acceptable and even cute in childhood, but are looked upon as strange and troublesome once a girl enters adolescence when she is expected to attract the male gaze (LaSala, 2010). Realizing one is gay, lesbian, bisexual, or transgender in the context of one's peers persecuting them for it is a certain pathway to emotional problems. So, it must be remembered, that when working with an LGBTQ person, there is almost always trauma related to this background.

For lesbians, one must be aware of the double threat of sexism and homophobia particularly among healthcare providers, as well as their increased risk for obesity, alcoholism, and breast cancer (Office on Women's Health, 2019; Poteat, 2012). Lesbian women have been found to be less likely to get preventative healthcare than heterosexual women, while bisexual and transgender women are more frequently victims of interpersonal violence (Office on Women's Health, 2019). Transgender people, like gay and lesbian persons, are harassed and stigmatized, and too frequently rejected by their families (Klein & Golub, 2016). If a trans person wants to physically transition so that their bodies are congruent with their gender identities, they must rely upon expensive medical procedures that may not be covered by health insurance. Transgender persons of low income too often put their health and lives in danger as they pursue silicone injections and hormones in unsanitary conditions without medical supervision (Williamson, 2010). Thus, among other things, it is important to ask transgender and gender nonbinary people if they have begun a physical transition and how they are pursuing it.

Latinx (Latino/a) people are from a variety of countries on two continents. There are some cultural similarities that cut across Latinx nations. If you perceive this diverse group monolithically, you would be overlooking language, cultural, and regional differences. Further, Latinx migrants and refugees, particularly those fleeing their home countries and seeking asylum, are likely to have experienced trauma both before and during the migration process. As of this writing, assaults of Asian and Asian descended people in the U.S. are on the rise (Zhang et al., 2021), because some Americans, including prominent politicians, believe that Chinese people are to blame for the Covid pandemic, rendering members of this population targeted and thus vulnerable and anxious.

African American people are overrepresented among the numbers of people experiencing almost all major health problems including hypertension, heart disease, influenza, asthma, diabetes, and work-related fatalities (Centers for Disease Control (CDC), 2013). Compared to Whites, African Americans suffer disproportionately higher rates of poverty, unemployment, incarceration, and stress-related illnesses (Boyd-Franklin, 2013) and their relative lack of access to healthcare could explain some of these disparities.

The Ongoing Pandemic of Racism

The widespread use of phone cameras and the ability to proliferate images through social media has brought incidents of racism to the attention of an increasingly wide audience. Currently, everyone has access to images of police officers killing unarmed African American men as well as Asian and Asian Americans being assaulted and even murdered on the street. This is traumatizing for us all, but even more so for those of us, our clients, family members, and friends who are members of these groups. Friends and students of mine fear for the safety of their young Black sons and older Asian relatives. Watching racist violence on social media and television is having traumatic effects on us which could explain our current polarizing debates about topics such as institutional racism, White supremacy, and critical race theory. In my classrooms, I have witnessed what could best be described as "the oppression Olympics" as people argue over whose suffering is worse and whose is (or ought to be) minimized. All of this has had a tremendous impact on our clients and ourselves.

Despite these pressures there is some evidence of what Wesley (2017) describes as a *race paradox* whereby African Americans as a group tend to have lower rates of mental health problems than their White counterparts. She has identified an immigrant paradox as well. This phenomenon suggests that *some* people are able to depersonalize and externalize the racism they experience. This *does not* mean that as clinicians, we excuse or ignore racism, but instead are advised to use such information to help our clients build the internal resources to cope with it. Such ideas are incorporated into the four clinical goals for members of oppressed groups described later in this chapter. It should be noted that when people from these populations *do* suffer from psychiatric disorders, they are more severe, long-lasting, and require more treatment (Smedley, Stith, & Nelson, 2003; Snowden, 2007).

This may be due to differences in access to mental health care along with the psychological impacts of historic and current racism.

White Male Theory Biases

I am writing this during a spike of the Covid pandemic and also as the nation witnesses the rise of the Black Lives Matter movement, arguably the most powerful civil rights movement since ACT UP in the 1980s. So, how do we work during these times?

First off, as therapists, we need to be mindful about the shortage of members of marginalized groups in our ranks. Social work educators can and must do a better job of recruiting people from oppressed groups. (As a clinician who works with transgender youth and families, I look forward to the day that I am "fired" and replaced by a transgender or gender non-binary/fluid psychotherapist.) Further, when you go to school, consider whose theories you are learning. Whose voices are included and whose are left out? It is worth taking notice how, in the clinical world, the most popular and widely cited contributors are male, White, and heterosexual. Freud's theories about "penis envy" (Freud, 1925), Bowen's ideas about fusion (Bowen & Kerr, 2009), and Minuchin's (Minuchin & Fishman, 1981) concept of enmeshment (among many others) are paradigms that have been developed by men and are thus male-biased. If you really think about it, you can see how these theories prioritize autonomy over connectedness, thus overlooking or pathologizing women's and non-White families' distinctive ways of relating (for example, see Boyd-Franklin, 2013; Walters et al., 1991). Psychotherapy theories are famous for "mother bashing" with little regard to the pressure women are under in a sexist world that expects mothers to be perfect while excusing fathers who are distant or absent. Family therapy theories tend to focus on the nuclear family when we know that many non-White, non-Western families rely on networks of nuclear, extended-family members, and even non-blood related kin. This does not mean that theories by White, straight men have no credibility and thus must be completely discarded. However, we must view them with a critical eye, understanding their contributions, acknowledging their shortcomings, and modifying them as needed. Clinicians from minoritized groups like Nancy Boyd-Franklin (2013), Elijah Nealy (2017), Ken Hardy, (2018), Insoo Kim Berg (DeJong & Berg, 2008), Rhea Almeida (2020), and Jose Szapocznik (Szapocznik & Hervis, 2020), to name just a few, add important perspectives to the clinical knowledge base. As we review their work, we must ask ourselves, how do their theories and interventions differ from those who are White, heterosexual, and male?

The terms etic and emic are from the field of linguistics and depict different frameworks to understand groups or communities (Pike, 1990). From the *etic* perspective, behavior is explained using theories that are believed to be applicable to all groups and cultures. Many of the theories we learn in graduate school, including Freudian, cognitive behavioral, and family systems, are examples of etic theories. However, etic frameworks are biased by the people who create them as well as the times during which they were developed. In the past, people engaging in same-sex sexual behavior, runaway slaves, and women who wanted more independence have all been pathologized using uncritically accepted emic perspectives among mental health practitioners. For example, during the era of slavery in the U.S., a physician named Samuel Cartwright (1851) coined the medical diagnosis drapetomania to pathologize slaves who ran away from their masters, thus defying, what was believed at the time, the natural role of Black people in relation to Whites. I will never forget a workshop I attended in the early 2000s, led by a famous author of a widely known etic theory, who showed a video from the 1960s of a session with a woman who spoke of taking care of her husband and children at the expense of her own needs. The presenter "diagnosed" this woman as being emotionally immature. Further, he seemed flummoxed when an audience member suggested that this woman was socially pressured to act in this way, particularly during the early 1960s. We must learn to be critical consumers of theories and suspicious of their potential to be used as ways to hold people to oppressive norms and for those in power to oppress others.

From the *emic* perspective, behavior and events are explained in terms of what they mean to members of the group being examined. When we see things from an emic perspective, we are prioritizing the view of the members of the group. Research and practice from an emic perspective tends to disparage etic theories in favor of emic viewpoints. As clinical social workers seeking to work effectively across difference, it is important for us to maintain an emic perspective. However, I do not believe that when we work with clients from oppressed or marginalized groups, we need to reject etic ideas and develop new emic theories from scratch. There is a downside to fully rejecting etic theories and their contributions simply because they might reflect some bias. Despite how wrong he was on gender, Sigmund Freud's theories have had a profound influence on not only our field but also our society. Our current understandings of the unconscious as well as what we know about therapeutic relationships are based on Freud's initial ideas. Murray Bowen articulated the important impacts of multigenerational family history on our current mental, emotional, and relationship difficulties; these ideas are relevant and clinically useful to clients across racial, ethnic, sexual orientation, and gender identity groups. Good clinical work integrates both emic and etic viewpoints. As stated by Sue: "All individuals in many respects are, 1) like no other individuals; 2) like some individuals; 3) like all other individuals" (Sue et al., 2019, p. 33). Thus, we should learn theories that purport to universally explain human behavior but with a critical consciousness that leaves open the idea that they need to be modified or sometimes, but not always, replaced to address the realities of people who are not White, heterosexual, able-bodied, cisgender, middle-class or born and raised in a Western European context. For example, in my own research, I have found that like their heterosexual counterparts, men and women in same-sex unions want to maintain relationships with their families of origin that allow for autonomy but also connection. However, what constitutes appropriate intergenerational boundaries for same-sex couples might look different from those described by traditional schools of family therapy (LaSala, 2002). Many gay male couples are able to achieve couple satisfaction without sexual exclusivity (LaSala, 2004), which challenges the prevailing norms about the importance of sexual monogamy in committed relationships. Further, family rejection and a history of bullying can have profoundly deleterious emotional impacts on LGBT youth (LaSala, 2010). There is not enough room on these pages to fully describe the impacts of discrimination, oppression, and disparities of access on all of our clients. However, we must always be as educated as possible about the social struggles our clients face. Structural inequities for people who are not White, not male, and not heterosexual are real and so are their impacts on mental health. The theories and interventions we apply need to reflect this understanding.

Clinician Self-awareness

As continuously emphasized throughout this book, self-awareness is vital, even more so when working with clients whose race, ethnicity, gender, sexual orientation, gender identity, or ableness is different from your own, and a self-inventory is a good initial step. We are all impacted by the messages we receive from our families, communities, peers, and institutions about various groups, and too often those messages are negative, reflecting societal prejudices. So, to begin, take a moment and think about what you have been taught and have absorbed over your lifetime. Do any of the following hit home?

"Gay men are promiscuous and thus unable to maintain a long-term relationship."

"Lesbians are jealous and possessive and get into relationships too quickly."

"Bisexual persons are oversexed and thus trying to maximize their sexual choices."

"Bisexuality does not really exist; bisexual people are really gay/lesbian people trying to avoid stigma ... or straight people trying to appear cool."

"Same-sex marriage is less legitimate than heterosexual marriage."

"All children need a mother and a father."

"Young people are being influenced by social media to be transgender."

"If you are unsure of your gender, pull down your pants and take a look."

"The gay community uses too many letters; I can't be expected to keep track of what they all mean."

"Women are biologically predisposed to be more emotional and less physical than men and therefore, not as qualified for certain positions."

"Heterosexual women who get HIV are 'innocent victims'."

"Women who want to move ahead in their fields need to put up with bad male behavior."

"Women should still be the primary parent because they are naturally better at parenting than men."

"Black men are dangerous, especially if they are angry."

"Black women are often angry."

"Black women are strong, independent, and do not need as much help as other women."

"The majority of people of color who got ahead did so due to quotas rather than qualifications."

"Racism is over as evidenced by the election of a Black U.S. president."

"Black therapists cannot really empathize with White clients."

"I use the term Negro because I'm old and cannot keep up with all the new names and labels people use."

"If Black people use the N-word, why can't White people?"

"People are poor due to their own fault. They're just not working hard enough."

"My own experience of oppression is worse than yours; my group is the most oppressed."

"Immigrants come to this country to commit crimes, steal jobs, go on welfare, and they refuse to assimilate."

"Why can't people from other minority groups be more like Asian Americans who have gotten ahead by their own hard work?"

"Education is key to getting ahead and is the great leveler. If people just worked hard in school, they wouldn't be poor."

"This used to be a home for delinquent Jewish boys? I didn't think Jewish kids misbehaved!"

"I'm uncomfortable sitting next to a Moslem man on a plane."

"Clients from oppressed groups do not want to talk about racism, sexism, homophobia, transphobia, ablism in therapy."

"Clients from oppressed groups want to talk about racism, sexism, homophobia, transphobia, and ableism as the main focus in therapy."

"I must be an expert on all oppressed groups and must share this information with each of my clients from these groups."

These quotes, uniformly representing uninformed, prejudiced, and oppressive viewpoints, are a compilation of the statements I have heard from colleagues and students (believe it or not), as well as clients. Perhaps we should not be surprised considering how we are all swimming in the same sea of oppressive social narratives. That is one of the reasons why it is so important to stay on top of not only the information related to diversity and oppression, but also one's own feelings and reactions. Thus, I am urging readers to periodically, take a moment and ask themselves the following questions:

1 How might your race, gender, ethnicity, sexual orientation, gender identity, and level of ableness impact your impressions of your client? Might you be consciously or unconsciously projecting your biases and prejudices?
2 What have you been taught about race, ethnicity, sexual orientation, sex, and gender identity growing up? What messages did you receive from your family, peers, teachers, and society? How have these messages changed over time?
3 How might who you are influence your client's feelings and impressions? Might they shield certain things from you as a result of your race, or sexual orientation (for example)? Might they project certain things onto you?
4 What do you think of the term "White privilege" and what is your relationship to it? Relatedly, how aware are you of health, education, wealth, and other disparities related to racial, ethnic, sexual orientation, and gender identity, migrant status, and ableness? What do you think drives these inequities? What is your role in fostering or ameliorating these inequities?
5 What gets in your way of listening, hearing, and working effectively with various groups? Are there some groups you might find easier or harder to work with than others? Why?

This list is no doubt incomplete but these questions begin to suggest what you need to be mindful of as you move forward in your career.

Working Across Difference

Making Mistakes

As stated repeatedly throughout this book, unrecognized and unchecked clinician anxiety can be a significant obstacle to good practice. Such anxiety is aggravated by the hostile and divisive public discourses surrounding the causes and solutions to police violence, the pervasiveness of racism, the teaching of critical race theory, and cancel culture. The ground beneath us is shifting as people from oppressed groups demand justice. Yet it can feel as if the consequences for making mistakes are dire. Wanting to be "a good social worker" and present to the client as such, adds to the fear of doing or saying the wrong thing. This anxiety could lead to interventions such as the following:

WHITE CLINICIAN: (a much younger me in the first moments with a Black client) Ms. Jones, I notice that we have a racial difference. How do you think that will affect our work together?
BLACK CLIENT: (startled) Wow. *I* don't think it will be a problem ... do YOU?

Unfortunately, this landed in a way that appeared to Ms. Jones as if I was suggesting that racial difference would be an obstacle. When neophytes make such mistakes, they are fueled by anxiety. Among other things, I was apprehensive about working with a client from a racial group different from my own, no doubt aggravated by the fact that I had been raised in a socially segregated White environment. I wanted to show that I was aware and sensitive to these issues, and perhaps get a pat on the head as a reward. However, this early agenda was based on *my* need, not that of my client.

Clinicians need to understand the extensive history of oppression perpetuated by social workers who, in the past, have enforced oppressive welfare rules and regulations that disproportionately hurt Black families, removed children from minority families without adequate cause, and misdiagnosed people of various sexual orientations, gender identities, and diverse levels of ableness. Also, social workers must understand that the systems they work with, such as schools, the courts, the criminal justice system and even some agencies, have histories of racist practices.

WHITE CLINICIAN: Ms. Washington, your son has been missing school and not following your curfew. You might consider filing a PINS (Persons in Need of Supervision) petition in family court to get the support you need from other agencies and also for a juvenile probation officer to hold him accountable.
MS. WASHINGTON: What? Are you kidding me? No way! You don't understand. Judges and the courts are never fair to a young Black boy. I would never *volunteer* to put him in front of a judge. That would be crazy!
CLINICIAN: (after a long pause followed by a regain of footing) Gosh, yes, I can see that now; you are right. I am glad you brought that up. As a White man there are some things I don't get or don't understand. Let's be sure to keep talking about such things as they come up in our work together.

This vignette illustrates how, when working across difference and making recommendations, it is essential to understand the various structural oppressions people face. Further, it demonstrates how to make a mistake and then recover. Following is another example of a recent mistake of mine, reflecting my own ableist bias. I was working with a Deaf client, and she was describing a new friend of hers:

ME: Oh, so it sounds like you recently met someone you hit it off with and who is becoming a new friend. Tell me, is this woman also hearing impaired?
CLIENT: Dr. LaSala! Hearing impaired is an inaccurate and hurtful term. There is nothing about me that is *impaired*. I identify as Deaf with a capital D. My deafness is part of my identity and connects me to a community. It is *not* a deficit or disability.
ME: Oh, wow. I'm sorry. I'm glad you corrected me. Now I know, I won't make that mistake again. Thank you for pointing this out. Should we process this further? Or do you want to continue with your story. Up to you.

It is difficult and embarrassing to be caught short by a client during a clinical interview, even more so if you are a beginner. For many clinicians, the first response is defensiveness ("How was *I* supposed to know 'hearing impaired' was no longer used?"), shame ("What a bad social worker I am for not already knowing this"), and also anger ("Wtf, really? Is it such a big deal? Everyone is so PC these days!"). The appropriate response to being caught committing a microaggression is humility, an apology, and a stated commitment to growing and learning. It is at these times, clinicians need to remind themselves they do not need to be all-wise and knowledgeable, and that ideas, language, and terms change over time as we hopefully all become more sensitive, and knowledgeable. Never be the person (like some of my previously quoted colleagues) who refuses to try to understand new labels and terms for minoritorized populations. My Deaf client actually gifted me with an opportunity to explore my own feelings and lack of knowledge about deaf and Deaf people, which I pursued outside of the session and still do. The correction might sting, but that is a small price to pay for such an opportunity. Acknowledge, apologize, commit to ongoing learning, forgive yourself, give the client the opportunity to process, and then turn the attention away from you and your gaff and back to your client. Resist the impulse to try to get your client to assuage your guilt. Focus/refocus on what the client wants; remember, that's why you're there.

Raising the Issue

As stated throughout this volume, it is often up to the clinical social worker to raise difficult issues in therapy. In my own practice, I have found that clients of color do not typically bring up issues of difference and oppression. This could be because as a White man, they might think I could not or would not understand these issues. However, once I introduce these topics, clients immediately respond, as if they were waiting for a signal. Discussions about oppression between White people and those of different races or ethnicities can be uncomfortable and contentious. Clients who are not White know that White people can get angry and defensive, and too often will attempt to invalidate their impressions and feelings. Thus, it is important to indicate to clients that you understand that these topics are important and that you can discuss this material without minimizing, dismissing, invalidating, or responding defensively.

Carlos and John are a couple that have been together for five years. Despite their agreement to be sexually exclusive, Carlos suspected John was having sex outside the relationship. In a reciprocal fashion, Carlos' jealous suspicion was aggravated by John's emotional distance and silence which might have been John's reaction to Carlos' jealousy. Adding insult to injury, John still maintained a friendship with a previous partner, which Carlos did not understand. Once you broke things off, contact should be severed, according to Carlos.

After getting the couple to talk about this with each other, there was no resolution nor movement in that direction. Finally, I wondered aloud:

CLINICIAN: Something I have been thinking about—do you ever wonder if some of these conflicting opinions relate to your ethnic differences? Carlos, as a Latino man, perhaps you have different ideas from your Irish American partner about expressing emotions and also maintaining relationships with ex-partners. Tell me if I'm right or wrong, but my impression is that in your culture, there is more emotional expression than in John's. Also, there is perhaps an emotional coolness to John related to his background that might, among other things, make relationships with previous partners possible.

CARLOS: Oh my God, you are so right. I love this country, but when I first moved here, I was struck by how cold people seemed. They were friendly and polite but it was hard to get to know them in any depth; they keep their feelings to themselves—like John! When we Latinos break up with someone, that's it for good. If you are still speaking, you are probably looking to get back together.

JOHN: You are right about Irish Americans. I was attracted to Carlos because of his warmth, affection, and emotional expression—so unlike my own family. However, sometimes I wonder if it is too much for me.

The good news is that this frame helped this couple move beyond this impasse, embedded in an old unhelpful frame that Carlos was "hysterical," "overemotional," and "insanely jealous" while John was "cold," "unemotional," and therefore untrustworthy. The framing of these cultural differences helped the couple externalize the cause of their difficulties rather than blame, personalize, and defend. As in virtually all couple and family therapy, the goal is to get people to be less reactive so they are freed up to better communicate and negotiate solutions, and this type of externalization can assist with that.

Dwayne, a 50-year-old African American man who was an accountant by trade was seeing me due to concerns about his excessive drinking. As we tracked his drinking behavior, it became clear that it was related to discomfort about his anger. Immediately prior to his last drinking binge, he got into a political argument with a friend who repeatedly dismissed him: "You don't know what you're talking about." After the argument was over, he wondered why he got so upset and couldn't just "get over" his feelings (translation: "I shouldn't be angry"), which then led him to drink in an attempt to numb them. Of course, in an argument, "You just don't know what you are talking about" inevitably generates reactivity rather than fruitful discussion. In therapy, we were able to identify how this phrase was something his mother would say during arguments and this provided additional reason as to why he became so distressed.

I asked Dwayne if the person he was arguing with was White. Turned out he was, and hearing this phrase from a White man was particularly galling for him. Dwayne then revealed how immediately after the murder of George Floyd, he isolated himself in his home and went on a three-day drinking binge, which we also identified as a symptom of his discomfort with feelings of rage. Through his telling of these experiences, we could identify a well of deep, concealed anger related not only to family-of-origin issues but also the racist climate in this country. In therapy, his reactions and feelings were validated and normalized, which helped Dwayne become more comfortable with his justifiable anger.

As these two case examples suggest, if you are of a different race or ethnicity than your clients, and particularly if you are White, you may have to introduce the subject of oppression. Once you do, it can open floodgates to feelings that the client has kept locked away, thinking the therapist would not be able to understand. That is why it is up to us to skillfully raise these topics when we see an opening. However, the clinical social worker should also understand that they might not always be correct in their assessment of the client's willingness to talk about their own experiences with oppression. As stated previously, as clinicians we must always know when to advance but also retreat.

Darlene is a heterosexual, cisgender, Latina clinician who was working with Frank and Tony, a same-sex couple struggling in the aftermath of Frank's recent infidelity during which he had a one-night stand with another man. Darlene was aware that a proportion of gay men are in relationships that are sexually nonmonogamous, so she knew it was important to raise this issue:

DARLENE: Tell me about your relationship agreement regarding monogamy. I know that some gay male couples prefer to have open relationships. Was that an option that you ever discussed?

Frank and Tony were surprised that a heterosexually-identified clinician would know about open gay couples and be willing to talk about them. It is not uncommon for gay men to believe they have to hide aspects of their sexuality from straight therapists for fear of judgement. While this couple might not be willing to alter their extradyadic sexual agreement, by raising the issue Darlene shows an openness to discussing the unique ways gay men experience and express their sexuality.

Of course, it is not uncommon for clients to belong to multiple oppressed groups. According to intersectionality theory, individuals who inhabit multiple social identities are shaped by the cultural and material experiences that result from their intersections (Crenshaw, 1989; Murphy, et al., 2009). Thus, for example, each gay Black man is impacted in complex ways by a combination of racism, sexism, and homophobia. I once had a colleague who was African American and identified as bisexual. He was not out at his job because, as he stated, "They can handle a Black man, and they might be able to handle a gay man, but can they handle a Black bisexual man? Or would that be too much for them—and therefore *for me*?"

Jake was a 40-year-old gay African American man who talked about feeling lonely as a result of what he felt was a compelling need to distance himself in personal relationships. We examined his history of being raised by a harshly critical mother and a distant father who failed to run interference, and how this might have set him up to be very sensitive and also fearing of criticism. However, I wondered if the issue of racial difference and racism might also play a role in his feelings.

CLINICIAN: You know, we have spent quite a bit of time talking about you feeling distant and afraid of being judged, and how this could stem from the history of your relationship with your parents. However, I am wondering if your race and sexual orientation or both might play a role in these feelings.

JAKE: (without any hesitation) Yes, I think that is true. I have spent my entire life in mostly White spaces, but I cannot say it has been comfortable for me. At the law firm where I work, I am only one of the two people of color among a staff of 50. People act one way to my face, but I always wonder what they are really thinking. I've dealt with continuous racial microaggressions for sure. Plus, I think my colleagues accept me as a gay man, but they are conservative. They might have a hard time with my social life as a single gay man.

CLINICIAN: Yes, I can see why that would make you distrustful and want to distance. These are necessary coping mechanisms that you have probably been using all along to protect yourself in certain environments, like your workplace. However, to some extent, they could interfere with your relationships—a real dilemma that would be good for us to continue to discuss.

Sexism and the Clinical Encounter

As stated by Jessie Bernard (1982): "There are two marriages ... in every marital union, his and hers. And his ... is better than hers (p.14)." Despite the changes in women's rights, marriage remains a gendered institution whereby women are expected to do the lion share of housework, childrearing, and emotional labor (Rosenfeld, 2018). Further, society still seems to go easy on men who do not share housework and childrearing and some of this attitude has wormed its way into family therapy. Decades ago, feminist family therapy writers rightly pointed out that therapists were not as confrontive with men in the belief that they would flee if pushed too hard (McGoldrick, Anderson, & Walsh, 1991), and there is good reason to think that this reluctance continues. These divergent expectations can create problems in the clinical encounter.

HUSBAND: I worry about my wife. She is constantly busy and she never seems to be available to me, for either sex or companionship.
WIFE: I don't know what's wrong with me; I am tired all of the time. I feel like all I do is work.
CLINICIAN: Tell me more about your day.
WIFE: Well, I work full time. Then on my way home, I pick up the kids from daycare. I come home, make sure they do their homework, and then I cook dinner. I clean up, put the kids to bed. Then I do some laundry before I go to bed.
THERAPIST: Wow! No wonder you are tired? How do you do it all? I can't imagine.
WIFE: I don't know; I just do it.
CLINICIAN: (to husband) What do you think of all of this?
HUSBAND: Well, I help!
WIFE: Yes, you do the dishes or the laundry sometimes. I appreciate that.

Note how this two-job couple normalizes unfairness. The husband responds to his wife's complaints with "I help" as if he is not a full partner, father, and co-owner of the home but instead is a "helper" which seems as if he is doing his wife favors. The wife seems apologetic for her tiredness and does not seem as if she will confront her husband to take on more of his fair share of household chores. Thus, it is up to the clinician:

CLINICIAN: Hmmm ... it seems your wife is grateful for your help, but I have to tell you both, "helping" is very different from sharing responsibility for household tasks. So, for right now, I would like to see the two of you discuss what you can do to make the housework more evenly assigned so you (the wife) are less tired and that you (the husband) get the companionship you seek. Go ahead and discuss this and I will listen.

As can be seen from this intervention, the clinician is pushing for the couple to change something they did not directly identify as an issue but is related to their complaints. The therapist also "sells" the solution to both members of the couple by mentioning the payoffs, namely a less tired wife and a less lonely husband.

Although sexist expectations around family roles can negatively impact men, women are usually the ones who seek out couples therapy and also initiate divorce (Rosenfeld, 2018). In my experience, in troubled heterosexual couples, women often complain about the lack of attention from the men in their lives. However, when a man calls for therapy, it usually means his wife or female partner has her bags packed and he is panicked by the sudden realization that he will lose her. This suggests that women are still the ones to manage the emotional aspects of their relationships with men, thus they are more likely to initially identify when there is a problem and take the steps to solve it. Men, who are not socialized to attend to their feelings, never mind talk about them, are often silent in the face of marital problems. For too many, only a threat of dissolution and its ensuing abandonment will get them to rise to action and face their couple problems head on.

Interestingly, men in troubled dyads will admit to being bothered by a lack of sex. Perhaps sexual desire is one of the few emotions that are okay for men to express. Many men are still willing to have sex with their spouses even after an argument, while for women, sex is the last thing on their minds when they are unhappy with their spouses. They can feel used and objectified in response to their husbands' request for sex following an argument. I help women in heterosexual couples communicate this to their male partners, while at the same time suggest the reframe that a man's sexual desire could be one of the few socially acceptable ways for him to request closeness. I in no way imply that the wife must comply and agree to have sex when she is not inspired to do so. However, seeing this request in light of a desire for closeness can dial down the reactivity, which is invariably a first step toward resolving conflict.

Making Client Perceptions Central

No matter what you learn in your diversity classes, our work is about our clients' distress and how *they* perceive their cultural backgrounds and experiences, not how "woke" you are. Since the previously described incident with the Deaf client, I have met people who have identified themselves as hearing impaired. I have overheard well-meaning clinicians, some of whom are White, complain that their clients from oppressed groups do not understand or do not want to address issues of oppression in their lives. Unfortunately, this leads to an "I know better than you" attitude on the part of clinicians which can get in the way of the vital task of learning client perceptions. Clients might or might not see the role of their difference and oppression in their lives in the same way as you or your diversity professor do, or they might not perceive any impacts at all. Client perceptions and agendas are always first and foremost in clinical social work. The most sensitive and empowering way to approach a client, no matter what oppressed group they come from is: "What is it you want to change?" This question underscores that they are in charge of their own destiny and empowers them in a way that is at least a partial antidote to structural oppression.

Therapist Match

It is reasonable to wonder how important it is that the therapist and the client be of the same racial, ethnic, or sexual orientation group for treatment to be effective. While there is no solid, consistent evidence that therapist matching on race, ethnicity, or sexual orientation affects treatment outcomes (Ertl et al., 2019), it does seem that people of color prefer therapists of their own race. Also, my gay male clients have sought me out because I am a gay man. It would seem logical that if the therapist and clinician shared membership in the same group, that conversations about experiences of oppression would be more spontaneous. However, as a gay man counseling other LGBT clients, I can tell you that this is not always the case. The tendency not to acknowledge oppression can remain, even in matched therapist-client relationships.

It is important to realize that clients do not always have the option to choose their own therapist particularly if they seek help from a nonprofit or public clinic. Thus, clinicians need to be as culturally aware and competent as possible and always willing to learn and grow in this area.

Clinical Goals for Members of Oppressed Groups

In my experience, happy and healthy clients from oppressed groups are able to do the following:

1 Explore and *express emotions*, including anger and sadness about the oppression they have experienced.
2 Cultivate a *critical consciousness* where they understand that societal messages about race, gender, sexuality, able-ness, and other oppressed groups are wrong.

3   Engage with a *supportive community* to gain support to help buffer the impacts of oppression.
4   Develop a thorough understanding and *appreciation of their own strength* and resilience, having a clear-eyed view of what they did to survive and how they managed to do so.

Emotional Expression

The term *safe space* has received some unfair derision in the media lately suggesting that young LGBTQ persons, people of color, youth with mental illnesses, and others who have been emotionally wounded, are fragile, and thus unable to handle the pressures of the real world. This is rather unfortunate, in part because in many cases, meeting the challenges of surviving as a member of an oppressed group actually builds resilience. For sure the therapeutic relationship needs to be the ultimate "safe space" where clients get to express their feelings about what they have been through without being met with defensiveness, judgement, or invalidation. If you are not finding an opening to raise these issues, you might either be missing something *or* the client might not be acknowledging or ready to acknowledge the influences of oppression—*or* perhaps there *is no* influence. It is recommended that at least once, after the initial relationship is established, the clinician checks in with the client as to the role of racism, homophobia (if gay), transphobia (if transgender), and so on in their difficulties, particularly when there is an opening.

"You spoke of being bullied in middle school. Do you think it had anything to do with you being gay? Tell me more about that? What did it feel like?"

"When you talk about your coworkers not taking you seriously as a Latina woman, I can really see your annoyance and frustration. Talk to me about that."

"You are about to send your son out into the world to attend college away from home. I'm sure this is an occasion of pride for both you and him, but as a mother of an African American young man, I am wondering if you have some concerns that you would like to share."

As previously suggested, once a level of trust is achieved between the client and the clinician sufficient to discuss these issues, the clinician can then help the client elaborate in ways that are validating and cathartic. This is particularly important in a world where discussions of such topics, particularly between people of different groups, is considered taboo—all the more reason why some of our clients might need a bit of a nudge.

Cultivating a Critical Consciousness

When clients raise issues around inequity and oppression, it is important to encourage them to develop a critical consciousness of societal norms and values, and relatedly to become aware of how these norms are overly restrictive and just plain wrong when it comes to race, sexuality, gender, and relationships. In our society, it is believed that an individual makes their own success or failure, and obstacles such as structural racism and homophobia are not acknowledged, even by those whom they harm. As a result, clients tend to internalize incidents of oppression. Like this mother of a gay son:

> "If Travis wasn't looking and acting so gay on the subway, he wouldn't have gotten beat up."

From this statement, it seems that the client is placing the blame for this gay bashing on her son, rather than the perpetrator or the society that enables it.

CLINICIAN: It must be awful to see your son so physically and emotionally injured. Yes, Travis might have been targeted because of his looks and his behavior. However, I do want to point out that he *should* be able to go wherever he wants and act and dress however he wants without being attacked. It's not fair that he cannot do so. Unfortunately, we live in a world that has some pretty strict and misdirected rules about how men and women present themselves. Let's discuss how you can talk to Travis and help him develop ways that he can be himself but also be as safe as possible.

Here is another example from a woman client who had been sexually assaulted:

CHRISTINE: I know I should not have been walking home alone at night. It's not safe to do that. I should have known better.

CLINICIAN: Christine, what happened to you was awful. I know this is a really hard time for you, but let me disabuse you of the notion that what happened to you is in any way your fault. This is a free country, and women should be able to walk wherever they want, whenever they want, and be safe. Sadly, that is not the case as your attack illustrates. So, as we continue to work on your recovery, let's try to keep this in mind.

Of course, males should be able to express cross-gender (aka gay) behavior, women should be able to walk wherever they want, dress however they want without thinking they are inviting someone to harm them, and Black men should be able to drive or shop without being followed or stopped. When clients come to understand this, they become angry, which actually indicates that they are getting healthier. As clients come to terms with how unfair things are, they learn to accept their anger and commit to doing something about it, like fighting social injustice in some way. Social action is a component of some forms of psychotherapy. For example, see the work of Michael White and David Epston (1990) to learn how narrative therapists encourage their clients with eating disorders to engage in political action as part of treatment.

Engaging in a Supportive Community

Another intervention that can be helpful for clients of oppressed groups is to connect them to supportive communities of like individuals. It is helpful for them to find their tribes—fellow members who can assist with developing that critical consciousness and externalizing the causes of their oppression. For example, young, urban/suburban Black gay or bisexual men or transgender/gender nonbinary women should be asked if they have connections to the ball community in their city. Ball communities are a network of families-of-choice for gay, and bisexual men, and transgender women of color (Arnold & Bailey, 2009). Though not related by blood, these families consist of people in the roles of mother and father who provide physical and emotional support for the youth, and sponsor fashion shows (balls) during which individuals and families compete. For members of other minorities, it is important to ask about affinity groups in the neighborhood or workplace. Is there a need to start one? Community support and validation can be an invaluable component of mental health.

Building Resilience

As stated earlier, clinical social workers must be lifelong students of resilience, and nowhere is this more important than when working with members of oppressed populations. For sure, it is vital to explore clients' feelings about their painful experiences of stigma and discrimination. However, as stated repeatedly in this volume, never leave a clinical conversation about painful experiences without some exploration of client strengths.

> Delores, you have been through so much, and I'm sorry this all happened to you. I can see how painful it has been for you—who wouldn't be hurt by all you have been through? But switching gears a bit, tell me, how did you survive? How do you continue to survive? What can we do in here to help you continue to survive and grow stronger?

It bears continued repeating; a client will not be ready to switch to resilience talk until they are sure you understand (or are trying to understand) their experiences as well as their pain and suffering. If you ask a question like the one above and the client does not give you an answer, or responds defensively, you can decide whether to gently push the issue further, or retreat for now and approach the topic later in the therapy.

Social work is always concerned with macro-level interventions to address social injustice and institutional racism, sexism, homophobia, ableism; and rightly so. We must continue to advocate for social justice, whether that be in our voting, policy analysis, and policy making, or advocacy, and it is worth noting that such action is further emphasized in the newest edition of the NASW Code of Ethics (2021). On a local level, we need to make changes in the settings where we work to ensure fairness and equity. For example, if there are racist policies in schools, such as a zero-tolerance suspension policy (U.S. Government Accounting Office, 2018), or if there is ongoing bullying of LGBTQ students, clinical social workers must advocate to school administrators to assess and alter the school environment (LaSala, 2006). We must also do what we can to make changes at the societal level. However, our clients cannot simply wait for these changes to occur, if they ever will. Emphasizing social inequities without attending to client coping and strengths could lead to a victim identity that is disempowering and not conducive to mental health. So, we must help these clients become as strong and as resilient as possible. As stated in Chapter 2, helping our clients improve their mental health is in and of itself, an act of social justice whereby mentally and emotionally healthy members of oppressed groups make powerful social justice warriors; all the more reason that reinforcing client strengths is essential.

Families Struggling with Biculturality

There are close to 48 million immigrants in this country (Kariuki, 2020). So, as a practicing clinical social worker, it is inevitable that you will find yourself working with a client or family born somewhere else and struggling with the stresses of biculturality. We always want to be respectful of the client's home culture and the desire for people to preserve their customs and language. However, it is virtually impossible to live almost anywhere in this world and escape the widespread reach of American culture. No doubt that influence began way before your immigrant client packed a suitcase. American music, television programs, and movies are broadcast throughout the world and export the myth that our streets are paved with gold and all one has to do is grab a pick axe and start chipping away. All myths contain some truth, so while American upward mobility might be exaggerated, opportunities in the U.S. are likely more prevalent than in the countries from which many are migrating. Personal freedoms exist here that do not exist in many other countries, including more equitable rights for women and the ability for LGBTQ people to live openly. I had a client who came out to his mother while they both lived in rural Panama. His mother had a very hard time with this disclosure as she harbored all sorts of culturally-based misunderstandings about LGBTQ people. As part of her reaction, she handed her son money and the name of a relative in the U.S. She said, "Mi hijo, I worry about your safety if you stay here. If you are going to be gay, you need to go to a place that is more accepting." We must not minimize the hardships migrants face when they come to this country, nor the oppression and violence experienced by women and LGBTQ persons here in the U.S. However, we must consider these issues relative to migrants' countries of origin.

As hard as folks try to preserve the pastimes and language of their homelands or, alternatively, fully assimilate to American culture, it is virtually impossible to do either completely. As clinicians, we must be sensitive to the needs and feelings of clients who chose to migrate to the United States to seek personal freedom, safety, and opportunity, but who also struggle with how to integrate the parts of themselves that remain attached to their homelands. A migrant family's ambivalence about living in two different cultures often gets played out between polarized generations. Following is an example of an intervention designed to get at this conflict.

Chair Exercise

In this exercise, the clinician places three chairs in a row. The first chair represents the client's identity based on their home country. The third chair signifies the part of themselves that has become, or is becoming American, while the middle chair represents the burgeoning integration of both cultures. Clients are to sit in each chair and describe these different aspects of who they are.

Franco was the 47-year-old father of Maria, aged 15; both of whom were immigrants from Mexico. Maria and her father had come into family therapy because they were having arguments about Maria wanting more freedom. Her father came from a strict Mexican background where respectable unmarried women could not leave the house without a chaperone, and certainly would not be hanging out at the mall unaccompanied by a trusted adult, preferably a family member. As he tried to impose these rules and expectations, Maria started to rebel at home, talking back to her parents, refusing to do homework or chores. Things were coming to a head.

FRANCO: No daughter of mine is going to be hanging around with other kids without adults around. That is how a girl develops a reputation and gets herself into trouble.

MARIA: Oh Dad, you are so old-fashioned. All my friends get to go to the mall or school dances, but I have to stay home, like I am some kind of nerd.

CLINICIAN: Hmmm ... this sounds like a difficult conflict here; it's as if you are having a Mexico/U.S. culture clash within your family, which must be painful and difficult to resolve. I would like to try something that might seem a little strange, but I think will help you. It is something I call the chair exercise. I set up three chairs like this (arranging chairs in a row), and you each take turns talking in each chair, taking on a different persona while seated in each chair. Dad, I'd like you to sit in the first chair.

DAD: Ok.

CLINICIAN: Ok, now this is the Mexican chair. So, as you sit in it, I want you to speak from the part of you that is Mexican. Tell me, what does it mean to be a Mexican man, a Mexican father?

FRANCO: A Mexican man is very family-oriented. He takes care of his family, provides for them, and he protects them, especially his daughters.

CLINICIAN: Ok, good. Tell me how.

FRANCO: He makes sure they are well-behaved and not out alone where someone can hurt them. It is not safe to walk the streets at night where we come from in Mexico. It is also not so safe here in the Bronx. Girls can be tricked and taken advantage of by boys, so fathers must be careful and make sure their daughters stay out of trouble and remain the type of ladies a man wants to marry.

CLINICIAN: So, I see that as a good father and a Mexican man you care deeply for your family and particularly your daughter, and so of course you worry about her safety and well-being, and also her future.

FRANCO: For sure.

CLINICIAN: Ok, great. Now let's seat you here. (Franco gets up and seats himself on a chair on far left) This is the "American" chair. Ok good, now talk about what it is like to be an American—including what you like and value about American culture.

FRANCO: Well, this is the land of opportunity. In Mexico, it was hard for me to get a job. Also, there were many gangs who were threatening me because I would not join, which made life dangerous. Here, my family is relatively safe; I can get work and make a better life for my children. That is the American way. That is what I came for. Things aren't perfect here but they are better than where I came from. However, I am not sure about American families.

CLINICIAN: What about American families?

FRANCO: Well, I have noticed that they are more permissive with their children. Their children are disrespectful; they talk back and disobey their parents, which I do not like. However, my daughter is very smart and, here in the U.S. women have more opportunities. Maybe they can go to college and make something of themselves—and not have to rely so much on a man.

CLINICIAN: Clearly you care very deeply for your daughter. I can see that not only in what you say but also by how you say it. Maria is fortunate to have a father as caring and committed to her well-being and success as you are. OK, now, I'd like you to sit in the middle chair. This is the chair where you integrate or combine your Mexican and your American parts. Kind of tough I know, but it is something important to think about, as being part of a family that is from Mexico but now lives here. How will you do that? How will you integrate America into your life?

FRANCO: I'm not sure. I want my daughter to be successful but I don't think girls and women are protected enough here. Basically, I want her to be happy and free to go to college and have a career, but I also want her to be safe and able to get married and have a family.

CLINICIAN: Again, your deep love and concern for your daughter really shines through, wanting her to take advantage of the best America has to offer. As you say, women have freedom and more opportunities here, but they are also less protected than in Mexico. You need to help Maria find ways to enjoy these freedoms while keeping herself safe. This is something you need to think about and also talk about with your family.

The therapist repeated the same exercise with Maria. Unsurprisingly, Maria had little trouble identifying as an American teenager when she sat in the American chair. However, when Maria was placed in the Mexican chair, she stated:

MARIA: I don't really think much about this part of me. But I guess I can say that I enjoy the food, the music and also, I miss my grandparents, who we've left behind in Mexico. I miss them a lot—but that's it. We are in America and I'm American now, and I wish my dad understood this.

Considering Maria's great desire to be an American teenager as well as the polarization in this family, it is not surprising that she was reluctant to speak about her Mexican side. The therapist pointed out that as much as she tried, she could not erase that part of her.

CLINICIAN: You know, you will never be able to fully divorce yourself from your Mexican background, and because your dad is older and has spent more of his life in Mexico, he will have a stronger Mexican side. However, as a bicultural person, you may always experience a tension between these two sides of you. (turning to Dad) You must remember this as you approach each other with disagreements; you must do so with the understanding how both sides play a role for each of you. Maria, you need to move slowly with Dad and find a gentle, patient way to talk with him about how this culture clash plays out with you and your relationships with your friends. Think about what you can do to bring Dad along to your way of thinking.

The benefit of this exercise is that it reframes family conflict as something beyond individual personalities but instead is a result of the pressure of deciding how much to assimilate and how much to hold onto the culture from one's country-of-origin. When family members polarize on this issue and take sides, the ambivalence each member feels about managing two cultures gets lost in the arguments. Interventions that reframe such ambivalence as a function of the difficult task of finding ways to integrate two different worlds can help lower the reactivity in immigrant families in ways that can lead to resolution.

Continuous Effort

> Showing respect for all types of diversity is more than a one-time activity or a treatment strategy. It is a state of mind. A feature of this state of mind is our willingness to explore the personal narratives and see life through the eyes of our clients.
>
> (Goldstein, 2007, p. 18)

Learning to apply an understanding of difference and oppression is not a "one and done" affair, but an ongoing effort that must continue throughout a professional lifetime. Commitment to growth in this area is not an educational issue as much as a personal value. The information presented here is only the tip of the iceberg, enough to get you started on a journey that you will never fully complete. I wish you Godspeed.

References

Almeida, R. (2020). *Expansions of Feminist Family Theory Through Diversity*. Routledge.
Arnold, E. & Bailey, M. (2009). Constructing home and family: How the ballroom community supports African American GLBTQ youth in the face of HIV/AIDS. *Journal of Gay and Lesbian Social Services*, 21(2/3), 171–188. doi:10.1080/10538720902772006.
Bernard, J. (1982). *The Future of Marriage*. Yale University Press.
Bowen, M., & Kerr, M. E. (2009). *Family Evaluation*. WW Norton & Company.
Boyd-Franklin, N. (2013). *Black Families in Therapy: Understanding the African American Experience*. Guilford Press.
Cartwright, S. A. (1851). Diseases and peculiarities of the Negro race. *DeBow's Review XI*. www.pbs.org/wgbh/aia/part4/4h3106t.html.
Centers for Disease Control (CDC) (2013). CDC Health Disparities and Inequalities Report United States. www.cdc.gov/mmwr/preview/ind2013_su.html#HealthDisparities2013.
Crenshaw, K. (1989). Demarginalizing the intersection of race and sex: A black feminist critique of antidiscrimination doctrine, feminist theory and antiracist

politics. *The University of Chicago Legal Forum, 139,* 139–168. doi:10.4324/9780429499142-5.

DeJong, P., & Berg, I.M. (2008). *Interviewing for Solutions* (4th ed.). Pearson.

Ertl, M. M., Mann-Saumier, M., Martin, R. A., Graves, D. F., & Altarriba, J. (2019). The impossibility of client–therapist "Match": Implications and future directions for multicultural competency. *Journal of Mental Health Counseling,* 41(4), 312–326. doi:10.17744/mehc.41.4.03.

Freud, S. (1925). Some Psychical Consequences of Anatomical Distinction Between the Sexes. *Standard Edition of the Complete Psychological Works,* 19, Hogarth.

Goldstein, E. G. (2007). Social work education and clinical learning: Yesterday, today, and tomorrow. *Clinical Social Work Journal,* 35(1), 15–23. doi:10.1007/s10615- 006–0067-z.

Hardy, K. V. (2018). The self of the therapist in epistemological context: A multicultural relational perspective. *Journal of Family Psychotherapy,* 29(1), 17–29. doi:10.1080/08975353.2018.1416211.

Huey, S. J., Tilley, J. L., Jones, E. O., & Smith, C. A. (2014). The contribution of cultural competence to evidence-based care for ethnically diverse populations. *Annual Review of Clinical Psychology,* 10(1), 305–338. doi:10.1146/annurev-clinpsy-032813-153729.

Kariuki, D. (2020). How many people are in the U.S? *World Atlas,* www.worldatlas.com/articles/how-many-people-are-in-the-us.html.

Klein, A., & Golub, S. A. (2016). Family rejection as a predictor of suicide attempts and substance misuse among transgender and gender nonconforming adults. *LGBT Health,* 3(3), 193–199. doi:10.1089/lgbt.2015.0111.

Kosciw, J. G., Clark, C. M., Truong, N. L., & Zongrone, A. D. (2020). The 2019 National School Climate Survey: The experiences of lesbian, gay, bisexual, transgender, and queer youth in our nation's schools. GLSEN.

Laird, J. (1996). Invisible ties: Lesbians and their families of origin. In J. Laird & R. J. Green (Eds.), *Lesbians and Gay Couples and Families: A Handbook for Therapists* (pp. 89–222). Jossey Bass.

LaSala, M. C. (2002). Walls and bridges: How coupled gay men and lesbians manage their intergenerational relationships. *Journal of Marital and Family Therapy,* 28, 327–338. doi:10.1111/j.1752-0606.2002.tb01190.x.

LaSala, M. C. (2004). Extradyadic sex and gay male couples: Comparing monogamous and nonmonogamous relationships. *Families in Society: The Journal of Contemporary Social Services,* 85, 405–412. doi:10.1177/104438940408500319.

LaSala, M. C. (2006). Cognitive and environmental interventions for gay males: Addressing stigma and its consequences. *Families in Society: The Journal of Contemporary Human Services,* 87(2), 181–189. doi:10.1606/1044-3894.3511.

LaSala, M. C. (2010). *Coming Out, Coming Home: Helping Families Adjust to a Gay or Lesbian Child.* Columbia University Press.

McGoldrick, M., Anderson, C. M., & Walsh, F. (Eds.). (1991). *Women in Families: A Framework for Family Therapy.* WW Norton & Company.

Miller, A. (2013). *Soul Food: The Surprising Story of an American Cuisine, One Plate at a Time.* UNC Press Books.

Minuchin, S., & Fishman, H. C. (1981). *Family Therapy Techniques.* Harvard University Press.

Murphy, Y., Hunter, V., Zajicek, A., Norris, A., & Hamilton, L. (2009). *Incorporating Intersectionality in Social Work Practice, Research, Policy, and Education.* NASW Press.

National Association of Social Workers (NASW) (2021). *Code of ethics of the National Association of Social Workers.* NASW Press. https://www.socialworkers.org/About/Ethics/Code-of-Ethics/Code-of-Ethics-English.

Nealy, E. C. (2017). *Trans Kids and Teens: Pride, Joy, and Families in Transition.* WW Norton & Company.

O'Brien, K. H. M., Putney, J. M., Hebert, N. W., Falk, A. M., & Aguinaldo, L. D. (2016). Sexual and gender minority youth suicide: understanding subgroup differences to inform interventions. *LGBT Health*, 3(4), 248–251. doi:10.1089/lgbt.2016.0031.

Pachankis, J. E., Rendina, H. J., Restar, A., Ventuneac, A., Grov, C., & Parsons, J. T. (2015). A minority stress—emotion regulation model of sexual compulsivity among highly sexually active gay and bisexual men. *Health Psychology*, 34(8), 829–840. doi:10.1037/hea0000180.

Poteat, T. (2012). Top 10 things lesbians should discuss with their healthcare provider. GMLA. www.glma.org/_data/n_0001/resources/live/Top%2010%20forlesbians.pdf.

Pike, K. L. (1990). On the Emics and Etics of Pike and Harris. In R. A. Proujansky & J. E. Pachankis (Eds.) (2014). Toward formulating evidence-based principles of LGB-affirmative psychotherapy. *Pragmatic Case Studies in Psychotherapy: PCSP*, 10(2), 117–131.

Office on Women's Health (2019). Recognizing the needs of lesbian, bisexual, and transgender women. U.S. Department of Health and Human Services, www.womenshealth.gov/30-achievements/29.

Rosenfeld, M. J. (2018). Who wants the breakup? Gender and breakup in heterosexual couples. In D. F.Alwin, D. H.Felmlee, & D. A. Kreager (eds.) *Social Networks and the Life Course: Integrating the Development of Human Lives and Social Relational Networks* (pp. 221–243). Springer.

Smedley, C. D., Stith, A. Y. & Nelson, A. R. (Eds.) (2003). *Unequal Treatment: Confronting Racial and Ethnic Disparities in Health Care.* National Academies Press.

Snowden, L. R. (2007). Explaining mental health treatment disparities: Ethnic and cultural differences in family involvement. *Culture, Medicine, and Psychiatry*, 31, 389–402. doi:10.1007/s11013-007-9057-z.

Sue, D. W., Sue, D., Neville, H. A., & Smith, L. (2019). *Counseling the Culturally Diverse: Theory and Practice.* John Wiley & Sons.

Szapocznik, J. & Hervis, O. E. (2020). *Brief Strategic Family Therapy.* American Psychological Association.

Violence Policy Center (2020). Black homicide victimization in the United States: An analysis of 2017 homicide data. https://vpc.org/studies/blackhomicide20.pdf.

U.S. Government Accountability Office. (2018). *Discipline disparities for Black students, boys, and students with disabilities* (GOA Publication No. 18–258). www.gao.gov/products/gao-18-25.

Walters, M., Carter, B., Papp, P., & Silverstein, O. (1991). *The Invisible Web: Gender Patterns in Family Relationships.* Guilford Press.

Wesley, K. (2017). Disparities in mental health care and homeownership for African Americans and Latinos in the United States. In S. Kelly (ed.). *Diversity in Couple and Family Therapy: Ethnicities, Sexualities, and Socioeconomics* (pp. 393–419). Praeger.

White, M., Wijaya, M., & Epston, D. (1990). *Narrative Means to Therapeutic Ends*. WW Norton & Company.

Williamson, C. (2010). Providing care to transgender persons: A clinical approach to primary care, hormones, and HIV management. *Journal of the Association of Nurses in AIDS Care, 21*(3), 221–229. doi:10.1016/j.jana.2010.02.004.

Zhang, Y., Zhang, L., & Benton, F. (2021). Hate crimes against Asian Americans. *American Journal of Criminal Justice*, 1–21. Advance online publication. doi:10.1007/s12103-020-09602-9.

Chapter 9

Ethics: Protecting the Healing Relationship

All professions, whether they be teaching, medicine, law, or social work, have the following five factors in common (Bisman, 1994; Regan, 2020). First, professions are publicly recognized. Second, each has a specialized knowledge base; books, articles based on theory and peer-reviewed research that is taught to students and professionals. Because social work is an interdisciplinary field, information and knowledge specific to social work might also apply to other fields. The knowledge we draw upon we share with psychology, sociology, public health, and public administration. The third characteristic of a profession is a service mission, and clearly social work meets this standard. The fourth component is that each profession has a set of practice skills specific to it, which is what this book is about. However, while social work has a unique perspective of practice within a social justice context, we share theory and interventions with the fields of psychiatry and psychology. Finally, each profession must have a set of values and ethics which guides practice and with which the profession regulates itself. For social work, it is the National Association of Social Workers Code of Ethics (NASW, 2021).

The primary purpose of the Code is to protect our clients. As stated throughout this book, we are establishing healing relationships with vulnerable, distressed people who seek our help. They place a sacred trust in our hands and in return we must give their faith in us the honor and protection it is due.

The Code consists of ethical principles, namely: *service, social justice, dignity and worth of the person, importance of human relationships, integrity, competence*, and *behaving in a trustworthy manner* that are operationalized by the standards, which are the meat and potatoes of the document. Every social worker should be intimately familiar with the NASW Code of Ethics, which are easily accessible (www.socialworkers.org/About/Ethics/Code-of-Ethics/Code-of-Ethics-English). In the following pages, I will bring the Code to life with explanations and examples from the field that you can also anticipate in your current and future experiences. I have copied and pasted some of the standards for clarification purposes,

DOI: 10.4324/9781003011712-9

while I refer to others without replicating them. It is a good idea to have the standards handy as you read this chapter, and also to know how to easily access them as you enter the profession.

Standard 1: Social Workers Ethical Commitment to Clients

> Social workers' primary responsibility is to promote the well-being of clients. In general, clients' interests are primary. However, social workers' responsibility to the larger society or specific legal obligations may on limited occasions supersede the loyalty owed clients, and clients should be so advised.

This seems self-evident, right? Of course, client interest and benefits are central to our work. However, there are times when we must act in ways that go beyond enhancing the well-being of our clients. For example, we are obligated to break confidentiality and risk rupturing our therapeutic relationships when we have to report clients to state child abuse registries because we suspect they might have abused or neglected a child in their care. On occasion, as discussed in Chapter 4, when a client is at risk of harming others, we must notify the police and also anyone whom the client has threatened.

1.02 Self-Determination

> Social workers respect and promote the right of clients to self-determination and assist clients in their efforts to identify and clarify their goals. Social workers may limit clients' right to self-determination when, in the social workers' professional judgment, clients' actions or potential actions pose a serious, foreseeable, and imminent risk to themselves or others.

Clients must be given the opportunity to "run the show," as much as is feasible. In clinical social work, it is *their* psychotherapy (not ours) and this is manifested in their active involvement in goal setting. Within reason, we must prioritize their voices and let them guide the work. Note, earlier in the book I describe an instructor who turned her class into a group therapy session (Chapter 7). Without giving them a choice, she is violating her students' right to self-determination.

However, things get shady when we must assert our professional authority and act in ways that are in the client's best interests, but with which they disagree. Examples are occasions when we recommend residential treatment or involuntary psychiatric inpatient care. Under such circumstances, we assert that "we know better" than our clients and act accordingly. However, we must be certain that we are acting in a client's best interest. When we are unclear, it is advisable to apply one of the many available ethical decision-making frameworks (Beauchamp & Childress, 2013; Congress, 1999; Gray

& Gibbons, 2007; LaSala & Goldblatt Hyatt, 2019; Levy & Slavin, 2013; Reamer, 2013; Strom-Gottfried, 2008). It is always advisable to get consultation when you are considering the extreme step of recommending removal of a child from their home, advocating for the involuntary institutionalization of a youth or an adult, or contacting protective services when a child is in danger. Note, each of these acts might cause clients pain but are good for them in the long run.

1.03 Informed Consent

This standard links to self-determination in that the client must be aware of exactly what they are getting into. They should be fully informed about fees, and what information is to be shared, particularly with their insurance companies (if relevant). They should also know the limits of confidentiality or the conditions by which the worker must break it, namely if a client is at risk of harm to self or others, such as circumstances involving child abuse, suicidal, or homicidal behavior. If clients do not have the capacity to initially comprehend verbal or written informed consent due to age, language barriers, or disability, the social worker is obliged to deploy methods, technologies, and any necessary accommodations to help them understand. Examples of such include but are not limited to foreign language interpreters including sign language interpreters, and verbal and written communication that does not use language beyond a clients' capability to understand. Of course, clients are never to be audio or video recorded without their consent.

As stated earlier (Chapter 4), it is best practice with involuntary clients to inform them as to what to expect in treatment and to whom the social worker needs to report. Not only is this an ethical responsibility, but mandated clients who come to us are already distrustful. You will have no chance of the client trusting you if they perceive you are not being completely forthright. Even involuntary clients deserve to know what they are getting into and signing on for.

Years ago, paradoxical interventions were popular, especially in the field of family therapy. When working with a family that was particularly stuck, the clinician would recommend something that on the surface seemed counterintuitive, such as actually *prescribing the symptom*: "Chiara, you need to keep misbehaving so that your parents have something to worry about besides their marital problems," or "Marta, you keep saying you cannot handle your son anymore. We suggest you march him right down to the child welfare department and apply to have him placed in foster care." Also, "Chad, you are telling your mother right now that you want to run away from home. We think you should go home, pack your bags and get started." The purpose of these interventions is to create a recoil effect whereby Chiara's parents would realize they did not need or want their daughter to act out for their benefit, Marta recognized that she did not really want to give up custody of her child but was simply expressing her exasperation, and that, when push came to shove, Chad understood that he did not want to leave home. (For more information on these types of interventions, see Selvini-Palazzoli & Boscolo, 1994.) While in graduate school, I had a professor who insisted that these interventions violated the ethical standard of informed consent, whereby the clinician was acting and intervening in ways that the client did not or could not understand and so they could not actually consent. An argument can be made that in some of these examples, the clinician is simply asserting what clients believe their wishes are. However, it is reasonable to believe that paradoxical interventions fall into an ethical grey area and beginners need to consult with their supervisors before applying them. They might also consider analyzing such situations using the framework for resolving ethical dilemmas, described at the end of this chapter.

Suffice it to say that according to this standard, the client should always be aware of the nature and type of psychotherapy they are receiving, and this should be addressed at the start of treatment. The name of the treatment is not as important as explanations as to what can be expected during sessions: "I like to work with client strengths," or "I help clients with their thoughts and feelings," or "I get people to talk together in my session to see how they communicate and help them figure out how to do it better." The clients will then recognize and understand what is happening, which enhances their trust.

Many agencies ask clients to sign forms in which the client states that they actively consent to receive therapy. However, clients are typically given a rash of paperwork that is generally about covering agency liability. They then dutifully sign these forms without reading them. This is not informed consent. Informed consent is an ongoing discussion and agreement between clinician and client that is revisited throughout treatment. One way to do this is to periodically check in with the client and ask, "How do you think it's going? What do you like? What do you like not so much?" What is recommended in a previous chapter (Chapter 4) is also a way of fostering informed consent: "Let's take a look at your original goals and see where we're at and what if anything we need to revise or add."

1.05 Cultural Competence

As has been emphasized in Chapter 8, social workers are obliged to learn all they can about various cultures and to incorporate this knowledge into their practice. According to this recently updated standard, social workers need to understand the many oppressions our clients face including but not limited to, racism, homophobia, transphobia, sexism, and ableism. Clinical social workers must commit to take action against these barriers. They must also self-reflect when working cross culturally.

1.06 Conflicts of Interest

> Social workers should be alert to and avoid conflicts of interest that interfere with the exercise of professional discretion and impartial judgment. Social workers should inform clients when a real or potential conflict of interest arises and take reasonable steps to resolve the issue in a manner that makes the clients' interests primary and protects clients' interests to the greatest extent possible. In some cases, protecting clients' interests may require termination of the professional relationship with proper referral of the client.

Here is where the Code gets into what is known as *dual relationships*. This is anytime a client and a social worker have any other relationship in addition to the clinical relationship. Embedded in this standard is the dictate never to engage in a sexual or romantic relationship with a client. No matter how hard you might try to establish a mutual nonhierarchic relationship with your clients, they will always be in a one-down position. Many will feel emotionally dependent on you, and therefore may not believe they have the *self-determination* to decline such an invitation. Relatedly, it is never acceptable to exchange services such as babysitting, house painting, or artistic work from a client in lieu of a fee. (As a matter of fact, there is invariably a question about this issue on almost all licensing exams.) That is because you cannot really function simultaneously in the dual relationship of social worker/client and client/babysitter. As asserted previously in this book, the unique healing power of the therapeutic relationship is that it is all about the client and never about you. Believe it or not, I have seen situations where therapists hire current or ex-clients and it rarely ends well. Keep those boundaries clean and find your babysitters, housepainters, romantic, and sexual partners elsewhere.

Sharing a social environment with clients can also be a challenge. I currently specialize in working with gay men and because the gay community where I live is somewhat circumscribed, I have run into clients in social situations, such as on the beach, at parties, in my gym shower (yes, while naked), and even online. It is inevitable that you will encounter clients outside of the session. When this happens, remain calm; you have done nothing wrong. You and your clients are human beings who go to the beach, the gym, and social events, and seek friends, and sexual and romantic partners online. You are not expected to hide out somewhere to avoid running into clients. However, if you do, it is strongly advised that you process these encounters during sessions. "Hey, we ran into each other at the gym showers (beach, party, mall, Grindr, Tinder) the other day. Let's talk about that. What was that like for you?" I use these occasions to remind clients that our relationship is professional and we will never be friends, but that also, if we run into each other in social situations, in order to protect their confidentiality, I will not acknowledge them unless they say hello first. I also let them know that by saying hello to me in a public space, my friends or my husband might guess that they are clients of mine, even though I never confirm this. The great majority of clients are ok with this. Interestingly, I have actually walked by clients in public spaces unrecognized; no doubt because they are not expecting to see me and also because I look different in these external settings.

One is never, no matter how tempted, to befriend a client. I have worked with several clients who might make good friends and no doubt, if you do this work long enough you will too. When clients and clinicians spend the session discussing common interests like movies or politics, this is a warning sign that the conversation is too social and needs to be directed back to the client problems. Remember, your relationship with your client is one-sided in the interest of *their* healing. A friendship is hopefully much more of a mutual exchange whereby both people share problems and help each other. I say "hopefully" because, as stated in Chapter 2, many social workers have been socialized from childhood to take care of other people, and thus may find themselves in one-sided personal relationships. Of course, this is problematic and needs to be addressed in one's own psychotherapy. The necessity of social workers procuring self-care is a recent addendum to the NASW Code of Ethics (NASW, 2021), and establishing nurturing relationships outside of work in which you can discuss your own problems is an important way to care for yourself.

Do not be surprised if your clients show up on your various social media sites as suggested friends. Some of your clients may try to follow or friend you, which is a bad idea. However, they may become hurt if you fail to respond or you block them without explanation. Let them know from the start that in the service of professional boundaries, you do not friend clients, and this policy is meant to protect their privacy—and yours.

1.07 Privacy and Confidentiality

This issue is addressed several times in this chapter and throughout this book, but here are some additional tips. If you present client information to a supervisor or during a case conference at your agency, you need to let your client know beforehand that you will be doing so and document their consent in writing. Of course, you also need written client permission to share any of your information about them to other providers such as probation officers, courts, psychiatrists, and substance abuse counselors. Once again, remember that permission to release information is not only about signing a form. The client should be clear what information you are sharing and why. If you are seeing children, it is important to know, particularly in single-parent or divorced families, who has legal custody and to get that (those) person('s)(s') permission. It is also important to remind clients of the limits of confidentiality, namely if they report something that suggests either child abuse/neglect or that they are at risk of harming themselves or others.

I have never experienced nor heard of a situation where someone violated the Code of Ethics with malevolence. Instead, infractions occur because the social worker has not fully thought through what they were doing. Examples include calling out a client's name in the waiting room of their agency (so others waiting will know their identity) or casually running into a referral source and sharing information without first getting client permission. A prominent colleague of mine was investigated by our state licensing board and found to have violated client confidentiality. He had written a letter to a family court judge about a minor client without getting written permission from both parents. What made matters worse was that the divorcing parents were involved in a bitter custody dispute. The clinician was advocating for continued family therapy, but this request fell into the maw of the parents' conflict. One of them complained to the licensing board and the therapist was found in violation of the Code of Ethics. Keep in mind, if he had not found himself in the middle of their conflict, he might have "gotten away" with this, as what he had disclosed was relatively minor—a recommendation for further therapy in this situation is not all that revealing. Clients tend not to complain about ethical violations unless they are angry. However, as clinicians, we must always be strict about upholding such standards.

I once worked in a psychotherapy office that was at one time a storefront, so several offices had large windows that looked out onto the sidewalk. When one walked by these windows they could see the therapist and the client inside. I had to beg my colleagues to close the blinds. Quite often, they responded by doing so, OR telling me that they had checked with their clients who stated that they did not mind as they appreciated the sunlight. It is true that sometimes our clients care less about their confidentiality and privacy than we do. At that same agency, the administration briefly asked clients to put their names on a sign-in sheet upon arrival until it was pointed out that this was a terrible idea as clients would see each other's names. When the agency initially switched to electronic records, there was a laptop (not password protected) stored in the waiting room with client information. Once again, I pointed out these potential ethical violations and the laptop was relocated to a locked closet. I once had a student submit a final paper for class with the names and contact information of all of her clients attached as an appendix. She of course received an "F" on the paper. However, she was given the opportunity to pass and continue in the program if she informed each of her clients of the breach and apologized. It is important to note that none of these actions were done out of maliciousness but instead were a result of carelessness and not thinking things through.

The Danger of the "Special Circumstance"

Some ethical violations are more egregious and those who commit them rationalize their behavior by believing that their situation is special and thus the rules do not apply. This is often at play in dual relationship cases, particularly when clinicians engage in sexual or romantic relationships with their clients. When I was director of the MSW program, I reviewed applications for admissions. Once, I came across an applicant who included a letter of recommendation from her therapist. In her personal statement, the applicant mentioned that she had overcome an eating disorder, and since then, had wanted to dedicate her professional life to helping others with the same problem. The candidate disclosed this personal issue without inappropriately revealing too many personal details. In agreeing to write the letter, her therapist was engaging in a dual relationship; client/clinician and that of professional reference. I cannot know for sure, but I am guessing that the clinician chose to write the letter because she herself was a social worker and thus believed this to be a special circumstance. Unfortunately, the therapist revealed way more than the client herself, and in a manner that read like a psychiatric case study that was inappropriate as a letter of reference for graduate school. It was hard not to feel sorry for the prospective student as she seemed to have better boundaries than her own therapist. Even though the client may have asked for the letter, it was the responsibility of the clinician to decline this request and explain why. It is never a good idea to write a professional reference for a client.

As stated previously, sometimes our clients care less about their privacy than we do. I have had children yell across a crowded hallway in school, "Hey everyone! My social worker is here! There he is!" In keeping with self-determination, if a client chooses to break confidentiality and identify you, that is their right. When things like this happen, try to act as natural and as friendly as possible.

1.08 Access to Records

Clients deserve access to their records and actually, such records belong more to the clients than the clinician or the agency. That said, I can count on one hand the number of clients in my 40-year professional history who have requested to see their records. In many ways this standard also relates to self-determination whereby the client has a right to know what is being written about them. Even though the chances of a client requesting to read their records are small, the social worker should maintain them as if the client will read them. Derogatory language about the client or their diagnosis should be avoided and there should be nothing in the case record that would surprise or insult them.

If a client requests their record, it is a good idea to have them read it in the presence of their therapist or another mental health professional who can answer questions and provide clarification. When done well, this could be a therapeutic exercise in and of itself because it requires both therapist and client to review the history of treatment, goal progress, and the future directions of treatment. It also enhances a client's sense of trust.

1.09 Sexual Relationships

Of course, this is never acceptable. As stated earlier, social workers who engage in these relationships often rationalize that their circumstances are special and warrant an exception. This is self-delusion, plain and simple.

However sooner or later we all find ourselves sexually attracted to a client. Because of the prohibition against sexual contact, I have seen some students become self-punitive when experiencing such an attraction—as if the feeling was somehow as wrong as the behavior, which of course it is not. We live in a society that views sex and sexual feelings as shameful. However, freaking out over your attraction to a client is not helpful and could even be harmful to the work. Sexual feelings are a natural component of being human. We are engaging in very emotionally intimate relationships with our clients so it is understandable that sexual feelings might emerge either on the part of the client or the clinician or both. When a clinician experiences such an attraction, like most therapist feelings, this is "grist for the mill." The best response should be an internal, silent statement to oneself along the lines of, "That's interesting. Now let me get to work to see what it means." Questions to ask oneself include: "How am I feeling about my own sex life and sexual relationships? Am I getting my sexual needs met? Why or why not? If not, what do I need to do to get them addressed so they do not interfere with my work?"

Questions targeting transference/countertransference in the clinical relationship are also relevant: "Do my feelings, fantasies, and impulses emerge during certain occasions in the session? What is happening at those moments?" Also, "Is the client acting subtly or not so subtly seductive toward me right now?" This can be very powerful. Even though I am a gay man, during a session with a teenage girl, I started to experience sexual impulses. Initially I wondered, "What the heck is wrong with me? Am I some kind of pervert now?" (Note the self-punitive self-talk here.) I paused, took a deep breath, and started to track my feelings during our meetings. I realized there were several occasions when she would lean in, bend over, giving me a view of her bra. I soon realized this young woman was testing out the power of her new sexuality. However, she needed to learn how to be more judicious in how she used it. She also needed to know that it was not necessary for her to interact with men in a flirtatious or sexualized manner to get her emotional needs met. This incident prompted me to ask her about how she related to boys, which turned out to be important as she was struggling with ambivalence about the newfound male attention she was receiving but was unsure how to handle it. During this process, I also learned that for me, the desire to nurture and sexual feelings go hand-in-hand. So, when I am experiencing an attraction to a client it might be a sign that I am feeling very close to them and at some level, wish to soothe and comfort them.

The takeaway here is that while we must *never* engage in a sexual relationship with a client, it is also important not to become anxious and distressed if you experience these feelings. Instead, consider them as portals to potentially important, concealed data that can enhance treatment.

Nancy was a student in her mid 40s who was doing her field placement at a substance abuse agency. She was seeing a client who was not following through with treatment and was somewhat inappropriate with staff, making inappropriate, often sexual jokes. He was discharged from the agency, but because Nancy was inexperienced and felt badly for the client, she agreed to keep meeting with him in a local coffee shop and eventually in his home. (Note, Nancy was a good hearted, well-intentioned student who probably saw this situation as exceptional and therefore felt justified to break the agency rules.) As their relationship continued, he indicated that he was romantically interested in Nancy. One night while at his home, this ex-client sexually assaulted her. What an awful situation this was. She was seeing a man who had been discharged from her agency and therefore no longer a client. Nancy was in violation of agency policy by continuing to see him, raising the question of whether or not she was engaging in a dual relationship. Then, he attacked her. No one *deserves* to be sexually assaulted. However, Nancy did not fully understand the risk she was taking by continuing to see a discharged ex-client outside of the agency and thus without its support or protection. When you are seeing clients at an agency and something goes wrong, you have the agency's resources to assist you, including their legal support. However, if the agency discharges the client and you continue to see them, you are on your own. Of course, the worker and the agency are obliged to find the client an appropriate referral so they are not abandoned, but the worker can no longer meet with the client. What makes this situation even sadder is that neither Nancy nor her supervisor engaged in a thorough discussion of Nancy's strong feelings about the client's discharge, which might have prevented this situation. Let this be a cautionary tale so that you can learn from Nancy's mistake.

1.10 Physical Contact

Up until Covid times, I would shake my client's hand at the end of a session to initially greet them or say goodbye. Now I ask if it is ok to shake, or I just offer a fist bump (I live in New Jersey where we take credit for inventing this greeting). If a client asks for a hug, and I have no reason to believe there are strings attached, sexual or otherwise, I will oblige. However, I am rarely asked. Perhaps at some indirect level, I am communicating that I do not regularly hug clients, so such requests hardly come my way.

1.11 Sexual Harassment

This is self-explanatory. No one should sexually harass anyone, especially clients. Period.

1.12 Derogatory Language

> Social workers should not use derogatory language in their written, verbal, or electronic communications to or about clients. Social workers should use accurate and respectful language in all communications to and about clients.

When working in an agency or a private practice, it is easy to slip into troublesome language without thinking. I have overheard colleagues say things like, "I have a borderline today at 1pm," or "My anorexic is not doing well." The problem with this is that the human being gets lost behind the diagnosis. I would argue that continuing to refer to clients in this way can affect the ability of the clinician to empathize. I have never known a person with a borderline personality disorder who was not in a great deal of emotional pain. The woman who is scheduled to see you at 1 pm has gifted you with her trust and granted you the sacred opportunity to help her. Seeing her as her diagnosis is a distancing technique, related to the clinician's countertransference, that is not helpful. So, get in the habit of catching yourself when you are having these thoughts or communications and remind yourself that your client is flesh and blood and more complex than their diagnosis.

I have also heard colleagues make fun of clients during case conferences and casual conversations in the hallways. They might call it "gallows humor" whereas day in and day out they are dealing with human suffering, so they rationalize jokes as harmless banter that lightens the load. I recall a well-meaning therapist in a public mental health clinic, who when asked about a particular client's strengths, jokingly responded, "Well, she's ambulatory." First off, if that is the only client strength you can find, you are not looking hard enough. Second, such joking dehumanizes the very people who seek our help. Third, it is possible that a clinician who does this is bringing some of this attitude into their sessions, hampering their ability to fully empathize with their client. So, don't do it. Here is a good guideline: think about how your client would feel if they heard you refer to them by their diagnosis or that joke you made about them. If they would be offended, then that's a sign—it's wrong. Further, consider why you might do such a thing. Is this a way to distance you from a client's pain? Or is it a sign that you are emotionally spent and need a break? (Remember, per recent updates to the Code, you are also ethically bound to care for *yourself* as well as your clients.)

1.13 Payment for Services

If your agency or practice requires that clients pay for services, then of course the fee must be fair. If a client seeks your services, and the fee is too expensive, it is your responsibility to suggest alternatives, while advocating in your agency for reduced fees for clients of limited means. Clients must be informed in advance of the fee requirements and what the consequences are for not paying, or if relevant, for canceling sessions without sufficient notice. This should all be in writing and discussed verbally with clients at intake to ensure that they understand.

I am of the belief that, in clinical social work, clients should pay some kind of fee, even if it is nominal (e.g. $5) as this enhances their commitment to the work. Giving something away for free, including psychotherapy, can diminish its value. I have worked with clients who have paid no fee. When I sensed therapy was going nowhere and asked if they wanted to continue, they would say "Sure, why not?" as if this was a sideline and not something about which they were truly invested. They would also cancel and fail to show up for their appointments at whim, largely because there was no consequence for doing so. Alternatively, I have also found that clients who do not pay a fee sometimes feel obliged to the therapist and perhaps overly indebted. For all of these reasons, I recommend clinical social workers set a fee, even if it is nominal as it represents commitment and in fact can increase their investment in the work.

1.14 Clients Who Lack Decision-Making Capacity

> When social workers act on behalf of clients who lack the capacity to make informed decisions, social workers should take reasonable steps to safeguard the interests and rights of those clients.

The way to think about this issue is that the social worker must act in ways that result in the least restrictive environments for their clients. So, if, for example, you are being asked to make recommendations for an emancipated minor, the client may not have full decision-making capacity, but the social worker should solicit their preferences and take them into account when developing recommendations. The same is true when working with clients who are mentally incapacitated. Always ask the client for their preferences and if feasible keep those preferences front and center as much as possible.

1.15 Interruption of Services

1.16 Referral for Services

1.17 Termination of Services

It makes sense to cover these standards together as they address similar issues. Sometimes you need to interrupt your work with a client because you are leaving a job temporarily or permanently. Or, you might find that you do not have the expertise needed to assist a particular client. A social worker who recognizes that the client needs something that falls outside of their skill set and makes a referral (and follows up on it) is operating in compliance with the standards.

For example, I have little expertise in the area of substance addiction. However, I am willing to work with these clients either after their substance abuse treatment or simultaneously. I *have* terminated my work with clients who have active addictions but who continuously refuse specialized help. In these circumstances I become concerned that I am enabling the client's addiction by not insisting they attend addictions treatment or, at the very least, 12-step meetings. Nevertheless, I make sure they are armed with addictions resources to pursue if and when they are ready. When a client with an addiction initially seeks help from a general psychotherapist, they are barking up the wrong tree. However, once a client addresses and manages their addiction, powerful, painful feelings can surface that are clearly in the wheelhouse of psychotherapy.

Termination ideally occurs when the client has met all of their goals. It is best if the clinician and the client plan termination in advance and proceed gradually, tapering down sessions that are increasingly further apart (biweekly, once a month to meeting in two months). As part of the termination process, it is advised that the client and the clinician review client goals, those met and unmet, along with the course of treatment and how it all felt for the client and the clinician (what went well and what did not). Future plans for the client such as a transfer to another helper or agency, should also be addressed if applicable. However, terminations often do not happen in this planful manner. Instead, clients decide on their own that it is time for therapy to stop and then cancel an appointment and not reschedule. It is always a good idea to try to follow up with these clients and have some kind of termination discussion. However, when you cannot reach them (as is often the case), you must respect self-determination and let them go, perhaps with some kind of "goodbye" letter and a reminder that they can come back at any time in the future, should the need arise. As an aside, if you are leaving an agency and trying to transfer your cases, do not be surprised if your clients use this as an opportunity to go forward without therapy. Be sure they have instructions on how to reengage in treatment in the future, should they decide to do so.

Standard 2: Social Workers' Ethical Responsibilities to Colleagues

Basically, we do not put down or gossip about our colleagues to our clients. Even if a client complains about a previous worker, we should empathize with the client's dissatisfaction but without joining them in negative banter. It is seductive and perhaps soothing to our ego for a client to praise us to the detriment of another service provider, but we must never encourage it. We can never know what has really happened between a client and a prior clinician without hearing the clinician's perspective, and so it is advisable to get permission from the client to contact that previous therapist. When you get a client who has worked for some time with a prior clinician, unless the client reports unethical or clearly incompetent behavior, frame the previous work as establishing a foundation upon which the two of you can now build.

As clinical social workers, part of our professional responsibility is to advocate for services for our clients as needed. Our work is about relationships, and we need to establish strong professional ties with colleagues in other agencies in order to help our clients. As stated earlier, if you have a conflict with a colleague or coworker, which occasionally happens, resist the impulse to send a nastygram or gossip about them to others. Instead, wait 24 hours before responding, try to tune in to what your colleague might be feeling and then approach them as professionally as possible. It helps if you can learn not to take your conflicts with your colleagues personally but instead see them as part of the business of social work. You are not under any obligation to love or even like your coworkers, colleagues, and supervisors. However, you must respect them and do everything you can to establish and maintain strong working relationships with them for the good of your clients.

As the standards that fall under this title state, we of course do not sexually harass, nor do we engage in sexual or romantic relationships with our colleagues or subordinates. This should already be covered in your agency policy and procedures manual, and hopefully there is related training at your workplace. If not, you should advocate for it.

Further, we respect each other's boundaries just as we would with clients. Years ago, when I was fresh out of MSW school, there was a job I had applied for that I really wanted. The position offered good supervision and excellent training in family therapy. I was interviewed in a relatively dark room by a rather imposing man who had a reputation as a local leader in the field. During the interview, he had asked me about the duration of my longest relationship. At the time I was only 23-years-old and I had been dating the man who would eventually become my long-term partner and husband for only nine months. In addition, it was the 1980s and while I was out to my close friends and family, I was not sure what the consequences might be if my sexual orientation became known in the professional circles I was trying to enter. So, I stumbled, hemmed, and hawed. After a few awkward moments, I decided to answer this question without revealing my partner's gender. Once I did, he replied, "At your age, that's pretty good.

Why did you seem so nervous and hesitant?" As an aside, he had a reputation for asking this question of all interviewees. Several of my older fellow students walked out of their interviews when that question was asked, informing him that it was illegal. One assumably heterosexual male colleague responded with, "Why are you asking me this? Is this a job interview, or are you looking to *date me*?" The point of the story is that as professionals, we must treat each other with respect, and part of that is knowing employment laws and avoiding intrusive, potentially illegal questions during employment interviews.

Another key takeaway from this section of standards is the importance of dealing with a colleague who is impaired (standard 2.08), incompetent (2.09), or behaving in ways that are unethical (2.10). Again, these standards are related so I will address them together.

Unfortunately, I have worked with two colleagues who were seeing clients while under the obvious influence of alcohol and drugs. Both of these social workers exhibited intoxicated behavior such as slurred speech as they were about to see clients. As social workers, we are obliged to address this when it happens, and trust me, this is not easy. The first step is to confront the impaired worker directly and privately, particularly if you are their supervisor.

CLINICIAN 1: Gee, Barbara, I have recently noticed that you have been coming to work smelling of alcohol and seemingly intoxicated. Several other workers here have noticed the same thing. I am worried about you; are you ok?

CLINICIAN 2: Yes, I'm ok. I am going through a rough time; my mother just died, and I have been having a few in the afternoon. But I'm sorry. This won't be a problem again.

CLINICIAN 1: I am sorry about your mother, that must be a terrible loss for you. However, you cannot show up to work intoxicated. Do you need to take some time off? I can certainly arrange that for you. Also, how about a visit with our Employee Assistance Program (EAP)? You know, it is one of the benefits here.

CLINICIAN 2: Yes, the EAP sounds like a good idea.

(If your agency does not have an EAP, a referral is in order.)

In this situation, I was the supervisor of record. In the other, I contacted the person's supervisor who then confronted the worker. Things get tricky if this first step does not resolve the issue and the person continues to demonstrate problematic behavior. In such circumstances, the worker is obliged by the Code to contact the state licensing board and issue a complaint. Of course, this is an act of last resort and hopefully you will never have to do this.

Standard 3: Social Workers' Ethical Responsibilities in Practice Settings

3.01 Supervision and Consultation

Social workers who supervise must do so in the purview of their expertise. In addition, the same ethical standards that apply to clients and clinicians apply to supervisors and supervisees (Shulman & Sayfer, 2005). There are to be no dual relationships, and the supervisor must be careful not to in any way exploit the power differential with the supervisee.

It is useful to have a contract with the supervisee. It can be verbal or written but includes an agreement about how often they will meet and the purpose of such meetings. Such agreements should include mutually agreed upon professional growth goals for the supervisee. If the supervisor is charged with doing an evaluation of the supervisee, there should be as much communication and transparency as possible about the supervisee's strengths, weaknesses, and professional goal growth.

The same standards apply between instructors and students when the social worker is in an educational role. Educators and field instructors are to avoid dual relationships. Further, when the student presents case material, it must be kept confidential. Supervision sessions should be private and out of earshot of anyone else, as confidential material is discussed. Also, as a supervisor, you will need to review your supervisee's records to ensure they are up to date.

Standard 4: Social Workers' Ethical Responsibilities as Professionals

4.01 Competence

> (a) Social workers should accept responsibility or employment only on the basis of existing competence or the intention to acquire the necessary competence. (b) Social workers should strive to become and remain proficient in professional practice and the performance of professional functions. Social workers should critically examine and keep current with emerging knowledge relevant to social work. Social workers should routinely review the professional literature and participate in continuing education relevant to social work practice and social work ethics. (c) Social workers should base practice on recognized knowledge, including empirically based knowledge, relevant to social work and social work ethics.

Social workers are not to practice outside of their areas of competence and expertise. However, this does not mean a social worker should refuse to see any client who has problems with which they are unfamiliar. Remember Jay, the child with the chronic cough in Chapter 4? Though I was no expert in psychosomatic coughing (nor could I find anyone who was), I consulted the literature on the topic, only to find very little that was helpful. Instead, I was able to rely on the assessment skills I already had to address this case.

Nevertheless, professional social workers (including social work students) must commit to expanding and continuously building their knowledge base by consulting the professional literature, seeking supervision and consultation, and engaging in continued education. For example, if you are assigned a client who is transgender, are unfamiliar with the treatment of such clients, but do not have the option to refer to an expert because none exist in the client's geographic area or budget, you must immediately begin educating yourself about this population and should seek regular consultation from an expert. Competence in clinical social work is not a destination, but an ongoing journey. Throughout your career, there will always be something new to learn, which is in fact what makes this field so exciting.

The standards around discrimination (4.02), private conduct (4.03), dishonesty, fraud, and deception (4.04), and misrepresentation (4.06) are self-explanatory. 4.07 states that we are not to ask our clients for endorsements, and this goes for quoted client statements on advertisements for our practice in print or online. According to 4.08, if you are a student and you plagiarize on an assignment, not only are you likely to get disciplined or even expelled from your college or university, but you are also violating the ethics of the profession. As a social worker, you must not in any way take credit for someone else's work or contribution, but instead must give credit where credit is due.

4.05 Impairment

4.05 addresses the issue of impairment of professionals and this standard warrants additional attention.

(a) Social workers should not allow their own personal problems, psychosocial distress, legal problems, substance abuse, or mental health difficulties to interfere with their professional judgment and performance or to jeopardize the best interests of people for whom they have a professional responsibility.

(b) Social workers whose personal problems, psychosocial distress, legal problems, substance abuse, or mental health difficulties interfere with their professional judgment and performance should immediately seek consultation and take appropriate remedial action by seeking professional help, making adjustments in workload, terminating practice, or taking any other steps necessary to protect clients and others.

As a group, social workers are highly committed professionals willing to go above and beyond to do what it takes to get the job done. This dedication of course is admirable. However, it becomes problematic when a worker has problems that impact or threaten to interfere with their responsibilities and do not attend to them. Illness, mental health problems (remember Chapter 1—we are prone to them), and other personal problems must be addressed through adequate professional treatment and self-care for our own good, and also for that of the clients we serve. As I have stated earlier, when the masks come down on the plane, you must put your own on first before assisting others.

Standard 5: Social Workers' Ethical Responsibilities to the Social Work Profession

5.01 Integrity of the Profession

Social workers should be good representatives of the profession and carry themselves as such. They need to keep this in mind as they conduct themselves in public and social media. Remember, you are a professional and your public image must reflect that. No one wants to see their clinical social worker acting foolish or looking messy. So, images on Facebook, Instagram, or TikTok that show you partying hard or acting silly with friends should be avoided unless access to your sites is very restricted. Refrain from online assertions of strong political positions to avoid alienating clients and colleagues. (Instead advocate and protest live and in person where you can make a difference). Keep in mind that even with careful application of filters, current, former, or future clients might be able to find you and your photos and statements on the internet. Clients want to see their clinician as kind, intelligent, mature, and nonjudgmental. Those characteristics should be reflected in your social media posts.

Once you have some experience, it is a good idea to start thinking about how you will give back to the profession. There are many opportunities to use your skills and knowledge to enrich the field whether it be through teaching, field instruction, conference presentations, or programs in the community. Eventually, it will be your obligation to explore these options.

5.02 Evaluation and Research

I strongly recommend that if an agency or individual wants to do evaluation research, they partner with a college or university so they can have access to an institutional review board (IRB). IRB's carefully review proposed research projects to ensure that whatever evaluation or research you want to do incorporates adequate protections for human subjects. Further, MSWs rarely have the training and experience necessary to do independent research. Having an affiliation with an academic institution will connect you with people who have the empirical experience and expertise you will need.

Standard 6: Social Workers' Ethical Responsibilities to the Broader Society

As stated earlier in the book, clinical social workers have an ethical obligation to understand and address inequality and to find ways to procure adequate resources for their clients. This could be in the form of political or social action and/or finding some way to shape and advocate for fairer social policies. Additionally, in the case of a local emergency such as a hurricane, earthquake, or attack like that of 9/11, social workers bear responsibility to be of assistance. So, be ready to pitch in during these sudden and disruptive incidents.

Resolving Ethical Dilemmas: The I CARE Method

While these standards are straightforward and their application might seem cut and dry, there are occasions when two or more ethical standards are in conflict, resulting in ethical dilemmas. When this occurs, it becomes clear that ethical standards cannot be uniformly prescriptive, and practicing in ways that are in compliance with these standards is not always clear-cut as conflicting values and obligations emerge. Several social work experts have created frameworks for analyzing and resolving ethical dilemmas (Beauchamp & Childress, 2013; Congress, 1999; Gray & Gibbons, 2007; Levy & Slavin, 2013; Reamer, 2013; Strom-Gottfried, 2008), which include: identifying the applicable ethical standard or principle, acknowledging the risks and benefits of several courses of action, consulting with experts, and evaluation. A colleague and I have developed a framework which goes by the acronym, I CARE (LaSala & Goldblatt Hyatt, 2019), and each letter of the acronym represents a step in the process:

1. Identification: Recognizing the ethical values and principles at stake.
2. Consultation: Seeking out available knowledge, including relevant literature, the advice of experts, and continuing education in the area of the ethical dilemma. You also must self-reflect on your own thoughts and feelings about the situation.
3. Action: Acknowledging the potential benefits of the proposed action or inaction.
4. Rebuttal: Identifying a counterargument while acknowledging ambiguity.
5. Evaluation: Assessing the outcome of one's action and documenting the entire decision-making process so that others could evaluate it as well.

Elsewhere, it is described how to apply this framework to resolving ethical dilemmas when working with transgender populations, as the gatekeeping role of the social worker for medical services for this population requires special attention (LaSala & Goldblatt Hyatt, 2019). However, following is an application of I CARE to a case involving a minor reporting child abuse to their social worker:

> Lina was an 11-year-old girl who regularly met with a social work field student, Amalia, at her school due to her behavioral problems in the classroom. During a session, Lina presented with a black eye and reddened marks on her arms. When Amalia asked about these injuries, Lina initially became uncomfortable but then disclosed that her mother slapped her face and squeezed and twisted her arm when she found out Lina had failed a math exam. Lina begged Amalia not to tell anyone about the incident, saying she did not want to get her mother into trouble, nor did she want to get into further hot water herself. In consulting with her supervisor, Amalia learned that the school had a policy dictating that all suspected incidents of child abuse be reported to the principle who would then decide whether or not to report them. When Amalia relayed what had happened, the principle ordered her NOT to call the state child abuse hotline.

In applying I CARE, the situation can be analyzed using each letter of the acronym.

Identification

Here is where we identify the ethical standards in play beginning with 1.07, privacy and confidentiality. Social work students are bound by the same ethical standards as professional social workers, so Amalia is obligated to keep her client's information confidential. Further, this situation could also be covered by the ethical standard addressing self-determination (1.02) which asserts that clients have the right to dictate the direction of the work. However, a social worker can limit client self-determination when in their professional judgment, not doing so would put the client at risk of harm. Lina is reporting something that could potentially put her physical (and emotional) well-being at risk. This situation also relates to Standard 1.14 which is about social workers needing to step in and use their professional authority when clients do not have the capacity to do so. As Lina is a young child, this standard applies.

Consultation

A good general guideline is that a fieldwork student or new worker should always first consult their supervisor whenever they are unsure of something. However, in this case the supervisor was part of an administration that enforced inappropriate and arguably illegal limits that interfered with the social worker's ability to act in ways that are in compliance with the values and ethics of the profession. Amalia was a good fieldwork student. She was liked by teachers, her supervisor, and the school's principal and assistant principal, and she believed these relationships would be helpful in her performance evaluations as well as her future career. However, in her practice class, Amalia remembered being taught that, when it comes to child abuse, she and all other social workers are *mandated reporters* whereby they are not only ethically, but also legally required to report incidents of *suspected* child abuse. As a field work student, Amalia was understandably intimidated by the prospect of going against school policy and potentially damaging her relationship with her supervisor and the principal.

First, she consulted with her practice professor who advised her that if she did not report this situation, Lina would remain at risk of serious injury and Amalia would be in violation of the NASW Code of Ethics (NASW, 2021). However, he also directed her to talk to staff in the social work department's fieldwork office.

Action

Amalia did just that. The field office informed her that no matter what her client's school policy was, she was obliged to report. Further, she was under no obligation to get permission or approval from either her supervisor or the principal to report the incident. However, she decided to inform them of her action after she contacted the hotline. Her university's social work fieldwork office contacted Amalia's field supervisor and principal to let them know that by law, as well as per the ethics of the profession, Amalia was required to report the incident to the state registry.

Rebuttal

Amalia could have chosen to follow the school policy. This would have prevented any potential disruption in the positive relationships she had carefully cultivated with her superiors. However, not only would this be a violation of the law and the ethics of her new profession, this would also result in Lina being unprotected and at risk for further abuse at the hands of her mother. When thinking this through, Amalia was confident that she had made the right decision.

Evaluation

Local child protective services interviewed Lina, her mother, and Amalia. As a result, Lina's mother admitted that she had struck her daughter out of anger. Child protective services mandated that Lina's mother attend anger management and parenting classes and kept the case open for six months so that they could continue to monitor Lina's safety. This is just what the situation needed, and if Amalia had not acted, Lina would continue to be in danger.

Fortunately, the principal and the supervisor learned some important lessons and changed their policy. The principal revised the school policy and requested that if a social worker or anyone in the building contacted the child abuse hotline, that he be informed if possible so he could be prepared for fallout from angry parents.

Conclusion

Social work students and social workers of all levels of experience must be familiar with the Code of Ethics and continuously integrate its principles in their work. These days, most licensing boards require some kind of continuing education in the area of ethics. This is something I support as it serves as a good reminder to social workers and also keeps us abreast of any changes to the Code which is periodically revised to address changes in the field. For example, consider the recent addition about social workers and self-care. Psychotherapy and self-reflection, recommended throughout this volume, along with other stress reduction activities are good ways for clinical social workers to take care of themselves. Self-care ensures that social workers are as strong and as competent as possible to face the challenges of this vital profession.

References

Beauchamp, T. L., & Childress, J. F. (2013). *Principles of Biomedical Ethics* (7th ed.). Oxford University Press.

Bisman, C. (1994). *Social Work Practice: Cases and Principles*. Wadsworth Publishing Company.

Congress, E. P. (1999). *Social Work Values and Ethics: Identifying and Resolving Professional Dilemmas*. Nelson Hall.

Gray, M., & Gibbons, J. (2007). There are no answers, only choices: Teaching ethical decision making in social work. *Australian Social Work*, 60(2), 222–238. doi:10.1080/03124070701323840.

LaSala, M. C., & Goldblatt Hyatt, E. D. (2019). A bioethics approach to transgender clients. *Journal of Gay and Lesbian Social Services*, 31(4), 501–520. doi:10.1080/10538720.2019.1653804.

Levy, C. S., & Slavin, S. (2013). *Social Work Ethics on the Line*. Routledge.

National Association of Social Workers (NASW) (2021). *Code of ethics of the National Association of Social Workers*. NASW Press. www.socialworkers.org/About/Ethics/Code-of-Ethics/Code-of-Ethics-English.

Reamer, F. G. (2013). *Social Work Values and Ethics* (4th ed.). Columbia University Press.

Selvini-Palazzoli, M. S., & Boscolo, L. (1994). *Paradox and Counterparadox: A New Model in the Therapy of the Family in Schizophrenic Transaction*. Jason Aronson, Incorporated.

Regan, J. A. R. (2020). The three pillars of the social work profession in the United States, Education, practice, and regulation. *Social Pathology and Prevention*, 6(2), 11–18. doi:10.25142/spp.2021.006.

Shulman, L., & Safyer, A. (2005). *Supervision in Counseling: Interdisciplinary Issues and Research*. Routledge.

Strom-Gottfried, K. (2008). *The Ethics of Practice with Minors: High Stakes, Hard Choices*. Lyceum.

Chapter 10

Healing Relationships in the Age of Covid

Wow, we've really all been through it, haven't we? As of this writing (winter of 2022), we are still reeling from the effects of Covid-19. It seems just as it was releasing its grasp, a new, virulent version emerged, seemingly out of nowhere. In the summer and fall of 2021, in-person attendance at theaters, houses of worship, restaurants and schools was resuming, some reimagined with masks and social distance. However, with Omicron, this progress has been halted and, in some ways, reversed. In the words of that Grateful Dead song, "What a long, strange trip it's been" and continues to be. My fervent wish is that, by the time this book gets into your hands, Covid is completely vanquished; that this pandemic is relegated to the dustheap of stories with which we will bore those yet to be born or too young to remember. However, we may have to deal with some aspect of this virus for some time, if not forever.

Pandemic Trauma

Many of us have been traumatized by the pandemic; how could we not? Seized by a long-handed, invisible villain intent on sickening and killing us, all we could do was hole up, frightened, in our homes, hiding from the disease, and each other. Repeated horror stories of freezer trucks filled with an overflow of cadavers only added to the sense of dread. Reports from the Centers for Disease Control (CDC), the World Health Organization (WHO), and the National Institute of Health (NIH) terrified us. The pandemic has had a profound impact on our relationships as loved ones died alone in hospitals, important social rituals including weddings, graduations, and funerals were canceled or postponed and seemingly everything that fostered community relationships such as religious worship, informal gatherings, theater, and restaurant dining was either canceled or moved online. No parent, student, or educator will ever forget the stress of home schooling. When we did not fully understand how the virus was transmitted, being outdoors took considerable courage as you wondered if the stranger walking toward you might infect and even kill you.

DOI: 10.4324/9781003011712-10

We have also had to cope with a lot more, namely a wildly controversial and contested presidential election and an insurgent attack on the US capital, all of which threatened the nation's stability. A rash of videos portraying police brutality against unarmed Black men meant we could no longer remain unaware or deny racism and police violence. The merciless and cruel killing of George Floyd looped continuously on television and social media, painful for all of us to watch but particularly traumatizing for those who are African American. This heinous act spurred a rise of political activism, the strengthening of the Black Lives Matter movement, but also the destruction of property, looting, and a backlash that spurred violence and divided the nation. Political divisions fostered anger and hatred among neighbors, friends, and family members. As if this wasn't enough to cope with, a war erupted in eastern Europe that threatened to politically and economically destabilize the world. The cumulative effects of the virus, racism, and politics has created a severe storm leaving us to figure out how to establish and maintain healing relationships amid the thunder and lightning.

This client lived in a major urban area that was devastated during the beginning of the pandemic, which is when this session took place:

CLIENT: Do you hear those sirens going off in the background?
CLINICIAN: Yes.
CLIENT: Those are ambulances taking Covid patients to the hospital, who are likely to die. We hear them all of the time.
CLINICIAN: Oh my God! That's a lot to live with day in and day out. What is that like for you?
CLIENT: Terrifying, I'm very scared.
CLINICIAN: I am too.
CLIENT: Really?
CLINICIAN: Sure, we therapists are human too. First off, these are such uncertain times and we are all having problems coping at some level—and under the circumstances, this is understandable. So, let's just normalize that.
CLIENT: OK.

Note that the clinician is not trying to explain away the client's feelings. Instead, they use self-disclosure to humanize and normalize the client's distress, so he does not feel so alone.

Thank goodness, the days of bodies in freezer trucks are no longer upon us, at least for now. However, the emotional and psychological fallout from the initial and ongoing trauma of Covid-19 remains. Thus far, we know that children and youth have been particularly hard hit by the psychological impacts of the pandemic. According to a recent report, depression and anxiety symptoms among youth have doubled since the beginning of the pandemic (Racine et al., 2021). For adolescents, visits to emergency rooms for suicidal behavior have increased and this rise has been particularly acute among teenaged girls (Yard et al., 2021). Reports from here and other countries indicate a similar, alarming rise of psychiatric disorders among adults (Dong & Bouey, 2020; Rodriguez, Litt, & Stewart, 2020).

Clinical Social Work During Covid-19

It is impossible to deny that the pandemic *has* rendered remote psychotherapy, also known as teletherapy, more commonplace. Clinical social workers and psychotherapists from other professions who in the past would eschew anything other than in-person sessions (including this writer) have been forced to adapt to a new reality. Necessity is indeed the mother of invention; our clients need us more than ever during the pandemic, and of course, we need our jobs. As of this writing, clients in private practices and agencies in my region are still not consistently being seen in person. In the agency where I work, the director has warned that she is eventually going to mandate that therapists come back to the office. However, this has yet to happen due to the rise of Delta and Omicron variant infections. As I am fully vaccinated and have received a booster, I offer the in-person option to my clients (provided they too are fully vaccinated) and about half take me up on it, stating that they prefer the physical connection. Others have declined this invitation due to logistics. They live a good distance from my office and it is simply more convenient to continue remotely than battle the traffic.

There are other practical advantages to teletherapy such as not being tied to an office, which in turn offers more flexibility for both the therapist and client. Before the pandemic, I saw my clients at a practice with limited office space. I was assigned Monday nights and was restricted to that evening. If a holiday fell on a Monday (many do), and I wanted to reschedule my clients for another night, it was extremely difficult, if not impossible. Now, I can see clients whenever it is convenient for both or all of us. Further, as stated previously, clients do not have to brave weather or traffic. These days, I generally see my clients in person and online on Mondays, toggling between the two methods in an evening. Nevertheless, when there is a holiday or some reason one of us can't make it to the office, I take advantage of the remote option. Recently, I had injured my foot and was not in condition to drive, so I moved my in-person clients to remote. During pre-Covid times, I would not have considered this, either toughing it out in person, or canceling sessions. The remote option makes it less likely that sessions will be canceled due to factors such as the client or the therapist traveling out of town, or inclement weather; we'll need to plan a funeral for snow days.

Online sessions make it convenient to switch screens and research resources on the web, while seeing the client, which helps with case management. I have been able to look up and recommend books, websites, and referrals to clients, and clients have been able to show me resources that they have found useful.

Though not my preference, effective psychotherapy is still possible to do remotely, more so than many of us hardliners originally thought. Nevertheless, in my opinion nothing compares to in-person psychotherapy. It is much easier to get a comprehensive picture of the client when meeting face-to-face where we can observe body language, gestures, clothing, and hygiene. Burgoyne and Cohn (2020) remind us that travel to and from the session offers downtime for the client to contemplate what had been discussed. Such an opportunity is lost when a person jumps online in the middle of the day and then quickly resumes other tasks when the session is over. There have been occasions where my clients have become distracted and even tried to do paperwork or answer texts during their remote sessions.

Nevertheless, there is good evidence that teletherapy can be just as effective as its in-person counterpart for a variety of mental health and relationship problems if good guidelines are put into place to ensure that the work is done in a meaningful and ethical way (Morgan et al., 2021; Probst et al., 2021). Here are some suggestions that are meant to maximize the effectiveness of your remote practice:

1. Investigate video and web conferencing platforms and choose one that is Health Insurance Portability and Accountability Act (HIPAA) (U.S. Department of Health and Human Services, 2020) compliant in terms of confidentiality and privacy—not all are. For example, Zoom was not previously but is now. SKYPE is not, nor is Facetime, but Lifesize (www.lifesize.com) is as well as Doxy (https://doxy.me). In time more HIPAA compliant platforms may emerge.

2. Prepare the room from where you are to remotely work. If it is in your home, make sure your background is tidy and professional. Wherever you do remote psychotherapy is technically your office and should look like it. Never work from a room that is visibly your bedroom as this can come across as either sloppy or seductive. There should be nothing distracting or too personal on the walls behind you. Remember, everything that the client can see imparts a message, so you want it to be as neutral and professional as possible.

    a. The room must be a space that is private, meaning that you can close the door and no one is going to barge in during the middle of a session. Let others who live in your home know that you are not to be interrupted. The vaudeville star W.C. Fields once remarked that he never shared the stage with animals or children, no doubt because they stole his thunder by redirecting the attention away from him. If you have a clingy, spoiled pet (as do I), after briefly introducing them, keep them out of the frame. Be sure to set a boundary with your children (do your best), so they know only to interrupt you in the event of an emergency. Ask your clients to do the same. The same advice applies for non-clinical professional meetings.

b   Make sure the lighting is adequate and that your microphone and camera are of good quality. These are the essential tools of teletherapy upon which you will be completely reliant.

3   If it is safe and feasible, it is important to see the client in person at least once in the beginning, before moving to 100% remote sessions. I was working with an adolescent boy who had body image issues, but on the screen, I could not see his body. It felt uncomfortable to ask him to show his body on camera. If we were meeting in person, this would have been a non-issue.

a   It is worth noting that you and your client are seeing yourselves on camera during the entire session. This could be awkward, particularly for clients who feel insecure about their appearances. The good news is that such feelings could be "grist for the mill" (a phrase I have used repeatedly in this volume) and should be explored and addressed during the course of therapy.

4   Make sure your client is also speaking to you from a private space. A client who shared a small apartment with a partner with whom he had conflict initially tried to meet with me from his bathroom. Unfortunately, his partner overheard parts of the session, so subsequent sessions were done from his car. A bar, restaurant, or coffee shop is never a good idea unless there is absolutely no alternative and it is an emergency.

a   If the client is remoting from their workplace, make sure they have secured a private space where they will not be interrupted or overheard.

5   Regarding eye contact, there is a weirdness inherent in teletherapy in that when you look directly at your client on the screen, it might appear as if you are peering over them because you are not looking into the camera. It might be possible to move a portable camera to the screen area (as opposed to the top of the screen) so that you can look into it as you are looking at the client (Burgoyne & Cohn, 2020). Nevertheless, I have found over time that clients (and therapists) get used to this eye contact discrepancy. If working with a couple, family, or group, you might need to say their names so they know you are addressing them.

6   When first meeting remotely, a good way to engage clients is to notice something in the background, like plants, pets, beautiful furniture, or an interesting photo on the wall. In many ways, a remote session is comparable to a home visit, so you can apply similar engagement tools.

7   Directly address distracted client behavior. If they seem inattentive or are allowing themselves to be distracted, address this gently but directly:

CLINICIAN: I have noticed, Roland, that when we started discussing how your mother abused you as a child, you seemed to withdraw into tidying up your desk.
ROLAND: (after a pause) Yup, you caught me (brief chuckle).
CLINICIAN: Are you finding this topic difficult to think about and talk about?
ROLAND: Yes, as a matter of fact I am.
CLINICIAN: Ok, got it. Let's discuss ways that we can make it at least a little more comfortable for you—maybe even slow things down a bit.

8   Couples therapy is possible with some adjustments. If the couple is situated far enough from the computer so that they are both in view, it can work. However, depending on the distance between the couple and the computer, they might have to squeeze together. Physical closeness for a couple or family in conflict could feel very uncomfortable. Therefore, it is a good idea to check in with them and if they feel awkward, coach them to rearrange the furniture in a way that allows for a more comfortable physical distance while still being seen on camera. In teletherapy, when setting up enactments, it might be more challenging as there may even be more of a tendency to direct communication to the onscreen therapist rather than each other. Additionally, therapists nervous about doing teletherapy might inadvertently encourage clients to talk to them directly. All in all, it may take extra effort on the part of the therapist to keep enactments going.

9   Family therapy might be even trickier, but is certainly not impossible. What does not seem to work well is to have each family member on a different device and in a different box on the screen. The clinician may have to see the family in twos and work with one dyad at a time in order for them to fit the screen. The good news is that clinicians and researchers are hard at work trying to determine what teletherapy technologies and methods work best and also are developing new ones. Thus, we can expect more information and tools in the near future.

10 Remote groups share some of the same benefits and weaknesses of other types of teletherapy. The therapist and the clients lose out on seeing each other's body language, there can be annoying and disruptive technical glitches, and getting people to talk to each other from their "boxes" can be tricky. However, I have noticed that in groups in particular, there is a marked tendency for clients to get distracted and to start doing other things, like check their phones, look at papers, clean their rooms. Some even put on wigs! (See Chapter 7.)

11 Even though body language is more difficult to gauge online, facial expressions are not, and I have been better able to notice looks on people's faces and thus, get them to talk about what they are experiencing.

CLINICIAN: Audra, I notice that when Roland was talking, you were rolling your eyes. Clearly, something he said struck a nerve. Would you be willing to share your reactions?

It can be tricky to determine whether a client is tearing up, or there is a distortion on the video, so it is important to closely observe the client's face. When you suspect a client is having an emotional reaction, it is best to investigate.

CLINICIAN: Felix, even though we are speaking remotely, I think I see you getting emotional. I have to ask, are your eyes tearing up?
FELIX: Yes.
CLINICIAN: Can you tell me what's happening? How are you feeling right now and what is setting it off?

12 After each session, ask your client(s) to take a moment and reflect on the session as they might during the commute after an in-person session. It would also be a good idea for the therapist to do the same. Zoom fatigue is real, so you might want to space out your sessions more than you would when working in person to allow for this reflection and also some rest.
13 As stated repeatedly in this book, do not forget about client strengths. After hearing about the difficulties and reflecting and empathizing with their feelings, ask your clients how they are coping. What are they doing to get through these difficult times? What is happening when things do not quite feel so bad? What coping strategies have they found that work, even a little bit? What can they reprise?
14 Finally, approach each online session with an attitude of flexibility and forgiveness. Things will go wrong; screens will freeze, the sound will sometimes not work, dogs and children will make surprise appearances. In early 2021, there was a hilarious video that went viral online that showed a remote legal hearing where one of the attorneys appeared as a cat, thanks to a tenacious image filter and his playful children. (You can Google this if you need a laugh.) Whenever you encounter these problems, try to fix the problem (reboot your computer) and do the best you can.

The Self of the Clinician

Throughout this volume, the reader has been continuously prompted to set aside time to self-reflect, and of course, these stressful times are no exception. During the worst parts of the pandemic, every therapist I knew had a filled schedule, some squeezed even more clients into their busy day, and we were all working harder than usual. Those not accustomed to working from home had to learn that working remotely did not mean you had to schedule sessions at all hours of the day or night just because you could. Boundaries needed to be set to allow one's batteries to be recharged. At the same time, we were also dealing with *our own* reactions to the pandemic and the civil unrest. I recall needing to remind myself to breathe, as I found myself holding my breath as I read the news. On top of all of this, we needed to do our work even when it was difficult to know what to say to clients to comfort them. It is advisable for clinicians to take a moment (and, for Pete's sake, take a deep breath!) and ask themselves the following questions:

1   How was I doing during the first 18 months of the pandemic? How has it affected me?

   a   What were the most difficult times for me? What were the feelings I experienced?

2   How did I survive? What coping methods worked well; which ones did not?
3   Did I reach out for help and support? Did I do this enough?
4   How did the stresses of those times affect my work? Are previous and current pandemic stresses affecting my clinical work now? What can I do to ensure that I am able to continue to be effective?

I had a recent conversation with a group of therapists who spoke about how clients expressed their fears and looked to them (us) for answers. As in the case example earlier in this chapter, many of us disclosed that we were also befuddled and afraid. While judiciously sharing our feelings with clients can be a good thing, we cannot stop there. Firefighters no doubt feel fear when they run into a burning building, but they do it because that is their calling. As professionals, we must rush in and attend to our clients.

Clinical Social Work During the Ongoing Pandemic(s)

As stated earlier, we are coping with a new variant and others may follow. Racism, and what to do about it is an ongoing dilemma, and our country remains as divided as ever about just about everything from the last presidential election, to how to fight Covid, and whether or how to talk about racism in our homes, schools, or workplaces. So, we must continue to be prepared to assist clients to cope with a myriad of difficulties and crises that lie in our future.

As I state throughout this book, we must first be sure the client knows we hear and understand their feelings before asking about and encouraging their strengths. Ongoing clients will see the relationship you have both built as a safe-haven to discuss their painful emotions and isolation, and also a resource for problem solving. Once you have successfully convinced them that you are hearing their suffering, help them gather an inventory of their strengths as well as effective coping methods they have used in the past. Finally, it is important to get them to reach out to others to break the isolation, even if it must be done remotely.

CLINICIAN: (after carefully helping the client to explore her fears and frustration) Of course, I see how hard this has been for you. But I would like to change course if I may. In the past, when you have faced a difficult problem or even a scary situation, what has helped you cope? What did you do to get yourself through?
CLIENT: Well, I distracted myself a lot, by reading, cleaning the house, and exercising.
CLINICIAN: OK, and how did that all help you?
CLIENT: It made me feel calmer.
CLINICIAN: Tell me more.
CLIENT: It calmed me down. It got my mind off negative things.
CLINICIAN: Great! Anything else?
CLIENT: I reached out to friends and family for support.
CLINICIAN: Hmmm ... do you think you could do some of that now to see if it would help?
CLIENT: On Zoom? That's all my friends and family want to do. Ugh, it's not the same.
CLINICIAN: Absolutely, for sure you're right, but it is all we have right now with this new variant, and people isolating to try to stay healthy. Do you think it might be worth trying?
CLIENT: I guess.
CLINICIAN: OK, I know every crisis situation is unique. But is distracting yourself in the ways you mentioned previously something you might give a try and see if it helps at all in this situation?
CLIENT: OK, yes. I mean, what have I got to lose?

With more information as to how to stop the spread, vaccines, and variants running their course, people may soon no longer fear so much for their own safety and that of others. However, traces of the trauma might still remain. I know people who are still terrified, despite being vaccinated and boostered, and some of this must be because the pandemic had touched upon client issues around safety and control. Thus, as we go forward during these difficult and uncertain times, it is a good idea to ask your clients how they made it through the storm, and, importantly, how they are coping now. Be sure to ask those questions of yourself as well.

References

Burgoyne, N., & Cohn, A. S. (2020). Lessons from the transition to relational teletherapy during COVID-19. *Family Process*, 59(3), 974–988. doi:10.1111/famp.12589.

Dong, L., & Bouey, J. (2020). Public mental health crisis during COVID-19 pandemic, China. *Emerging Infectious Diseases*, 26(7), 1616–1618. doi:10.3201/eid2607.200407.

Morgan, A. A., Landers, A. L., Simpson, J. E., Russon, J. M., Case Pease, J., Dolbin-MacNab, M. L., ... & Jackson, J. B. (2021). The transition to teletherapy in marriage and family therapy training settings during COVID-19: What do the data tell us? *Journal of Marital and Family Therapy*, 47(2), 320–341. doi:10.1111/jmft.12502.

Probst, T., Haid, B., Schimböck, W., Reisinger, A., Gasser, M., Eichberger-Heckmann, H., ... & Pieh, C. (2021). Therapeutic interventions in in-person and remote psychotherapy: Survey with psychotherapists and patients experiencing in-person and remote psychotherapy during COVID-19. *Clinical Psychology & Psychotherapy* 28(4), 988–1000. doi:10.1002/cpp.2553.

Racine, N., McArthur, B. A., Cooke, J. E., Eirich, R., Zhu, J., & Madigan, S. (2021). Global prevalence of depressive and anxiety symptoms in children and adolescents during COVID-19: A meta-analysis. *JAMA Pediatrics*, 175(11), 1142–1150. doi:10.1001/jamapediatrics.2021.2482.

Rodriguez, L. M., Litt, D. M., & Stewart, S. H. (2020). Drinking to cope with the pandemic: The unique associations of COVID-19-related perceived threat and psychological distress to drinking behaviors in American men and women. *Addictive Behaviors*, 110, 106532. doi:10.1016/j.addbeh.2020.106532.

U.S. Department of Health and Human Services (2020). Your rights under HIPAA. www.hhs.gov/hipaa/for-individuals/guidance-materials-for-consumers/index.html.

Yard, E., Radhakrishnan, L., Ballesteros, M. F., Sheppard, M., Gates, A., Stein, Z., Hartnett, K., Kite-Powell, A., Rodgers, L., Adjemian, J., Ehlman, D. C., Holland, K., Idaikkadar, N., Ivey-Stephenson, A., Martinez, P., Law, R., & Stone, D. M. (2021). Emergency department visits for suspected suicide attempts among persons aged 12–25: Years before and during the COVID-19 pandemic - United States, January 2019–May 2021. *Morbidity and Mortality Weekly Report*, 70(24), 888–894. doi:10.15585/mmwr.mm7024e1.

Epilogue
Some Closing Thoughts

If after completing your social work education (or this book), you are overwhelmed by all you do not know, do not worry; this is a common feeling among new professionals and actually a good sign. An MSW by no means fully prepares you for independent practice; you will need to continue to be supervised and further trained; important things to keep in mind as you search for employment. In the long run, good training and supervision at the onset of your career will mean more than salary and benefits, so prioritize these factors in your job search. If the agency you are considering does not offer clinical training, is there support for pursuing training elsewhere, including funding and/or education time-release? State licensing boards require ongoing continuing education, so consider this obligation an opportunity to extend your clinical training. Do not just fulfill those requirements simply to check off a box. Instead, use those credits to get education in various theories and clinical techniques. There are scores of models of psychotherapeutic treatment available and if history serves, more on the way.

As you now know, this volume is not a survey of multiple models of clinical practice. For good compilations of various methods of psychotherapy, see Nichols (2017) and Turner (2017), and I am sure there are many others. The exclusion or inclusion of treatment paradigms in this book is in no way a rejection or exclusive endorsement of any of them. However, what is essential is that no matter what model you use, the relationship between clinician and client is the most important element of the psychotherapeutic work. Herein, the interventions I describe are steeped in the common factors, along with Rogerian, solution-focused, and systemic thinking, all of which match my personality and worldview, and that I have found to be effective. However, do not just take my word for it; try these things out for yourself and see if they work for you and your clients. After trying them for a while, alter, discard, or replace as you see fit.

If you are fortunate enough to be employed or placed in an agency that works from a specific model, by all means immerse yourself in it, uncritically at first. As you pursue continuing education on your own, find a model of clinical practice that attracts you and study it in depth, absorbing everything it has to

DOI: 10.4324/9781003011712-11

offer. Keep an open mind with a minimum of initial questioning as you try it on for size. After you have done this for a year or so, it is time to do some critical thinking. What have you found works well, what doesn't work; does it work better for some clients than others (like a lot of models)? Does the model fit the type of clients you are seeing? Does it fit well with *your* personality and worldview? Does it allow for modifications for clients of different racial, ethnic, gender, sexual orientations, income levels, or able-ness? How might you alter the model to better suit your own personal style and the clients you are seeing? Generally, clients who are intellectual, highly educated, and/or seeking insight are more likely to be customers for models of practice that are insight-oriented as they seek deep understandings of the role of familial and historical factors in their problems. As stated to me once by a new client, "I wasn't ready to explore my relationship with my mother before, but I'm ready to dive in now." For clients in a great deal of pain, or who are looking predominantly for symptom relief at least initially, symptom-based models may work best. That said, it is advisable to use some integration of both relationship and symptom-oriented models in your work and to lean into one more than the other, depending on the situation.

If you find a model that suits you, great, however some cautions are in order. Psychotherapy paradigms can be like religions, with their own priests, bibles, apostles, evangelizers, and practitioners—who do not take kindly to having their ideas challenged. I have seen experts in the field of psychoanalytic psychotherapy suggest that people who disagree with them suffer from a personality disorder. I was once at a family therapy conference led by a giant in the field where a participant asked a question. In front of a 500-plus person audience, this leader asked this person if she was divorced. She replied that she was, and based on this response the leader accused the participant of being unable to think systemically and suggested she leave the conference. At another conference, when a panelist questioned a component of the philosophy of a long-deceased leader in the field, another panelist started banging on the desk saying he would not tolerate such a criticism. Jungian and Freudian teachers will point to excerpts from books that are over 50 years old as "proof" of the validity of their assertions, a clear sign that the model is not changing and growing with time and is thus calcifying. The point here is to remain open and curious, and remember that no one person or model has all the answers. Always seek to learn new things, for yourself and of course for your clients.

Finally, psychotherapy has its limits. Sometimes a client will get to a point in treatment where they ask questions such as, "Why did this happen to me? Why was I born into such a family?" "Why did I have to lose my child at such a young age? Why are we experiencing this pandemic?" Healing relationships in clinical social work can only go so far. Such questions are intended to be addressed in a relationship to one's higher power. So don't be surprised if some of your clients get to a place where they are asking questions that are better answered by a spiritual source. See if they are open to this by gently asking if they have a spiritual or religious belief or practice. It is not uncommon for psychotherapy to be a springboard for a spiritual quest.

The most important thing is to continue self-reflecting, searching, and growing throughout your career. Ongoing personal and professional growth will not only benefit you but the people you have been called to serve. Best wishes to you and your current and future clients.

References

Nichols, M. (2017). *Family Therapy: Concepts and Methods* (11th ed.). Pearson.
Turner, F. J. (Ed.) (2017). *Social Work Treatment: Interlocking Theoretical Approaches* (6th ed.). Oxford University Press.

Appendix: Questions for Individual Self-Reflection and Class Discussion

Chapter 1

1   Based on what you know about yourself now, what types of client problems might you be particularly well-suited for?
2   At this point in your career, what client issues might be difficult for you to work with?
3   What action can you take to enable you to work more effectively with these clients?
4   How might your race, ethnicity, sexual orientation, gender identity, ableness, or other demographic factors influence your perspective as you work with clients?
5   What possible biases might you harbor? How might you address them?
6   What is your reaction to the notion that social workers might have more difficult family and childhood backgrounds than those from other professions?
7   Do you believe clinical social workers should be required to enroll in psychotherapy as part of their training? Why or why not?

Chapter 2

1   What is the definition of clinical social work according to the licensing board in your state? What professional activities does it include or exclude?

    a   What are the requirements for clinical licensure in your state?

2   From reading the chapter, you know that some believe that social workers who practice psychotherapy, particularly in private practice, are abandoning the mission of the profession. Break up into two teams (or work with a partner) with one arguing this position, and the other arguing against it. Afterwards, what have you learned from the experience?

3   Like many social work students, are you interested in eventually developing a private practice? If so, how will you do so in a way that maintains the profession's commitment to social justice, and diverse and oppressed populations?

Chapter 3

1   Find a partner and practice engagement. Start with small talk and then get them to talk about something a bit more personal. Notice what seems to work and what doesn't based on your partner's body language, facial expressions, and how much they talk. Then ask them to describe what it feels like to sit across from you and talking to you.
2   Think about who you are. How might your age, size, sex, race, ethnicity, and gender expression play a role in how clients of various backgrounds might see you? How will you use who you are in your work?
3   Consider the issue of advice; when is it a good idea to give advice, and when is it better simply to listen?

Chapter 4

1   Clive, a 65-year-old depressed Black man is pursuing psychotherapy. At your first session, when you ask him what he would like to change in his life, he replies:

> I feel so low all of the time, so sad. When I wake up, it feels as if a boulder is on my chest and it takes everything I can to get out of bed. I have trouble getting going, getting ready for work. Sometimes it is so bad, I feel like I cannot take it. I just don't know what to do.

How might you respond in a way that demonstrates empathy?
What questions would you ask to try to get at possible causes of his depression?
  i   Would you do a suicide assessment? Why or why not?
  ii Would you refer him to a psychiatrist for a medication evaluation? Why or why not?
2   How would you proceed to elicit treatment goals from Clive?
3   What potential strengths do you see?
4   Recall the last time you were very upset about something. Use this incident to complete a dysfunctional thought record (DTR). Have you noticed any change in how you now feel about the incident after completing this exercise?

5   Break up into pairs or small groups. One person should be chosen to play the role of the client and describe a problem (it can be real or a role play of a client situation.) The others are to take turns complimenting the client and asking questions that get at their strengths (adapted from De Jong & Berg, 2002).

Chapter 5

1   Couples work requires that the clinician (and ultimately the couple) move away from individually-based understandings of the couple problem ("Our problems are all *your* fault!") to a systemic framework where both members of the couple understand that they each play a role in the difficulties. For you, what might be the limits of such a perspective and why?
2   Infidelity was not addressed in this chapter, but how might you frame such behavior using systems thinking and reciprocity? (See the work by Esther Perel (2017) about this topic.)
3   Think about your own couple relationships. What are your partner's actions that really make you angry? Thinking systemically, and incorporating the idea of reciprocity, what role do you think you might play in your partner's annoying relationship behaviors?

   a   As an experiment, would you be willing to change the ways you interact with your partner to see the impact on your relationship? Why or why not?

Chapter 6

1   Watch several episodes of the television program *Finding Your Roots* by Professor Henry Louis Gates, Jr. (www.pbs.org/show/finding-your-roots/). What conclusions can you draw about his celebrity subjects based on their family histories? What strengths or obstacles get passed down from generation to generation?
2   Consider your family three generations back. What do you know about your grandparents, great grandparents, great-great grandparents, aunts, uncles, and cousins? What information do you have and what is missing? Go a step further, and ask your relatives about any missing information. (If you are feeling ambitious, consult McGoldrick, Gerson, & Petry (2008) or Monica McGoldrick's videos on YouTube to assemble your own genogram.) Overall, what are the strengths and liabilities you have inherited from the previous generations of your family? How might they assist you in your clinical work?

Chapter 7

1 Think of a group situation you are currently in. If you are a student, consider a classroom. If not, think about a committee or an informal group to which you belong.

   a   What are the formal and informal rules of the group? Who has established them?
   b   Can you identify problematic behaviors in the group? Is there a dominator, distractor, or people pleaser in the group?
   c   How does this "group" handle conflict, painful topics, or other difficult subjects?

2 Using the guidelines from this chapter, lay out a plan for a group that you would be interested in running. Choose a subject, or population. Will it be a support, educational, or therapy group? Open or closed? Time-limited or ongoing? How will you recruit clients? What will the rules of the group be? How will you start the group?

Chapter 8

1 Each of us, no matter who we are, have been impacted, positively or negatively, directly or indirectly, by the various oppressions and inequities in our society. Talk about how you have been personally affected by the following "isms." Address each topic no matter what your race, sex, sexual orientation, gender identity, or level of ability is:

   a   Racism
   b   Sexism
   c   Homophobia
   d   Transphobia
   e   Able-ism

2 We all commit microaggressions. Are you willing to share the last time you committed one? What would make it more difficult or easier to talk about this with your peers, supervisor, or classroom instructor? Discuss with a partner or in a group. You may choose to talk about this on a meta level: "What would make this topic easier to discuss is ..." with or without describing the actual microaggression.

3 We live in a segregated world. So, find someone from a different race, ethnicity, sexual orientation, or gender identity to interview *or* go visit a space where people from one of these groups is the majority. Become an expert on the group with which you are now least familiar.

Chapter 9

1 Review the NASW Code of Ethics (2021). Which standards do you think would be the most difficult for you to adhere to and why?
2 Think of the current population you are serving in your field placement or workplace. What is a possible ethical dilemma you might face? How will you address it? If you have already faced such a situation, discuss it with a partner.

Chapter 10

1 During the initial period of the HIV/AIDS crisis, when AIDS was a fatal disease, it had been said that gay men who chose to be sexually active became on-the-spot philosophers, weighing pleasure and freedom against the risk of disease and death. The same could be said for anyone who steps out of their home during this global pandemic. Answer the following questions:
    a What is *your* philosophy about Covid risk? How do you make decisions about mask wearing, social distancing, isolation, vaccines, and sending children to school?
    b What do you think of people who make different decisions?
    c How will you handle working with clients who hold philosophies and decisions different from your own on this issue?

Epilogue

1 What are your plans for supervision, training, and continuing education once you graduate and in your first years as a clinician?

References

De Jong, P., & Berg, I. K. (2002). *Instructor's Resource Manual With Test Bank: Interviewing for Solutions* (2nd ed.). Brooks/Cole.

McGoldrick, M., Gerson, R., & Petry, S. S. (2008). *Genograms: Assessment and Intervention*. WW Norton & Company.

National Association of Social Workers (NASW) (2021). *Code of ethics of the National Association of Social Workers*. NASW Press. www.socialworkers.org/About/Ethics/Code-of-Ethics/Code-of-Ethics-English.

Perel, E. (2017). *The State of Affairs: Rethinking Infidelity: A Book for Anyone Who Has Ever Loved*. Hachette UK.

Index

12-step programs 162–163
20 second rule 170

abandonment, fears of 125, 138
ABCD model 81
adult relationships 71, 73–74, 75, 125
adverse childhood experiences (ACEs) 3, 8
advice to clients 55–56
advocacy 29, 99, 203
African Americans 27, 136, 156, 184, 186, 235
agoraphobia 79
Alcoholics Anonymous (AA) 162–163
all or nothing thinking 82
American Board of Clinical Social Work 13
Anderson, R. 2
anger management 49, 72–76, 129, 130–131, 169
antecedent events 79, 81
anxiety 10, 22–23, 39, 62, 191–192
assessment and treatment 14; between-session homework 124; biological predisposition 127; coaching 120–124, 146–152; couple, joining with relationship of 113–114; couples and context 127–128; enactment conversation 118–122, 144–146; family-of-origin questions 124–127; process questions 122; scaling questions 114–118, 124; strengths, mining for 122–123
attachment theory 58, 125
attack, intervention in 172
avoidance 63
avoidant attachment 125

Beck, A. 81
Beck, J. 81

beginning social worker 34; communicating authority 35–36; compliment the clients 39–40; dress code 34–35; engagement skills 38–39; goal setting 40–41; listening, importance of 37; sense of control 36; self-correcting mistakes 36; setting up the space 37–38; sexism 43–45; sitting posture 38; space for reflection, finding 37; therapist matching with the client, issue of 41–43
behavioral therapy 78–80; classical conditioning 78–79; operant learning 79–80; *see also* cognitive behavioral therapy (CBT)
behaviorist school approach 16
Berg, I. K. 27, 64, 84, 124
Bernard, J. 197
biculturality 203–207
Big Book 163
biological predisposition 156
Black, P. N. 2
Black Lives Matter 187
Bowen, M. 125, 134, 155, 188
Boyd-Franklin, N. 16, 27, 136, 156
broader society, ethical responsibilities to 229
Burgoyne, N. 237, 238

Cartwright, S. 188
case management 17, 28–29, 99–101, 236
cathartic venting and problem-solving session 98, 200
chair exercise 204–207
childhood trauma 3, 72–74, 124–125, 126
children 94; and adults, relationships between 71–72; adverse childhood

experiences (ACEs) 3, 8; behavioral problems of 139–140; child protective workers 96; as co-therapist 155; family boundaries with 136–138; groups for 181–182; rigid hierarchy 139; LGBT children 154, 189; neglect of 94–95, 139; and parent, relationship between 17, 41–43, 58–59, 71–76, 134–159 ; parentified 2–3, 5, 8; physical abuse 94, 139; protection from harm 94–96; rejection of 155; sexual abuse 94–95; subsystem 136–138; *see also* parent–child relationships
child therapy 91–93; *see also* family therapy
Chodron, P. 6
cisgender 180–181, 189
classical conditioning 78–79
client–clinician relationship 77; *see also* clients, ethical commitment to
client resilience 27–28
clients, ethical commitment to: cultural competence 214; derogatory language 221; informed consent 213–214; lacking decision-making capacity 222; payment for services 222; privacy and confidentiality 216–217; records, access to 218–219; self-determination 212–213, 215; sexual relationships 219–220; special circumstance, dangers of 217–218; termination of services 222–223
clinical assessment *see* assessment and treatment
clinical social work definition 17
clinician: anxiety 24, 26, 41, 191–192; issues facing 75–77
closed group 167
coaching 120–124, 150; for abusive relationship 148–149; family therapy 146–152; person with a motivation to change 120; for same-sex couples 128
cognitive behavioral therapy (CBT) 80–84; ABCD model 81; advantages and disadvantages of 84; dysfunctional thoughts 81–82
Cohn, A. S. 237
colleagues, ethical responsibilities to 223–225
community support 202
compassion 3, 6–7, 13, 73
competence, professional ethics 226–227

compulsive behaviors 63, 162
confidentiality, of client 170, 216–217
conflicts of interest 215–216
consultation 14, 230–231
consultation ethics 226
Coombes, K. 2
corrective emotional experiences 74
countertransference 4–6, 47, 75, 180
couples therapy 104–132, 194–195, 197–198; assessment and treatment 113–128; and constructive negotiation 104; enactments 118–124; power 128–131; problematic agendas 107–111; and problem-solving 104; and reactivity 105; remote practice 239; resolving conflict 108; safety contract 130; self-awareness, importance of 105–107; systems thinking 111–113; violence in 130–131; *see also* family therapy
Courtney, M. E. 17–18
Covid-19 pandemic 234; clinical social work during 236–240, 241–242; and self of the clinician 240–241; and trauma 234–236
critical consciousness, development of 201–202
critical race theory 186
criticism, of clinical social work 17–18
cultural competence 214

defensive responses 193
definitions, of clinical social work 13–15, 17
De Jong, P. 64
Depression Bipolar Support Alliance (DBSA) groups 162
derogatory language 221
De Shazer, S. 27, 84
differences, working across 191–197
diverse and oppressed groups 184; biculturality struggles 203–204; chair exercise 204–207; client perceptions, centralization of 198–199; clinician goals for 199–203; and clinician self-awareness 189–191; continuous effort 207; critical consciousness, development of 201–202; emotional expression 200; impacts of oppression 185–186; and race 186–187; raising the issue 193–197; resilience building 202–203; and sexism 197–198;

supportive community, engagement in 202; therapist match 199; and White male theory biases 187–189; working across difference 191–197; *see also* groups
diversity, definition of 184
domestic violence and screening 130
drapetomania 188
dual relationships 215, 9219–220, 226
dysfunctional patterns identification 112
dysfunctional thought record (DTR) 81, 83
dysfunctional thoughts 81–82

educational approach 168
educator, clinician as 168–169
emic theories 187, 188
emotional expression 200
empathic reflection 76
empathy 3, 29–30, 46, 60–63, 173
enactments: couples therapy 118–124; and family boundaries 144–145; family therapy 144–153; same-sex couples therapy 128
end of the session coping questions 67
enmeshment 138, 145, 187
Epston, D. 202
Erickson, M. 84
ethics 211; broader society, responsibilities to 229; colleagues, responsibilities to 223–225; commitment to clients 212–223; dilemmas, resolving 229–232; practice settings, responsibilities in 226; professionals, responsibilities as 226–228; social work professional impaired responsibilities to 228
etic theories 187–188
evaluation and research, in profession 228

facial expressions, gauging online 239–240
family boundaries: with adolescents 137–138; with children 136–138; and enactments 144–146; external 135, 138; with older adolescents 149–152; and tracking 143–144
family-of-origin: issues with 66–67, 134; questions about 126–127
family psychopathology 3
family therapy 45, 104–105, 134–158; assessment 140–146; for biracial families 19–20; child as co-therapist 155; coaching 146–152; enactments and intensity 144–146, 152–153; engagement 140–142; family boundary issues 135–139; family therapy with one person 156–158; feminist 197; goal setting 142–143; intergenerational influences 155–156; and LGBT children 154–155; no-violence contract 131; reframing 153–155; and relationship 164; remote practice 239; setting boundaries and abuse 139; subsystems 136–138; symptoms and 139–140; tracking 143–144; and trauma 2–3; triangles 146; *see also* children; couples therapy; parent–child relationships
filtering 81–82
flexibility 21–22
fortune telling 82
foster care prevention program, case example for 45–46
Freud, S. 59, 188

Gelso, C. I. 69
genogram 3
goals, behavioral 64–66
goal setting 65
Goldstein, E. G. 207
grief 160
groups: 160–182; characteristics of 165; for children 181–182; communication, getting started 169–171; and compliments 169; and confidentiality 170; guidelines for starting 164–169; negotiating rules and guidelines of 170; participant's introduction in 170; problematic group behavior 171–181; professionally facilitated support groups 163; purpose of 160–162; supervision groups 163–164; support groups 162–163; termination of 182; therapeutic groups 164; types of 162–164; *see also* diverse and oppressed groups

Hanna, E. A. 3
harm to self or others: child protection 94–96; duty to warn 99; suicidal clients 96–99
Hartley, E. K. 2
Hayes, J. A. 69
healing relationships 58–79; assessment of history 66–67; concealed feelings,

pushing for 63–65; cultural curiosity 70–71; empathic connection, establishing 60–63; genuineness 69–70; goal consensus 64–66; good listening skills 60; parent-child relationship, considering 58–59; positive regard, unconditional 67–69; transference, working with 71–75; *see also* couples therapy; Covid-19 pandemic; diverse and oppressed groups; ethics; groups
Health Insurance Portability and Accountability Act (HIPAA) 237
Hendrix, H. 124, 125
heterosexual relationship: role of romance and sex in 116–117; sharing household chores in 111–112, 117, 119
holding environment 59, 73, 74, 164
Hollis, J. 2, 3
home visits 22–27; accepting food and gifts during 26; anxiety about 22–23; benefits of, 22; and compliments 25; dangers in 23–24; and family boundaries communication 24–25; and fear 25; important others in attendance during 27; important source of data 24–26; taking charge in 25–26; tips for 23–27

I CARE method 229–230; action 231; consultation 230–231; evaluation 231–232; identification 230; rebuttal 231
identified patient 141
idiot compassion 6–7
impairment, professional ethics 227–228
informed consent 162, 165, 213–214
insecure attachment 125
insider outsider dynamics 181
instead questions 66, 109, 143
institutional racism 19–20, 186
institutional review board (IRB) 228
intergenerational influences 155–156
intermittent reinforcement 80
intersectionality theory 196

Jeffreys, D. 2

knowing thyself/self-analysis 8–9

Lackie, B. 2, 3
Laird, J. 184

Lambert, M. J. 58, 59
Latinx (Latino/a) people 16, 17, 185–186
Leszcz, M. 161, 164
LGBTQ people 162, 185, 189, 200, 203–204
licensed clinical social worker 14
low intensity questions 141

magnification 82
male-biased theories 187–189
member participation 160–161, 179
Meyer, I. 185
microaggression, response to being caught committing 192–193
Miller, A. 70
mindreading 82
minority stress theory 185
minority therapist, role of 45–48
Minuchin, S. 17, 187
mistakes making, and recovering 192–193
multigenerational transmission process 155
mutual aid 162

National Association of Social Workers (NASW) 13, 15, 50
National Association of Social Workers (NASW) Code of Ethics 50, 77, 165, 203, 211–229; *see also* ethics
negligence of children 94–95, 139
New Jersey Division of Consumer Affairs 14–15
New York State Licensing Board 13
New York State licensing law 13, 15
Norcross, J. C. 58, 59

ongoing continuing education 244
online sessions 236–240
open group 167, 171
operant learning 79–80
oppression 184–187, 192; *see also* diverse and oppressed groups

Pachankis, J. E. 185
panic attack 37, 84
parental subsystem boundary 136–139, 145–146
parent–child relationships 71–76; handling 58–59; strengthening 17; *see also* children; family therapy
parentification: of clinician as child 2, 3, 5–6, 8

parents-of-transgender-youth group 163
partner, relationship problems with *see* couples therapy
payment for services 222
perseverance 57
personalization 82
person-in-environment 6
PFLAG group (Parents, Family, and Friends of Gay (LGBT) people) 167
physical contact, between social worker and client 220
politically minded client, handling 54
poor, services for 17–18, 21, 99
positive regard 67–69; and compliments 68; and long-term client 67; and self-criticism 68
power 128–131; domestic violence 129–131; financial power 128–129
practice settings, ethical responsibilities in 226
privacy, of client 216–217
private practice 1, 18, 20
problematic agendas 107–111; change 109–110; fix him! 111; I'm leaving, so take care of him 110–111; refereeing 107–108; social agenda 108; specification obsession 110; "you always" "you never" 109
problematic behavior of clients, acceptance of 68–69
problematic group behavior 171–177; distractor 174–175; dominator 171–173; example 180–181; fleeing pain 176–177; ignore nothing 177–181; people pleaser 175–176; silent one 173–174
problem-solving skills, inducing 84, 104, 123
process questions 122, 128, 155, 157
profession: ethical responsibilities to 228; integrity of 228
professionally led support groups 162, 163
professionals: ethical responsibilities as 226–228; working with other 29–30
projective techniques 182
Proujansky, R. A. 185
pseudo-over-closeness 138
psychological goods 18
psychotherapeutic skills 18
psychotherapy: 50-minute office session 17, 21–22; and clinical social work, difference between 15–16; counseling 14–15; need for participating in own 9–10; paradigms 245–246
psychotherapy plus 16

race paradox 186
racism 17, 19, 46–47, 186–187, 196, 200, 235, 241
reciprocal interaction pattern 112, 140, 194; *see also* reciprocity
reciprocity 157, 164
records, client's access to 218–219
reframing 153–155
reinforcement schedules 80
relationship reactivity 105–106, 115, 124, 153, 195, 198, 207
relaxation techniques 79
reminding couples of exceptions 109
remote practice 236–240
resilience building 27–28, 69, 200, 202–203
Rogers, C. 59, 69
roles and responsibilities, of clinical social work 13–30, 226–228
Rompf, E. L. 2
Royse, D. 2
Rule-breaking in clinical social work 50–55; accepting gifts 51–52; closed-ended questions 50–51; self-disclosure 53–55

safe space 200
Saleeby, D. 27
same-sex couples 72, 73–74, 106, 127–128, 131, 194–195
scaling questions 114–118; desired changes and goal setting articulation 115; end of the relationship assessment 117; and reactivity 114–115; reassessment of goals 117–118; romance and sex based 116–117
scope, of clinical social work 13–30
self-awareness, clinician 105–107, 189–191
self-blame 3
self-care, importance of 30, 216
self-criticism 3, 62, 80
self-determination 165, 212–213, 215
self-disclosure 50, 69; guidelines 53–55; related to clinical relationship 54
self-esteem, low for client 18, 52; for clinician 3, 5, 10

self-growth 57
self-harm *see* harm to self or others
self-help groups 162
self-knowledge 8–9, 105, 106
self-narration 80
self of the clinician 1–2, 43–48, 240–241
self-reflection 50, 77
self-reflection and class discussion questions 247–251
self-silencing behaviors 173–174
self-talk 80–81, 84
self-talk phrases 169
sexism 43–45, 197–198
sexual attraction to clients 77–78, 219–220
sexual harassment and assault 171, 221
sexually compulsive behaviors 72–73
sexual relationships ethics 219–220
short-circuit suffering, cultural zeal to 6–8
Shulman, L. 30, 162
Siebert, D. C. 3
social justice: advocacy for 203; issues, impact of 17–20; understanding of 18
social workers' relationship to themselves 1–11; knowing thyself 8–11; self as instrument 1–2; short-circuit suffering, cultural zeal to 6–8; wounded healer, path of 2–6
social work/social justice perspective 19–20
solution-focused therapy 27, 84–92; adolescents and children 91–92; approaches to 88–89; and compliments 87; mandated clients 88–93; miracle question 87–88; precepts of 84–85; probation 90–91; and relationship question 87–88; solution-generating questions 85–87
Specht, H. 17–18
speech impediment 47
strength-based approach 27, 122–123, 173; *see also* solution-focused therapy
substance abuse 100–101, 139, 160, 162, 223
subsystems 136–138; child subsystem 138; parental subsystem 136–137

Sue, D. W. 188
suicide: assessment 67; ideation, treatment for 96–99
supervision: ethics 226; in groups 163–164, 165, 180–181; use of 5, 44, 46, 49, 56–57, 153
symptom-focused treatment: behavioral therapy 78–88; cognitive behavioral therapy (CBT) 80–84
systematic desensitization 79
systemic thinking 111–113, 128, 135–140, 145, 157
Szapoznik, J. 16–17

Tarasoff vs. Regents of the University of California 99
teletherapy 236–240
termination of services 168, 182, 222–223
theory biases 187–189
therapist feelings as clinical data 48–50; anger 48–49; poor hygiene 49–50; sexual arousal 49; sleepiness 48
therapist match 41–43, 199
therapy sessions, cancellation of 64
time-limited groups 168
traditional psychotherapy 15
transference 71–74, 125
transgender groups 162, 163, 178–181,
trauma 27, 160; childhood 3, 72–74, 124–125, 126; and family therapy 2–3; feelings related to 63; healing of 59; and pandemics 234–236
trauma care, and resilience 69–70
treatment *see* assessment and treatment

unfaithful angels' paradigm 17–20

Wakefield, J. 18
Wesley, K. 186
White, M. 202
White clients 46–47, 70
White male theory biases 187–189
White supremacy 186
Winnicott, D. W. 59, 74, 101, 140

Yalom, I. D. 161, 164, 170, 176

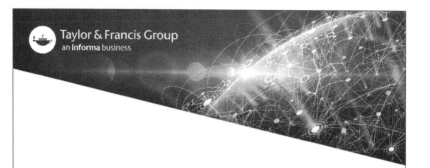

Printed in the United States
by Baker & Taylor Publisher Services